After the Vote Was Won

After the Vote Was Won

The Later Achievements of Fifteen Suffragists

Katherine H. Adams *and*
Michael L. Keene

McFarland & Company, Inc., Publishers
Jefferson, North Carolina, and London

LIBRARY OF CONGRESS CATALOGUING-IN-PUBLICATION DATA

Adams, Katherine H., 1954–
After the vote was won : the later achievements of fifteen suffragists / Katherine H. Adams and Michael L. Keene.
p. cm.
Includes bibliographical references and index.

ISBN 978-0-7864-4938-5
softcover : 50# alkaline paper ∞

1. Suffragists — United States — Biography. 2. Suffragists — United States — History — 20th century. 3. Women political activists — United States — Biography. 4. Women intellectuals — United States — Biography. 5. Women — United States — Biography. 6. United States — Politics and government —1919–1933. 7. United States — Social conditions —1918–1932. 8. United States — Intellectual life — 20th century. I. Keene, Michael L. II. Title.
JK1898.5.A33 2010
324.6'23092273 — dc22 2010019558

British Library cataloguing data are available

Front cover: The Valentine's Day deputation to the president, photograph from National Woman's Party Records (Library of Congress Manuscript Division)

Manufactured in the United States of America

McFarland & Company, Inc., Publishers
Box 611, Jefferson, North Carolina 28640
www.mcfarlandpub.com

MLK: For Claire

KHA: For Willie

Acknowledgments

We wish to thank Pat Doran, the interlibrary loan officer at Loyola University, for her constant kind help. Kate can be a challenge, but Pat never mentions that fact. We would also like to thank librarians at several university archives: Accacia Flanagan and Laurie Ellis of the Schlesinger Library at Radcliffe, Christine Connolly at the Sterling Memorial Library of Yale University, Ronald Patkus and Dean M. Rogers in Special Collections at the Vassar College Library, and Helen Selsdon of the Helen Keller Archives at the American Federation for the Blind.

Contents

Preface

When we were writing a book about Alice Paul, we researched the lobbying, parading, picketing, and hunger striking that members of the National Woman's Party undertook in order to gain the vote. While we were coming to recognize that Alice Paul deserved more attention, we also came upon another suffrage story that also deserved to be told: the story of what her supporters did after the vote was won and, as a result of their actions, what was going on in the women's movement in the U.S. during the years after suffrage was attained.

Scholars before us had looked only at the suffragists' impact on traditional politics: at whether these women sought elected office beginning in the 1920s, and whether they encouraged other women to do so. Given that means of assessment, since women certainly did not gain an equal footing in politics in those years, these suffragists have repeatedly been judged as failures, their efforts denigrated as the temporary efforts of a meek first wave who sought the vote and then went home, with their movement stalling out metaphorically in the sand.

But were these critics who focused on women's place (or lack thereof) in traditional politics asking the one right question? Were they concentrating on what these women sought to achieve?

It is certainly true that the most active of the suffrage campaigners did not dedicate themselves to the suffrage effort solely to gain the vote or to enter political careers. As they state in their journals and articles, some of them didn't even vote after 1920. However, for American women, the suffrage campaign provided a necessary and important platform not just for entering traditional politics, but for seeking the right to pursue a wide range of opportunities. Shown by Alice Paul what was possible, and tempered by their experiences following her, these women were able to rewrite what women could be and do in fields as diverse as art, education and especially adult education, science, writing and publishing, and civil rights. And it was the suffrage experience itself— the organizing, picketing, and hunger striking — that had honed such goals. These women left the suffrage campaign with a changed view of themselves: as strong individuals and group members who could envision change and enact it regardless of the forces amassed against them.

This book thus tells the story of many of the women who made the greatest sacrifices for the vote — especially by standing on picket lines and entering American jails — and of what they did with those lessons after the vote was won. These women include Louisine Havemeyer, Louise Bryant, Dorothy Day, Mary Church Terrell, and others, some well known and some much less so. What they all deserve is not dismissal (because they did not seek political office) but rather serious consideration (for the many remarkable things they did). We were attracted to this story because these militant suffragists deserved recognition as a dedicated and effective group.

To study these women, we looked carefully at the journals that they kept during and after the suffrage campaign, at their autobiographies, and at their other published works. In conducting this research, we were lucky to be able to call upon the resources of the Schlesinger Library as well as collections housed at Yale and other universities. We also relied daily on interlibrary loan to bring to us these women's writing and artworks as well as scholarship concerning them.

Though women did not have the impact on American political life that should have come with suffrage, it is not fair to say that suffrage activists failed in what they sought. Indeed, this experience made women both wary of the American political process and more determined to wield their influence outside of it. This book considers their lives of courageous activism and the impact of that activism on this nation.

Introduction

In Book III of *Gulliver's Travels*, when Gulliver arrives at Glubdubdrib, he has a chance to meet both with historical figures and with those who have written about them, ghosts called out magically at night. He finds that not many of the leaders of ancient or modern times are quite like he had been taught in school. Why had some figures been disparaged and others exalted? His answer was the "roguery and ignorance" of historians, writers bent on securing a reflected glory for their own social group or, more specifically, for themselves (185).

Swift understood that history has always served rhetorical purposes. As Joan Wallach Scott notes, the meaning of human experience is "always contested, always therefore political, always a construct in a retelling that is put to some cultural use" ("Experience" 37; Ardis and Lewis 2). When it comes to the campaign for woman's suffrage in the United States, such a rhetorical retelling certainly occurred over the course of the twentieth century. For different reasons, and in different generations, historians have told a changing story about the group of women who worked so hard to achieve the vote.

One rhetorical choice concerns the group of women that receives attention. Susan B. Anthony, Elizabeth Cady Stanton, and Lucretia Mott are certainly the best known figures of the woman's suffrage movement in the United States. By 1906, however, they had all died, and women did not achieve the vote until 1920. Who, then, carried on their work and secured the passage of the Nineteenth Amendment? The most common answer would be Carrie Chapman Catt and Anna Howard Shaw, leaders of the largest suffrage organization, the National American Woman Suffrage Association (NAWSA), an amalgam of two associations that formed after the Civil War. After Anthony's death, Catt and Shaw led the difficult state-by-state fight for woman's enfranchisement, working through a national council and local affiliates that involved two million members.

The official story, depicting a triumphal march of early pioneering leaders and later organizational leaders, appeared in many books by and about these women published before 1930, and it still persists in the public consciousness. Friends and associates of Anthony, Stanton, and Mott wrote laudatory biographies, such as Anna Davis Hallowell's *James and Lucretia Mott: Life and Letters* (1890) and Ida Husted Harper's *The Life and Work of Susan B. Anthony* (1898). The women themselves also wrote autobiographies and histories of the suffrage movement: Elizabeth Cady Stanton's *Eighty Years and More* (1898), Anna Howard Shaw's *The Story of a Pioneer* (1915), and Carrie Chapman Catt's *Woman Suffrage and Politics: The Inner Story of the Suffrage Movement* (1923). Stanton and Anthony worked with Ida Husted Harper, NAWSA's historian, on a six-volume *History of Woman Suffrage*, published between 1881 and 1922, which featured the contributions of the first leaders along with NAWSA's yearly progress. Following the lead of these early biographies and histories, subsequent publications told the same two-part story. Books with all-encompassing titles, like *American Feminists* (Riegel, 1963), *The Woman Movement* (W. O'Neill, 1969), and *One Half the People: The Fight for Woman Suffrage* (Scott and Scott, 1975), as well as many textbooks, repeat this familiar construction of women's history.

After these women, especially those in the first inspirational group, became the accepted heroes of the American suffrage movement, they gained further status through official forms of commemoration. For example, a portrait monument of Mott, Stanton, and Anthony was placed in the Crypt of the Capitol, the large circular area on the first floor, on February 15, 1921, Susan B. Anthony's birthday. This statue is now in the Rotunda. The post office issued stamps with Susan B. Anthony's picture in 1936 and 1955, and one featuring Stanton, Mott, and Catt in 1948. And in 1979 the Susan B. Anthony dollar appeared. With the publicly awkward issue of her sexuality avoided, she ultimately became the one powerful symbol of the movement.

Missing from this story centered on Anthony was much mention of other groups and other leaders instrumental in obtaining the vote for women, perhaps most notably, Alice Paul and the National Woman's Party (NWP). After Paul moved to Washington, D.C., in December of 1912 when she was twenty-seven, she devoted all of her time to achieving a federal amendment, which she judged the most direct route to suffrage for American women. With Jane Addams' help, Paul talked NAWSA into appointing her as head of a subcommittee charged with introducing a federal suffrage amendment in the Congress each year. Because NAWSA was emphasizing state-by-state campaigns, this committee had been serving a ceremonial function. Instead of accepting that limited goal, Paul created an active congressional committee in 1913, formed the Congressional Union (CU) later that same year to expand her campaign throughout the nation, separated her group from

NAWSA in 1914, and instituted the NWP in 1916, first involving members only from states where women could vote but later including women from all states. Although many suffragists preferred state-level work, Paul insisted that her organization's only focus would be federal adoption of the plainly written Susan B. Anthony Amendment:

Section 1. The right of citizens of the United States to vote shall not be denied or abridged by the United States or any State on account of sex.
Section 2. Congress shall have power, by appropriate legislation, to enforce the provisions of this article.

While changing state laws could go on interminably, Paul felt, passage of this legislation would signal the country's recognition of women's equal status in all states, for all elections, concerning all issues.

The CU and then the NWP planned and executed a series of actions that shocked the government, the press, and even fellow suffragists. In states where women already had the vote, members conducted boycott campaigns against Wilson and other Democrats because his majority party opposed a federal amendment. In Washington, these women staged mass protests, lobbied legislators, picketed the White House and Capitol, burned Wilson's speeches on democracy, and then burned him in effigy. As the jail terms resulting from these actions stretched from a day to seven months, with Paul at one point placed in a psychiatric ward to demonstrate—or cause—her mental instability, suffrage prisoners chose to initiate hunger strikes that led to their being force-fed, with tubes shoved down their mouths and noses. On one "Night of Terror," November 15, 1917, they were beaten, pulled down halls by their hair, and handcuffed to beds.

Only within the last twenty years have historians begun to include the hard work of Paul and the NWP in the suffrage story. Unlike Mott, Stanton, Anthony, Catt, and Shaw, Alice Paul did not seek to have her own story told although her colleagues Doris Stevens and Ida Haynes Irwin did record their own experiences. Instead, following the ratification of the Nineteenth Amendment, Paul immediately turned her attention to securing passage of the Equal Rights Amendment, which she authored with fellow NWP member Sue Shelton White in 1923. Paul was not interested in publicizing her role in suffrage, and no group had a reason to do so. She had represented a minority of suffrage advocates, and the details of her story disparaged both Democrats and Republicans while revealing dirty truths about American police and jails as well as the president.

Only at the end of the twentieth century did two books, Christine A.

Lunardini's *From Equal Suffrage to Equal Rights: Alice Paul and the National Woman's Party, 1910–1928* (1986) and Linda Ford's *Iron-Jawed Angels: The Suffrage Militancy of the National Woman's Party, 1912–1920* (1991), finally provide a fuller picture of the NWP's activities. Our own *Alice Paul and the American Suffrage Campaign* (2007) attempted to analyze her visual public rhetoric. At the Democratic Convention in 2008, Hillary Clinton further created interest in these suffragists as she spoke about determined heroes of the suffrage campaign who "looked into their daughters' eyes, imagined a fairer and freer world, and found the strength to fight. To rally and picket. To endure ridicule and harassment. To brave violence and jail." The story of picketing and going to jail took a long time to be told perhaps because it revealed dirty truths about American justice and it complicated the iconic depiction of Susan B. Anthony and her colleagues.

While historians have recently begun to fill in the larger story of the suffrage movement, they have also begun to reexamine earlier judgments of its effect on women and on the United States. Secretary of State Colby, interviewed the day he signed the amendment into law, compared the moment to Admiral Dewey's entry into Manila harbor. Dewey had supposedly said, "When you are ready, you may fire, Gridley." Thus Colby said after the signing, "So I turn to the women of America and say: 'You may now fire when you are ready. You have been enfranchised'" ("Colby Proclaims").

Developing almost immediately was the view that these suffragists weren't ready and they failed to fire: that the women who had sought the vote with such determination abandoned their goal of equality and just went home. This thesis appeared in the popular press, with provocative titles. In early 1924, a presidential election year, criticism seemed particularly virulent as the mainstream media sought to define this cultural change as endurable. In the *Atlantic Monthly* in February, George Madden Martin claimed that "American women generally are not interested in public affairs, national or local, in the concrete or in the abstract" (170). In March, the anti-suffrage *New York Times* noted that at least with this failure, "one bright ray of sunshine illumines the drab picture": women are "still as gentle, as feminine, as lovable as ever" ("How Woman Suffrage Works"). In March also, in a *Century Magazine* article entitled "Is Woman-Suffrage a Failure," Charles Edward Russell concluded that "no wonder the politicians are happy" because "women would not vote for women" (725–26). In an article in *Literary Digest* on April 12, 1924, called "Woman Suffrage Declared a Failure," the author began with key questions that the title answered: "Is it true that 'women will not vote for a woman'? That they are a negligible quantity in local politics? That voting women have done nothing but double the votes of men? That they are apathetic regarding public matters?" (12). In "American Women's Ineffective Use of the Vote" in *Current History* that fall, sociologists Stuart A. Rice and Malcolm M. Willey argued that women were not voting as the same rates as men and that they had not penetrated the "inner circle of party machinery" because of their lack of interest and lack of aggression (647).

During the Depression and the war years, the lack of women's political participation seemed of less media interest as women were needed to do the country's work and as other stories occupied the nation's attention. And certainly during the 1950s, with men returning to work and to societal control, writers did not focus on the need for women to take a greater role in government. But in the 1960s, this thesis again arose in historical studies, with the beginning of a new women's movement and thus more attention to women's history.

In those uncertain times, some scholars seemed determined, like those in 1924, to prove that women's activism had not altered American life. William L. O'Neill's *Everyone Was Brave: The Rise and Fall of Feminism in America*, from 1969, strongly stated the thesis that with the vote won and with an array of issues facing Americans in the 1920s on which feminists did not agree, they never achieved any political goals and made no impact on American life. In the preface, he summed up the argument that the book defended: "The struggle for woman's rights ended during the 1920s, leaving men in clear possession of the commanding places in American life" (vii). Not only did he write that with the vote "the feminist movement ended," but he also claimed, as a basic principle guiding his historical presentation, that he could not judge whether gender equality had even been an appropriate goal: "To begin with, I have avoided the question of whether or not women ought to have full parity with men. Such a state of affairs obtains nowhere in the modern world, and so, since we do not know what genuine equality would mean in practice, its desirability cannot fairly be assessed" (vii–viii).

Many women writers of the 1960s did not question women's right to equality, but they had another purpose for depicting those who went before as ineffective: by this imagery, they could position themselves positively, as the true radicals. In 1968, in the *New York Times Magazine*, journalist Martha Weinman Lear used the term "second wave" to describe her own generation and its efforts at seeking equality in employment and law. She reserved "first wave" for the suffrage generation, castigated for seeking just one narrow right and politely going home. Further employing her metaphor of ocean waves, she thus declared that the first wave "ebbed after the glorious victory of suffrage and disappeared, finally, into the great sandbar of Togetherness" (24).

Although Lear commented only briefly on the first wave and then turned her attention to the second, subsequent texts created a more negative depiction of the first wave, with the effect of further glorifying the qualities of the second. In *The Female Eunuch* (1970), an international bestseller, Germaine Greer used the following description for the women who fought for the vote: "The old suffragettes," as she named them, were women "who served their prison term and lived on through the years of gradual admission of women into professions which they declined to follow, into parliamentary freedoms which they declined to exercise, into academies which they used more and more as shops where they could take out degrees while waiting to get married" (11). These women, in Greer's analysis, wanted no social change and advocated for no other group; they just sought the chance to join meekly in the male-defined status quo: "In the old days ladies were anxious to point out that they did not seek to disrupt society or to unseat God. Marriage, the family, private property and the state were threatened by their actions, but they were anxious to allay the fears of conservatives, and in doing so the suffragettes betrayed their own cause and prepared the way for the failure of emancipation" (12). Greer attributed women's lack of progress since the 1920s to the narrow thinking of this group: "The cage door had been opened but the canary had refused to fly out" (2). Continuing with this bird imagery, Greer argued that "the conclusion was that the cage door ought never to have been opened because canaries are made for captivity; the suggestion of an alternative had only confused and saddened them" (12). Here is a stringent judgment, one that depicted the suffragists as an affluent and conservative group accepting current institutions and just seeking to be given a bit of a place in them, the suffrage campaign having been for them a short, fun outing leading to a flapper's short skirts and a mother's tight corsets.

While writers from the 1960s and 1970s situated the ineffectiveness of the suffragists as beginning with the very passage of the amendment, other later writers continued this theme of failure, but placed the end of the movement's efficacy at other points. In "Separatism as Strategy" (1979), Estelle Freedman argued that 1920 signaled the end of the movement; in "Separatism Revisited" (1995), she revised her judgments and maintained that the Cold War led to the death knell of activism. Similarly, in *Beyond Suffrage Women in the New Deal* (1981), Susan Ware identified a network of women who played an important role in shaping and implementing New Deal programs, their influence ending with World War II.

Only recently have some studies focused on an ongoing influence on politics of the suffrage generation and of subsequent decades of voting women though with the emphasis on limited impacts, less than what should have occurred. *Survival in the Doldrums* by Leila J. Rupp and Verta A. Taylor, from 1990, explored the persistence of women's political influence throughout the twentieth century. Focusing on women who saw themselves as heirs of the suffrage movement and who were, in many cases, participants in the campaign, Rupp and Taylor chronicled the choices of activists who maintained their commitment by building a small, supportive community of mostly white, middle- and upper-class, like-minded women. Six months after the Nineteenth Amendment was ratified, they noted, the NWP was refounded and dedicated itself to the elimination of women's legal disabilities. Initially it drafted model bills for states to pass, but soon decided that this strategy was too slow and uncertain. Alice Paul oversaw the preparation of another constitutional amendment, the Equal Rights Amendment, in 1923. Her group lobbied for changes to state laws as well as the inclusion of equal rights for women in the United Nations Charter in 1945 and for the addition of "sex" to Title VII of the 1964 Civil Rights Act, which prohibited discrimination in employment. But the social homogeneity of the movement, Rupp and Taylor argued, robbed it of any chance of launching a broad-based challenge on behalf of women's rights, its victories far between and its impact thus minimal. The group remained isolated, small, and exclusive — in the authors' words, "elite-sustained" (196).

In 1996, in *After Suffrage: Women in Partisan and Electoral Politics before the New Deal*, Kristi Andersen further altered the judgment of suffragists: she focused on a political contribution made in the 1930s that has continued ever since, involving allegiance to candidates over parties, a focus on social issues, and a use of new political techniques such as lobbying, all of which helped to redefine modern politics for both women and men. Thus, they conclude, these women "helped to solidify the movement from the highly partisan politics of the nineteenth century to the increasingly nonpartisan, candidate-centered, interest group politics of the mid-twentieth century" even though they did not achieve the participation levels that they sought (2).

From these books, readers have gotten a changing sense of the political and legal influence of suffrage activists. But what all of these histories and cultural studies have omitted is a thorough look at the actual women involved, especially those that risked their reputations and their lives through NWP activism. When historians and social reformers anticipated a certain sort of voting record or level of political involvement from women and then judged the suffrage movement for whether that result was delivered, they may have missed what these women wanted to achieve and what they did achieve. Ironically, the failures with which these women have been branded, especially in the 1920s and 1960s, concerned narrow political goals that most of these women didn't have. They joined the campaign because their experiences taught them that they lacked the power and civil rights needed to do the varied sorts of work that they sought to do. And indeed, whatever the judgment of their voting records, they did matter to American history, far beyond the votes that they cast. Dale Spender, in *There's Always Been a Women's Movement This Century*, wrote that she had been indoctrinated, through texts from the 1920s forward, to see women's suffrage protest as "a fleeting — and flighty — phase" and to ignore the ongoing process of education and influence that these women engendered (12). But in various fields such as art, science, education, publishing, and social activism, they made their mark, their choices shaped by the life-changing experiences, in parades, on the picket line, and in jail, that they shared.

To study the greater impact of the suffrage generation, we will first examine these women's formidable experiences, describing what was for them profoundly transformative. In subsequent chapters, we will move from the group to the lives and careers of suffragists like Louisine Havemeyer, Helen Keller, Mary Church Terrell, Dorothy Day, Louise Bryant, Rhoda Kellogg, Betsy Reyneau, Hazel Hunkins Hallinan, Mary Agnes Chase, Helena Hill Weed, and Sue Shelton White, through whom we can see more clearly what the Nineteenth Amendment wrought. Like earlier generations of scholars, we approach history, no doubt, through our own roguery and ignorance, as Jonathan Swift would claim, but also with what we believe to be a worthy rhetorical purpose: to evaluate these women by their own goals — to look at what they wanted and what they achieved.

1

In America: Picketing, Jail, and Torture

In the drive to gain the Nineteenth Amendment, two million women worked through NAWSA, an organization formed after the Civil War, with varying levels of involvement. At the beginning of the twentieth century, many suffragists felt that this organization and their struggle had been gaining no ground. In 1902, Elizabeth Cady Stanton died; in 1906, Susan B. Anthony. Although the state of Washington granted woman suffrage in 1910, California in 1911, and Illinois a limited presidential suffrage in 1913, a state suffrage referendum failed in Oregon in 1910; in Ohio, Michigan, and Wisconsin in 1912; in North and South Dakota, Nebraska, and Missouri in 1914; and in New York, New Jersey, Massachusetts, and Pennsylvania in 1915. With this very mixed track record, and no headway made in the South, state-by-state campaigns had begun to seem to many a slow and arduous means of getting a national right to vote, doomed to failure especially with a world war looming and other priorities filling the American consciousness.

Among advocates of abandoning the state campaigns were Alice Paul, Lucy Burns, and members of the National Woman's Party (NWP) that they formed. This small group worked assiduously for suffrage, taking risks to get the public's attention and create change, beginning with meetings and moving to parades, boycotts, picketing, and even burning the president in effigy, acts that led to jail terms and torture. As they took on these challenges, they formed a strong group, risked their reputations and their lives, and stood up to their government. Their dedication would greatly alter their own lives and those of Americans, what they did after the vote was gained being determined by the huge sacrifices they made to obtain it.

To the American suffrage movement, Alice Paul brought a superior education in political reform. She graduated from Swarthmore College, worked in a settlement house in New York for a year, obtained master's and doctoral degrees in political science at the University of Pennsylvania, and stud-

Left: **To begin her own campaign for women's suffrage, Alice Paul moved to Washington, D.C., in December 1912, and there devoted her time to passage of a federal amendment. Photograph dated 1913. Original copyright by Taylor Studio, Washington. Source: Library of Congress Prints and Photographs Division.** ***Right:*** **Lucy Burns joined Alice Paul in early 1913. Their group was formed as the Congressional Union, which separated from NAWSA in 1914 and became the National Woman's Party in 1916. Her first arrest, made while she was picketing on the sidewalk, was for "obstructing traffic." Photograph by Harris & Ewing, Inc., dated 1917. Source: Library of Congress Prints and Photographs Division.**

ied in England at the Woodbrooke Quaker Study Centre and the London School of Economics. In London, to contribute to the English campaign for suffrage, she worked with the Pankhursts and their Women's Social and Political Union (WSPU), planning meetings, questioning politicians, and hunger-striking in jail. Lucy Burns attended Vassar and Yale, went to Germany to study language, and then to Oxford. Burns met Paul in England where they joined in the protest for the vote (Adams and Keene 11–12).

In 1910, Paul wrote that the Pankhursts' WSPU was providing an opportunity for women to "throw off their mental bondage. It had kindled in their hearts a great spirit of rebellion against their subjection. It has developed a self-respect, a respect for their sex, unknown before. On all hands one hears it said: 'A new race of women is developing before our eyes'—a type which has discarded the old ideal of the physical, and mental, and moral depend-

When word came that Tennessee had ratified the suffrage amendment (August 18, 1920), Alice Paul unfurled the Woman's Party ratification banner from the balcony of their headquarters. Photograph originally published in *The Suffragist,* 8, no. 8 (1920), n.p. Photographer National Photo Co. Source: Library of Congress Prints and Photographs Division.

ence, and has substituted the ideal of strength" ("The Woman Suffrage Movement" 27). Paul wanted to begin her own American campaign similarly, by altering the prevailing view of women, as weak, insufficiently educated, hysterical or temperamental, and dependent on men, thus not worthy of the vote, judgments that women themselves all too commonly believed. With a new sense of self-respect, Paul felt, women could achieve all.

To mount this campaign for suffrage based on a new definition of the American woman, Paul moved to Washington, D.C., in December 1912, and there devoted her time to a federal amendment. Burns joined her in early 1913. Their group — formed as the Congressional Union (CU) that separated from NAWSA in 1914 and as the NWP in 1916 — certainly never rivaled NAWSA in size. Paul's organization never had more than 70,000 members, a number reduced to 50,000 during wartime picketing in 1917 (Josephson 94). But low numbers did not overly concern members; what they sought was a dedicated and moveable force, formed generally of younger NAWSA

Alva Belmont donated the building which became headquarters of the NWP. She is seen here speaking at the building's dedication, May 21, 1922. In 1895, when she divorced her first husband, William K. Vanderbilt, president of the New York Central Railroad Company, she received ten million dollars and several estates. Photograph by National Photo Co. Source: Library of Congress Manuscript Division.

members and working class women who had not been involved in other suffrage organizations.

This woman's party drew women looking for a more effective means of securing the vote, a more radical path than NAWSA seemed to provide. Some of them were older widows from the social elite, a group especially incensed by the Sixteenth Amendment, ratified in 1913, which established Congress' right to impose a federal income tax, for them taxation without representation. When Alva Erskine Belmont, a prominent multi-millionaire, divorced her first husband, William K. Vanderbilt, president of the New York Central Railroad Company, in 1895, she received ten million dollars and several estates; the death of her wealthy second husband, Oliver Hazard Perry Belmont, in 1908, further increased her personal wealth and real estate holdings. In 1909 she joined NAWSA and was named an alternate delegate from New York to the International Women's Suffrage Association meeting in London, where she observed the commitment of Emmeline

Top: The Valentine's Day Deputation to the President: (L to R) Jessica Henderson, Anne Archbold, Mrs. Wm. Draper, Sallie Hovey, Hazel MacKaye (who designed tableaux for the NWP), Gail Laughlin, Mrs. Ernest Schelling, Mary Kelly McCarty, Louisine Havemeyer, and Elsie Hill. Photograph from National Woman's Party Records. Source: Library of Congress Manuscript Division. Louisine Havemeyer. *Bottom:* Louisine Havemeyer with Vida Milholland, being welcomed to Syracuse by an unnamed policeman upon the arrival of the Prison Special. She and her husband had built the premier collection of impressionist art in the United States. Photograph dated March 8, 1919. Photograph from National Woman's Party Records. Source: Library of Congress Manuscript Division.

Pankhurst and her followers. In 1913 when the CU separated from NAWSA, so did Belmont. Joining in also was Louisine Havemeyer, who with her husband, Henry O. Havemeyer, owner of the American Sugar Refining Company, had built the premier collection of impressionist art in the United States. Harriot Stanton Blatch drew Havemeyer into the suffrage movement and the CU after the death of Henry Havemeyer.

The CU also attracted younger women, many well educated, seeking activist participation not quite offered by NAWSA. Doris Stevens graduated from Oberlin College in 1911. She worked as a teacher and social worker in Ohio and Michigan before she became a regional organizer for NAWSA. In New York, she became friends with leading members of the Greenwich Village radical scene, including Louise Bryant. In 1914 Stevens worked as a full-time organizer, as well as executive secretary, for the CU. Inez Milholland, who went to Vassar, became a labor lawyer before she devoted herself to suffrage, first through NAWSA and then the CU.

Additionally, especially after the United States began waging World War I, more immigrant and blue-collar workers joined the CU and NWP, a site to protest a government that did not consult women on the crucial decision to enter a war, perhaps against their own family members. Born Ruza Wenclawska in Poland, Rose Winslow came to the United States as an infant with her immigrant parents. Winslow's father worked as a coal miner and steelworker in Pennsylvania. She began working as a mill girl in the hosiery industry in Pittsburgh at eleven and was also employed as a shop girl in Philadelphia but was forced to quit work at age nineteen when she contracted tuberculosis, which left her disabled for the next two years. Winslow became a factory inspector and a trade union organizer in New York City with the National Consumers' League and the National Women's Trade Union League. She brought her speaking and organizing powers to the CU and then to the NWP by addressing gatherings on the streets, in union halls, and at suffrage rallies.

Although the majority of the members were white and some African Americans, like Ida Wells Barnett, felt alienated from the NWP because suffrage was its only goal, many African Americans joined its ranks. Nell Mercer, for example, who became a small hardware-store owner in Norfolk after moving there from Buell, Virginia, joined her state's NWP and the picket lines in 1919. Mary Church Terrell, who taught at a black secondary school in Washington, D.C., was appointed to the District of Columbia Board of Education as the first black woman in the United States to hold such a position and served as the first president of the National Association of Colored Women's Clubs, marched in parades and stood on picket lines with her daughter Phyllis.

Left: **Doris Stevens graduated from Oberlin College in 1911 and worked as a teacher and social worker in Ohio and Michigan before she became a regional organizer for NAWSA. In 1914 Stevens worked as a full-time organizer, as well as executive secretary, for the CU. She later wrote one of the first accounts of the NWA and the suffrage movement, *Jailed for Freedom* (New York: Boni and Liveright, 1920). Photograph from National Woman's Party Records, dated ca. 1919. Source: Library of Congress Manuscript Division. *Right:* Inez Milholland Boissevain, labor lawyer and graduate of Vassar. She died while giving a suffrage speech. Her last words were said to have been, "Mr. President, what will you do for woman suffrage?" and "Mr. President, how long must women wait for liberty?" Picture was published in the program of the Woman Suffrage Procession, Washington D.C., March 3, 1913, and in *The Suffragist*, 4, no. 50 (December 9, 1916): 10. Photograph from National Woman's Party Records. Source: Library of Congress Manuscript Division.**

To secure legitimacy for the new organization, the CU enlisted influential supporters for an advisory council, members of which were immediately listed down the left-hand side of CU stationery, a strong visual symbol of support that would soon take up two columns and leave little room for writing. Early choices for the council, consisting only of women, included activists with standing in the suffrage community such as May Wright Sewall and Bertha Fowler, associates of Susan B. Anthony. Well-known luminaries such as Belle Case LaFollette, Helen Keller, and Charlotte Perkins Gilman added their names. Paul also sought out academics such as Maria Montessori, Emma Gillette, dean and founder of the Western College of Law, and Clara Louise Thompson, a Latin professor at Rockford College, as well as labor activists like Florence Kelley.

By the end of 1916, NWP suffragists, led by Paul and Burns and their advisory council, had tried a variety of aggressive and hazardous techniques to achieve a federal amendment. They had staged a parade involving 5,000 participants on the day before Wilson's inaugural parade in Washington in 1913, in which they "politely but firmly asserted their entitlement to use the political space of Washington as they saw fit" (Barber 45). In the next three years, they lobbied state and federal legislators assiduously while also meeting with Woodrow Wilson within the White House and without. They held parades in Washington and around the country, mounted tableaux near the White House, traveled cross-country by car and train in publicity campaigns, staffed a booth at the 1915 World's Fair, and planned a stirring memorial service in the Statuary Hall of the Capitol on Christmas Day 1916 for their compatriot Inez Milholland who collapsed while speaking for suffrage and died that fall. In 1912 and 1916, they boycotted the Democratic Party and Wilson himself. In all of these efforts they sought to influence other women, men, the media, legislators, and ultimately the president himself. As Lousine Havemeyer noted, dealing with the entire population was not more difficult than dealing with this one man: "The President dominated in Washington; he had a Democratic Congress supinely yielding to his will. We were opposed by a President who felt himself absolute, and to whom the thought of mobilized

Rose Winslow was born Ruza Wenclawska, daughter of a Polish miner and steelworker from Pennsylvania. She helped lead the hunger strikers when they were imprisoned and smuggled out a note that said, in part, about forced feeding: "Yesterday was a bad day for me in feeding. I was vomiting continuously during the process. The tube had developed an irritation somewhere that is painful.... Don't let them tell you we take this well." Photograph dated ca. 1916, published in *The Suffragist*, 4, no. 42 (October 14, 1916): 5. Photograph from National Woman's Party Records. Source: Library of Congress Manuscript Division.

Left: **Many African American women joined NWP's demonstrations. Nell Mercer, for example, who became a small hardware-store owner in Norfolk after moving there from Buell, Virginia, joined her state's NWP and the picket lines in 1919. She was arrested for taking part in one of the Watchfire demonstrations. Photograph dated ca. 1910, from National Woman's Party Records. Source: Library of Congress Manuscript Division.** ***Right:*** **Mary Church Terrell's parents were former slaves. She graduated from Oberlin College in 1884 and became the first president of the National Association of Colored Women. Later she was involved in founding of the NAACP and in picketing for suffrage. Photographer Addison N. Scurlock. Dated "between 1920 and 1930," photograph is from Visual Materials from the National Association for the Advancement of Colored People Records. Source: Library of Congress Prints and Photographs Division.**

woman-power was as a red rag to an infuriated bull. His education and commitment to suffrage was a long and difficult task" ("The Prison Special" 662).

At the beginning of 1917, the NWP still had not secured a federal amendment, and no technique these activists had tried before seemed likely to alter that impasse. The organization's leaders felt that they needed to instigate a new technique that might engage the populace and secure results: something dramatic, something that would prove that these women would not go away, that they had the physical and emotional strength to persevere. Paul later recalled the logic of that January as based on this question: "We had had speeches, meetings, parades, campaigns, what new method could we devise?" (Younger, "Revelations" Oct., 12).

At a large meeting, of the advisory council and members, what the

On January 10, 1917, the first picket line left NWP headquarters to march to the White House. L to R, Berta Crone, Vivian Pierce, Mildred Gilbert, Maude Jamieson, Joy Young, Mary Dowell, Gertrude Crocker, Bessie Papandre, Elizabeth Geary, Frances Pepper, Elizabeth Smith, and Pauline Floyd. Photograph from National Woman's Party Records. Source: Library of Congress Manuscript Division.

group decided upon was a dangerous and daring new form of visual rhetoric—using women's bodies day after day to literally stand up to the president and for the cause. They decided to picket the White House, the first time a citizen group had done so. As Maud Younger wrote, these women thus decided to begin "visualizing to the world the long waiting of women for justice" ("Revelations" Oct., 12). Because of its possible strong effect, NWP members believed, this picketing would result in "the saving of many years of women's energy, when it is so greatly needed" (Stevens, *Jailed for Freedom* 89).

On January 10, 1917, the first "silent sentinels," twelve women in white dresses, left the NWP headquarters on Lafayette Square at ten in the morning and walked to the east and west entrances of the White House, six for each entrance standing three on each side, "demure and unsmiling and silent," as the NWP magazine, the *Suffragist*, described the scene ("Suffragists Wait"). With different shifts coming out, women stood silently from 10:00 to 5:30, holding banners in their suffrage colors of purple, white, and gold. They did not speak unless they answered a question; then they replied quickly and returned to their silent standing. This first day's group included suffragists from California, Illinois, Pennsylvania, Virginia, and Arkansas as well as the District of Columbia ("President Ignores").

From the first day, pickets held banners as large as four feet by six feet, decorated in suffrage colors, with long sashes and fringes adorning them. The first banners read "Mr. President, what will you do for woman suffrage?" and "Mr. President, how long must women wait for liberty?" questions from Inez Milholland's last speech. In the next few days, pickets also began carrying banners with well-known sayings from Susan B. Anthony, including "The right of self-government for half of its people is of far more vital consequence to the nation than any or all other questions" as well as "Resistance to tyranny is obedience to God."

After Wilson asked the Congress to declare war on April 2, the NWP had a difficult decision to make about picketing. NAWSA began devoting itself to the war effort even though many of its leaders and members opposed it. Both Carrie Chapman Catt and Anna Howard Shaw, neither of them war supporters, accepted appointments on the Women's Committee of the Council on National Defense and abandoned direct suffrage advocacy. In England, even the Pankhursts suspended their activism and turned their attention to war work. But the NWP decided to continue seeking suffrage by picketing during war (Resolution Passed). In circular letters through which members tried to maintain allegiance after this controversial choice, they spoke in patriotic terms: "we must stand now for the establishment of a true democracy in this land" and "we are showing our highest patriotism." On April 21, an article in the *Suffragist* entitled "Mutual Responsibility" reminded readers that this country, which expected so much of women during wartime and needed the full participation of every American, was not willing to treat them as citizens and thus they had to fight for change. On June 9, 1917, in "The Indomitable Picket Line," Lucy Burns wrote that lowering the banners, especially during wartime, would be an abandonment of women's claim to liberty.

As pickets continued to march to the White House each day, the war brought up an unprecedented rhetorical opportunity—to point out the contradiction between Wilson's advocacy of democracy worldwide and his failure to support it at home, a controversial choice requiring great bravery to carry out. To emphasize the president's shocking contradictions, pickets began presenting excerpts from his speeches on their banners. From his war message on April 2, favored choices were the short "make the world safe for democracy" as well as the long "we shall fight for the things which we have always held nearest to our hearts—for democracy, for the right of those who submit to authority to have a voice in their own governments." Even years later, Paul believed that these quoted phrases had been an especially powerful choice: "It was really a big turning point. That's when the militancy really began. This going out and standing there with our beautiful banners wasn't anything very militant. But this [using Wilson's own lines] really was, I would say, the beginning of the militancy" (Fry, Conversations).

Banners featuring his war rhetoric challenged Wilson through the spring, and then the NWP sought and achieved an increased level of aggression and publicity, with a "To the Russian Envoys" banner. On June 20, 1917, as representatives of the new Kerensky government of Russia drove up to the White House, Lucy Burns and Dora Lewis held out a large banner, with the following text: "To the Russian Envoys: We the women of America tell you that America is not a democracy. Twenty million American women are denied the right to vote. President Wilson is the chief opponent of their national enfranchisement. Help us make this nation really free. Tell our government it must liberate its people before it can claim free Russia as an ally" (Stevens, *Jailed for Freedom* 74). Edith Bolling Wilson wrote in her autobiography about this action that seemed to her so disrespectful to her husband and especially about the violent response of the crowd: "I was indignant, but apparently no less so than a crowd of onlookers who tore the pickets' banner down" (138).

This event had a great potential for criticism and controversy, as the NWP well knew. Beginning in March of that year, after the abdication of Tsar Nicholas II, Alexander Kerensky had risen through the positions of minister of justice and minister of war to provisional prime minister. His assumption of power at home and his friendship with the United States mattered a great deal to Wilson, for Kerensky intended to continue Russian involvement in the war and to subdue Bolshevik leaders who were encouraging soldiers to withdraw from battle. For pickets to be standing outside the White House carrying a sign arguing that Russian diplomats could not trust Wilson—and that Wilson did not even have the support of his own citizens—generally appeared as incendiary, even traitorous, an affront to the war effort and to plans for worldwide postwar democracy.

Such highly public opposition to the president, especially during wartime, became a daily target of the media. Many articles hyperbolically allied the suffragists with socialism and with Germany. The *New York World* noted, "The militant suffragists are exercising no right whatever unless it is the right to make fools of themselves. No less offensive than the I.W.W., the professional pacifists and the pro–German propagandists, they are serving the Kaiser to the best of their ability and calling it a campaign for equal suffrage" (Comments of the Press). In a letter sent to the editor of the *Chattanooga Times* and other papers, Ida Harper of NAWSA, perhaps exaggerating somewhat, estimated that over seven hundred editors had taken a similarly critical stance (Letter to the Editor).

After the Kerensky banner appeared at the White House gates and the negative press response escalated, women began to be arrested for the picketing that had been going on since January. On June 21, a District of Columbia police captain called on Alice Paul and ordered her to stop the picketing. But Paul refused and the group went out as usual on June 22. Lucy Burns and Katharine Morey were then arrested for obstructing traffic, a charge that Paul found ironic because the NWP did plan, through the picketing and the suffrage that would result from it, to obstruct the patterns of Washington's political traffic.

In the next few days, the pickets continued to challenge the district police. On June 23, the police warned the NWP that pickets would again be arrested if they went to their regular posts. On that day, four were arrested. On Sunday, June 24, the police captain again telephoned headquarters to say that the group could no longer hold banners of any kind before the White House. And Paul said to him in reply: "Well, I think that we feel that we ought to continue and I feel that we will continue" (Fry, Conversation). On June 25, twelve women were arrested as they carried banners with quotations from the president and from Susan B. Anthony as well as suffrage flags from those states where women had the vote. Twelve were arrested and ordered to appear for trial when summoned.

Because these women were now picketing in violation of a governmental order, the police offered them no protection from the large crowds assembling in the wake of the Russian banner, and the physical risks escalated. On June 26, when Lucy Burns and Alice Paul carried the banner declaring "Democracy should begin at home" by the lower White House gate, a few boys destroyed it, with the police "looking placidly on." A great crowd began to surge up and down the street while Burns and Paul "stood motionless." Later that day, another mob charged upon other pickets and tore their banners to shreds while the women remained silent and still. Nine pickets were arrested but no members of the crowd were charged.

In this contest of wills, from which the NWP refused to withdraw, the government next took the unprecedented step of imprisoning pickets. During the trial of six of those nine who had been arrested on June 26, the pickets attested that they had refused to desist when told to do so because picketing was legal under the Constitution. The court was violating basic rights of citizens, these pickets claimed, when it convicted these women not for picketing, which wasn't illegal, but for "obstructing the highways." These women refused to pay the twenty-five dollar fines and were the first to be incarcerated, for a period of three days. Charges on the preceding days had all been dismissed ("Prison—and the Reaction").

As courts issued sentences for picketing on subsequent days, the NWP began orchestrating visual scenes that caused larger crowds to gather, greater numbers of women to be arrested, and longer sentences to be meted out. On July 14, Bastille Day, sixteen suffrage leaders picketed, including many women of high social status: Betsy Graves Reyneau, painter and granddaughter of a chief justice of the Michigan Supreme Court; Alison Turnbull Hopkins, wife of J.A.H. Hopkins, an influential member of the Democratic National Campaign Committee of 1916 and a close associate of Wilson; Florence Bayard Hilles, daughter of a former ambassador to Britain and secretary of state; and Eunice Dana Brannan, daughter of journalist Charles Dana and wife of the president of the board of trustees of New York's Bellevue Hospital ("Protest for Liberty Answered"). On that day, the banners included "Liberty, Equality, Fraternity, July 14, 1789" and "Mr. President, how long must American women wait for liberty?"—another combination of a historical plea for freedom with their own. As these pickets went out to celebrate the tradition of democracy, police arrested them for unlawful assembly and for obstructing traffic. On July 17, the government went further than before by meting out sentences of sixty days. When the judge decided that a twenty-five dollar fine would suffice instead, these protestors opted for prison.

As NWP leaders had done before, they soon decided on a further increase of the danger and controversy. On August 10, they unfurled a new banner: "Kaiser Wilson, have you forgotten your sympathy with the poor Germans because they were not self-governing? 20 million American women are not self-governing/Take the beam out of your own eye" ("Kaiser Wilson"). Two other banners more specifically compared Wilson to the German dictator: "He rules over them (Am. women) by sheer autocratic power — the very type of power he denounces in Austria and Germany" and "A President is a duly elected representative. For 20,000,000 American women Wilson Is NOT a President. A Kaiser is an autocratic ruler. For 20,000,000 American women Wilson is a Kaiser" (Faber 163). Of course with the nation at war against Germany, and Kaiser Wilhelm constructed in the national press as an evil villain, many critics viewed this banner not as an intellectual plea for equality but as a vicious attack on the president, one tantamount to treason.

On August 10 through August 16, as pickets walked out with Kaiser banners, the police offered them no protection against mounting violence and even gunshots. On August 10, when Wilson was driving by, three sailors, part of a "mob" of 5000, sprang onto Lucy Burns and dragged her to the curb. On each subsequent day, the pickets stood together silently as they faced repeated "attacks of excited boys and United States sailors" ("Kaiser Wilson"). Then, on August 14, after the women returned to headquarters with torn banners and placed them on the second and third floor balconies, three sailors brought a ladder and tore down the "Kaiser Wilson" banner and an American flag, and a bullet was fired through a second-floor window, all without any police response ("President Onlooker"). On August 17, police major Raymond Pullman told NWP leaders that pickets would again be arrested because Wilson had lost patience with their new offensive banners. Pullman hoped that the threat would keep pickets away, but they returned to their posts. On that day, police arrested six women, who were sentenced to thirty days at Occoquan Workhouse in rural Virginia. Their assailants, like attackers from previous days, faced no charges ("The Administration Versus the Woman's Party" 7).

Even after the NWP retired the Kaiser banner, arrests continued, and suddenly the government chose to impose increasingly harsh sentences. On September 4, in punishment for banners that reminded the president that women's sons were fighting the war—"Mr. President, how long must women be denied a voice in the government that is conscripting their sons?"—thirteen women were arrested and sent to Occoquan Workhouse for sixty days (Irwin, *The Story of* 245). For picketing on September 22, four women received thirty-day sentences. On October 6, the day that Congress adjourned, Paul was arrested along with ten other women who protested the legislature's continuing inaction on suffrage. Their sentences were suspended. On October 15, four of the women under suspended sentences, including Rose Winslow, went out again and for this repeated offense got a sentence of six months in the Workhouse. On October 20, Paul went out with three others carrying a banner quoting words Wilson had recently used on posters for the Second Liberty Bond Loan, words that applied to their campaign as well as to the war: "The time has come when we must conquer or submit. For us there can be but one choice. We have made it" (Irwin, *The Story of* 255). Paul was sentenced to seven months in jail.

As women kept returning to the picket line, they entered prisons in large numbers. In October, for example, there were seventy women in two jails, some for just a few days on their first sentences, others for thirty or sixty days, and six for seven months. In total that fall, 168 women served jail sentences and at least 500 were arrested, not for picketing but for violations like "obstructing sidewalk traffic."

As difficult prisoners refusing to go home, they often faced harsh, retributive treatment, in parts of jails not in regular use. Matilda Hall Gardner talked with her attorney and later provided the *Suffragist* with details from Occoquan Workhouse in rural Virginia, about having her clothing removed, being sent into showers with open doors, eating wormy food, living in enforced silence, and working long hours each day. A complaint filed by Lucy Burns in September also concerned harsh conditions: "The water they drink is kept in an open pail, from which it is ladled into a drinking cup. The prisoners frequently dip the drinking cup directly into the pail. The same piece of soap is used for every prisoner" (Irwin *The Story of* 276). Similar horrid details came from prisoners at the District of Columbia Jail, a second site used so that large numbers of suffragists would not be able to congregate and act in concert. In press bulletins, Sarah Colvin described specifics about the District Jail that she also recalled in her 1940 autobiography: "It was full of rats. I minded them more than anything else. I can still hear them squealing and fighting, and the sound they made as they fell from the table to the floor and scurried away" (137).

The NWP expected more of these women than just to forego bail and endure such difficult prison conditions. Pickets asked, when they entered courts and then jails, for political prisoner status, for recognition that they were being jailed because they had opposed the government and not because they had interfered with sidewalks or streets. Through this choice, the NWP wanted to make clear that women were being denied the basic rights of citizenry, including freedom of speech. When this status was disallowed, and indeed it had to be because the United States does not recognize that category of prisoner, the jailed suffragists refused to accept work details and to wear prison clothing. They also went on hunger strikes and endured the forced feeding that occurred as a result. Affecting details reported by Rose Winslow at the District Jail and smuggled out by friends and sympathetic prison employees depicted this harsh reality: "Yesterday was a bad day for me in feeding. I was vomiting continuously during the process. The tube had developed an irritation somewhere that is painful.... Don't let them tell you we take this well. Miss Paul vomits much. I do too. It's the nervous reaction, and I can't control it much. We think of the coming feeding all day. It is horrible" (Stevens, *Jailed for Freedom* 118–19).

A next ordeal concerned the psychopathic wards that women knew could extend their term of imprisonment indefinitely; in the District of Columbia, as in many states, women could be placed in these facilities indefinitely with the agreement of a physician and a family member — or of two physicians when family members were not present, as they would not be when a woman was incarcerated. Prison officials threatened that if Alice Paul did not end her hunger strike at the District Jail she would be transferred to the prison system's psychopathic ward in St. Elizabeth's Insane Asylum, a state institution for the insane. When she refused, she was taken to a cell in the prison's psychopathic ward and there placed in solitary confinement and treated like a mental patient. The specific details of this treatment, which she reported as soon as she could, frightened her comrades: "There were two windows in the room. Dr. Gannon immediately ordered one window nailed from top to bottom. He then ordered the door leading into the hallway taken down and an iron-barred cell door put in its place. He departed with the command to a nurse to 'observe her.'" Each hour, even during the night, a nurse flashed a light in her face: "This ordeal was the most terrible torture, as it prevented my sleeping for more than a few minutes at a time" (Stevens, *Jailed for Freedom* 117). Doctors then came to tell her that she was not in a stable mental condition and needed thorough examination, and when she continued her hunger striking she was force-fed three times a day—a further display of administrative force. Although Dr. White, the head of St. Elizabeth's Insane Asylum, would not consent to having her transferred to his hospital after the prison doctor provided the first signature, prison doctors treated her as an unstable mental patient where she was.

At Occoquan, suffragists had to fight against the same threat of psychopathic wards used against Paul in the District Jail. When Ernestine Hara Kettler went to visit Peggy Johns at the Occuquan Hospital, where she had been sent because the poor food had made her ill, Kettler found Johns in civilian clothes, made ready for transfer to a psychopathic facility in Washington, D.C. Immediately Kettler gathered women walking in the yard, and they forced their way into the superintendent's office, claiming that Johns could not be sent to a mental ward unless she was accompanied by her lawyer, because without such guardianship "we had no assurance what would happen to her." Superintendent Raymond Whittaker, Kettler claimed, tore the phone out of the wall to keep them from dialing their headquarters, and then he called in other prisoners and they "beat the hell out of us. I was so little that I was scared to death to get in the crowd and I was on the outside. I saw some women on the floor, being trampled" (259). Although Johns did go to a hospital in Washington because of her weakened condition, this altercation kept her from a psychopathic ward.

As Kettler noted of this altercation, women faced violence in jail along with poor conditions, separation from each other, and the threat of long-term psychiatric placements. When pickets entered Occoquan Workhouse, one well-publicized incident of horrendous treatment occurred on November 15, 1917: the women later called it the "Night of Terror." Under orders from Raymond Whittaker, the superintendent, as many as forty guards with clubs brutalized the jailed suffragists. According to many affidavits, women were grabbed, dragged, beaten, kicked, and choked. In the *Suffragist* and in press bulletins, Mary Nolan of Jacksonville, Florida, a seventy-three-year-old woman crippled by a lame foot, as well as other women, created powerful accounts of that night, of cruel, uncontrolled men beating and terrorizing women.

When the women entered the workhouse, as Nolan reported, they asked to be treated as political prisoners and to see the warden. After keeping them waiting for hours, Superintendent Whittaker "burst in like a tornado," followed by a crowd of men, many not in uniform. When the women rose to address him, Whittaker said, "You shut up. I have men here to handle you." Men grabbed Nolan and dragged her through the corridors; she could hear women crying out as they suffered similar treatment, incurring injuries as they were dragged to dark and filthy cells. Nolan wrote that as guards carried Dorothy Day, "a frail girl," they twisted her arms above her head and twice banged her arm down on an iron bench (7).

In accounts that appeared in the *Suffragist*, newspapers, and circular letters, as well as autobiographies, other participants added their own details to this horrifying story. Dorothy Day, then a writer for the *Call* and the *Masses* who had come down to Washington to join the picket line at the urging of a friend, recounted her own path to the cells: "I have no doubt but that I struggled every step of the way from the administration building to the cell block where we were being taken. It was a struggle to walk by myself, to wrest myself loose from the torture of those rough hands. We were then hurled onto some benches and when I tried to pick myself up and again join Peggy [Baird] in my blind desire to be near a friend, I was thrown to the floor. When another prisoner tried to come to my rescue, we found ourselves in the midst of a milling crowd of guards being pummeled and pushed and kicked and dragged, so that we were scarcely conscious, in the shock of what was taking place" (*The Long Loneliness* 76). As they could, weakened from their Night of Terror, some of these women began a hunger strike to protest their treatment as well as Paul's placement in a psychopathic ward. During the rest of their sentence, they tried to help each other since no physicians came to see them.

For those women who came to Washington to picket in the summer and fall of 1917, entering the picket line was certainly a very difficult choice. In her autobiography, Sarah Colvin discussed her husband's negative reaction to her being jailed. An army officer at Ft. McHenry, he opposed her plans to picket and accept a jail term because these public actions could be embarrassing for him and become a career liability. Given his oft-expressed contempt for pickets and their jail terms, she did not tell him of her intentions before she left to join the picket line one morning. They did discuss her choices, in their own way, when she returned home from jail: "The morning I was released I went back to Baltimore, and Dr. Colvin and I had a very full and frank discussion of the whole situation. After the first shock of his learning that I could possibly consider anything of more importance than his career, which had caused him really great distress, and further that, according to his estimation, I had misused the word 'principle,' we did as we have always done, finished the subject and never discussed it since. It has made no difference in our lives" (142).

Many women found their participation shocked their families and made them suspect members of their communities; the reactions that they experienced went beyond those of Dr. Colvin. Louisine Havemeyer told fellow suffragists, and later said in her speeches, that telegrams from her family expressed their extreme shock and distaste when she marched and entered jail: "From them I gleaned I had stripped the family tree, I had broken its branches, I had torn up its roots and laid it prostrate in the sorrowing dust. What had the whole treeful of innocents ever done that I should treat them thus?" ("The Prison Special" 672). Dollee Chevrier, whose Franco–Catholic family in Manitoba opposed woman suffrage, objected to her participation in the picketing; both her parents and her fiancé thought it might be better if she didn't return home after local papers reported that she had entered a Washington jail (Payment).

Since longer sentences resulted from repeated picketing, many busy wives and workers picketed once and accepted short sentences, but then did not return to the line: they had other commitments, they faced negative judgments, and they also knew what terror might await them. Ernestine Hara Kettler told an interviewer that when she left jail she stayed in Washington for a week or two: "I was even tempted to go back again on the picket line, but I just couldn't stand the thought of going back to that workhouse again. After thirty days of that dreadful food and the fear of what might happen to the next contingent that was arrested, I just wasn't courageous enough to go back again. I felt horrified by the different things that could happen to you in prison" (261–62). Although Paul encouraged women to feel strong and involved, and she worked at getting them to Washington, she knew that each one had to make her own decision about appearing on the line and returning to it.

When the Senate failed to vote for suffrage in January 1918, after a year of picketing and a fall of jail terms, NWP members felt shocked that their sacrifice had not been enough. They were then moved to more drastic actions in response to their government's denial of their rights.

The NWP chose a monument of warfare and freedom, the statue in Lafayette Square of Marquis de Lafayette, the fierce French warrior for liberty during the Revolutionary War, as a site for large protest meetings. On August 6, 1918, one hundred women gathered at the statue bearing the Milholland banner as well as others condemning Wilson and the Democrats as hypocrites and liars, enemies of democracy: "We deplore the weakness of President Wilson in permitting the Senate to line itself with the Prussian Reichstag by denying democracy to the people" (NWP Press Release). One by one, women came up to speak against Wilson and the Senate, and one by one they were taken away. In all, the police arrested forty-eight women, "acting under the orders of Colonel Ridley, President Wilson's chief military aide," as the NWP wanted clearly pointed out. The charge was "congregating in the park" ("Suffragists Again Attack President"). As their well-known leader, Paul was arrested as she stood "perfectly still" in the street ("Women's Protest").

To make it clear that their protest would continue regardless of the consequences, women boldly went out to the monument again. On August 12, police arrested thirty-eight suffragists there and took them to police headquarters where officers attacked them fiercely: "When released the women appeared with tears streaming down their faces, bruised throats, swollen, twisted wrists, and sprained fingers." On August 14, speeches at the monument connected these police actions to the Senate's disrespect for women and for democracy. Elsie Hill's speech involved a comparison that NWP speakers frequently reiterated, that the Senate resembled the German Reichstag: "On the days our boys in khaki won their first brilliant battle in France, we, their women at home, were forced to see a few made-in-Germany Senators viciously defeat the cause of human liberty here" ("The Later Demonstrations"). On that day, while Hill was speaking, thirty women were arrested on the charge of "holding a meeting without a permit."

At this point, the courts no longer chose to give out sentences of several months; these twenty-four women received sentences of ten to fifteen days. This time, officials decided to isolate the women so they would not get information to the press. They were "sick, cold, shut off from the world" for five days in a District prison abandoned in 1909, in underground cells that had been declared too unsanitary for ordinary criminals. Since these women had made contacts with sympathetic wardens at both Occoquan Workhouse and the District Jail, court officials chose a solitary, and more frightening, place to lodge them this time. In this locale, the women were denied mail; they could visit with lawyers but not with friends; they had to endure the foul odors of this abandoned structure. As soon as they entered this facility, they initiated a hunger strike to secure their rights as political prisoners ("In Prison"). With their supporters protesting, these women were released after five days ("Women's Protest").

On September 16, the NWP initiated a new level of aggression in Lafayette Square. Suffragists burned copies of Wilson's "war for democracy" speeches in urns, and they dubbed the fires "Watchfires for Freedom." Lucy Branham, a Columbia Ph.D. who had hunger struck in the District Jail, first stepped up to burn Wilson's words — to "symbolize the burning indignation of women." He gives "words, and words, and words," she claimed, words that did not indicate real support for suffrage, words that he never backed up with real action ("President's Words Burned" 7). On that day, several suffragists gave speeches to reinforce the message of the burning quotations.

Next NWP members sought a new type of daily reminder of the lack of justice for women, and thus they decided to use urns not just for burning Wilson's words but also for maintaining a perpetually lit "watchfire." Many years later, Paul described this rhetorical act to an interviewer:

> We had a sort of perpetual flame going in an urn outside our headquarters in Lafayette Square. I think we used rags soaked in kerosene. It was really very dramatic, because when President Wilson went to Paris for the peace conference, he was always issuing some wonderful, idealistic statement that was impossible to reconcile with what he was doing at home. And we had an enormous bell — I don't recall how we ever got such an enormous bell — and every time Wilson would make one of these speeches, we would toll this great bell, and then somebody would go outside with the President's speech and, with great dignity, burn it in our little caldron [Gallagher 93].

These women endeavored to keep a continual fire, first near Lafayette's statue and then in front of the White House, as a signal that they still had to war against a repressive government, still had to fight for even the basic rights of citizenship, standing witness for democracy. With this fire and with this name of watchfire for it, Paul was associating her suffragists with heroic soldiers at war. During the American Revolution, towns along the coast had frequently used fires to signal the position of British ships or British troops; towns along the Western frontier had also used them to protect themselves from Indian attack. The term watchfire thus implied the actions of a group not moving offensively, but staying alert to observe the opposition's movements and its treacheries.

This new level of opposition began as a New Year's Day event to signal the beginning of another year in which women could not vote. As the *Suffragist* and press bulletins reported, women marched to the White House and then to the Lafayette Monument. In an urn that they placed near the statue and dedicated to Lafayette and to liberty, they built a watchfire. It rained, but they kept the fire going. Then, in the night, to increase the danger of the event, Rose Conlan went to an ornamental urn, a large and permanent fixture on a pedestal near the White House, and lit a second watchfire, angering the police, who immediately claimed this urn was too near to the president. Police immediately arrested Conlan and tossed out her fire. But as they took her away, Alice Paul increased the blaze with fresh wood. When she refused to desist, police arrested her. Then two more women went up to relight this fire as they also kept a blaze going in the urn by the Lafayette Monument (Morris).

With publicity increasing, NWP members kept the fires going for four days, with succeeding relays of women on duty ("The Watchfire"). Participants came from across the United States as they read publicity about the effort; college suffrage groups, like one from the University of Minnesota with whom student Rhoda Kellogg came to Washington, helped to forward the effort. Soldiers and sailors frequently overturned the urn near the White House and stamped on the ashes, but as soon as they took action another fire would blaze up from the urn by the monument. At least one was kept continually burning even though women were arrested — on the charge of lighting bonfires between sunset and sunrise (Morris). On the third day, police began using chemicals to put the fires out, but the women relit them. Then on Sunday, January 5, suffragists brought out asbestos coils to start fires more quickly. That day, four women received five- to ten-day sentences for trying to start a fire in the White House urn; in the District Jail, they again insisted on their rights as political prisoners and began to hunger strike ("Guilty of—?"; "Impressions").

In February of 1919, the amendment again going down to defeat in Congress, the NWP instigated a more radical and threatening act: burning Wilson in effigy, using a cardboard likeness. Paul wrote about this choice to Louisine Havemeyer: "We have to do something drastic, or they — the administration, who are beginning to feel uneasy under criticism of their treatment of American women — won't fight us." Effigies had commonly been used to demonstrate disapproval for leaders and their policies, especially during wartime, another NWP reference to the American Revolution. In 1765, the newly formed Sons of Liberty burned Boston's stamp agent in effigy, destroying his office to get wood for the fire, an event that led to instant recruitment of members and fame throughout the colonies. This form of protest, against stamp agents and other British officials, soon spread to other towns. After the war, Independence Day celebrations often featured a likeness of George III that was paraded through a town and then burned in a central square. Although burning an enemy in effigy was an accepted and even lauded part of American history, the NWP's choice of this protest technique, employed right in front of the White House, seemed traitorous to many.

On the afternoon of February 9, 1919, the eve of the last senatorial vote on suffrage in the Sixty-Fifth Congress, a column of thirty-six suffragists, led by Havemeyer, left the NWP headquarters and marched to the White House, where they burned their effigy of Wilson. The statement that Sue Shelton White read to begin the proceedings once again depicted the president as a tyrant: "We burn not the effigy of the President of a free people, but the leader of an autocratic party organization whose tyrannical power holds millions of women in political slavery" ("Suffragists Burn Wilson"). The suffragists told the crowd that quickly gathered that they had to deal with Wilson in effigy form because he had left for Europe in December in the falsely assumed role of international savior of democracy. In front of the White House, women put the "little figure," about two feet tall, into an urn, and then the crowd erupted. Louisine Havemeyer's depiction of the moment included the harsh police response: "They grabbed at the women and dragged their resisting leaders across Pennsylvania Avenue to the curb" ("The Prison Special" 665).

That day, Lucy Burns, Helena Hill Weed, Sarah Colvin, and Louise Bryant, and thirty-five other participants were arrested. As the NWP requested, Louisine Havemeyer had kept throwing bundles toward the urn to assure her own incarceration and the negative press that would result from it ("The Demonstration of February 9 '10). When the women appeared in court, they were given the choice of five days in jail or a five-dollar fine, and they refused to pay. They were then taken to the abandoned jail where women had been incarcerated the previous August.

That February, the NWP looked for additional rhetorical actions that would focus on women's betrayal and their need for continued forms of radical action: "The great club of publicity was in our hands and we were only waiting for an opportunity to brandish it" ("The Prison Special" Feb. 1). To shape that publicity, the membership decided on a national campaign by a reserved train, dubbed the Prison Special. The prison wrappers, shapeless calico dresses with washrags pinned at the belt, and the oversized brogans that women had to wear at Occoquan Workhouse served as their uniforms. Their itinerary at stops across the country followed a general plan: Havemeyer spoke first, on party methods and on the dramatic arrests; Elizabeth Rogers followed with a history of woman's suffrage; Vida Milholland sang the "Women's Marseillaise," a protest song from the British suffrage movement; Mary Winsor told of the terrible conditions in jail; Josephine Bennett spoke on the status of the amendment; and Mabel Vernon asked for contributions. The train's slogan was "From Prison to People," and its appearances were quite successful ("The Prison Special" Feb. 22).

In Boston, Prison Special travelers participated in a meeting with the sixteen women who had been jailed for a public protest there. When Wilson had returned from Europe, landing in Boston on February 24, Presidents' Day, women unfurled banners for suffrage; at that point they had been arrested for speaking on Boston Common without a permit and given ten days in jail; some of their associates were charged with loitering in the picketing area for more than seven minutes ("Reminding the President"). At a March 9 meeting, the Prison Special travelers gave these women prison pins, small brooches with bars to represent the front of the prison cell, a symbol of dedication given in Washington to the women jailed there. Then the combined group of prisoners marched in a well-advertised parade, between lines of Marines that tried to hold the crowds back. Twenty-one women were quickly arrested for loitering and most were sentenced to eight days in the Charles Street jail.

After all of this sacrifice, over so many years, involving picketing and jail terms as well as hunger striking and terror, the effort finally paid off. The Sixty-Sixth Congress convened on May 19, 1919, with the president at the Peace Conference in Versailles. The NWP worked on getting pro-suffrage Democrats and the president to influence those senators who still opposed the amendment. On the night of May 20, Wilson cabled a message of support for the amendment to the new Congress, and he even praised "women and men who saw the need for it and urged the policy of it when it required steadfast courage to be so much beforehand with the common conviction" (Irwin, *The Story of* 428). On May 21, 1919, the new House passed the suffrage amendment by 304 votes to eighty-nine, forty-two more than the required two-thirds. On June 4, 1919, with little debate, the Senate passed the amendment by a vote of 56 to 25. Immediately after the Senate vote, the NWP and NAWSA began working on securing the necessary ratification by thirty-six of the forty-eight states. By March 1920, thirty-five states had ratified, and only one more was needed. The motion failed in Delaware in May. In a packed Nashville, housing anti-suffrage as well as suffrage forces, suffrage was ratified on August 18.

In a three-year period, these women had stood up to the American government in ever more radical ways after they began to see that regular meetings and parades were having little effect: they instituted picketing, even in wartime, burned the president in effigy, served lengthening jail sentences, demanded political prisoner status, hunger struck in jail, fought against placements in psychopathic wards, suffered punishments inflicted by police and prison wardens, and endured the negative response of family, friends, employers, and the press.

These women who gave so much of themselves to see this fight to the end were a generation removed from Stanton and Anthony, and most even from Catt and Shaw, the iconic figures of suffrage. What this younger and lesser known group saw, what they suffered, awakened them to a type of injustices that they would have just read about otherwise — they saw what could happen to people deemed as Other, even within a democracy. As Elizabeth Stuyvesant, who was struck by a soldier, arrested, and sentenced to three days in jail for picketing on July 4, 1917, wrote of her fellow suffrage prisoners, "There was not one of us who did not come out of that experience with less awe of policeman, judge, and established ideas and with a clearer understanding of the true nature of authority" (97). That through the suffrage campaign these women recognized societal realities and took risks to change them ultimately would have a tremendous impact on their lives and on their country, not just in the narrowly political realm of elections but in a larger political realm, involving the expansion of respect and opportunity in art, education, writing, and law.

2

Suffragists as Collectors and Artists: Affecting a Cultural Future

After participating in this movement, in which they faced the realities of picketing, jail, hunger striking, and violence, many women acknowledged that they were changed, that they left the suffrage campaign ready for paths of activism that stemmed from self-respect and the power of the group. Suffrage had given them firsthand knowledge of what could happen to those that a society judged as disruptive or unimportant, and it had emboldened them to envision and seek systemic change.

Some of these women thought of art, and not of traditional politics, as the key element of an independent and full life, one free from older restrictions, and they felt able to explore the transformative possibilities that art could have not just for themselves but for Americans. Three of these women, who left picketing and jail inalterably changed, were Louisine Havemeyer, Rhoda Kellogg, and Betsy Reyneau, women who would enlarge the most basic of American artistic definitions.

Louisine Havemeyer (1855–1929)

Before entering the suffrage movement, Louisine Waldron Elder Havemeyer had a full life in art collecting, the works shown in her home to members of her select circle, an involvement and direction that ended when her husband died in 1907. It was suffrage, and especially the jail experience, that made her into an American social activist and donor, bringing to the nation access to a new generation of art. She certainly did not seek public office after the suffrage campaign: she sought an influence involving an entirely different sphere — modern art.

Havemeyer was born in New York to wealthy merchant George W. Elder and his wife, Mathilda Adelaide Waldron. Shortly after her father's death, when she was eighteen, her mother took Havemeyer and her sister on a tour of Europe. While attending a boarding school in Paris, Havemeyer met American artist Mary Cassatt who engaged her in learning about new art trends. She met Edgar Degas through Cassatt and bought one of his pastels; she also quickly bought her first Pissarro and Monet. A lifelong friendship developed between Havemeyer and Cassatt, who later made several pastels of Havemeyer and her children and continued to serve as her artistic advisor.

From the beginning of her many years as a collector, Havemeyer considered emerging art movements and price in making decisions, but she was also drawn by the sheer power of great art, regardless of artistic prestige or fads. Of an 1873 Manet painting, *Gare Saint-Lazare* or *The Railway*, of a girl outside the St. Lazare train station, combining rails and steam with a starkly portrayed child and mother, she responded to a question about why she bought it: "I answer art, art, art. It is there appealing to you, as it appealed to us. You must feel it. You must hear the voice calling to you, you must respond to the vibrations Manet felt, which made his heart throb and filled his brain, which stirred his emotions and sharpened his vision as he put his brush upon the canvas" (*Sixteen to Sixty* 239). When Manet first exhibited the painting at the official Paris Salon of 1874, as art critic Isabelle Dervaux wrote, "Visitors and critics found its subject baffling, its composition incoherent, and its execution sketchy.... Only a few recognized the symbol of modernity that it has become today" (1). Among those few, and the collector bringing the painting to the United States, was Louisine Havemeyer.

Together with her husband, Harry Havemeyer, owner of the American Sugar Refining Company whom she married in 1883 and with whom she shared this pursuit, Louisine built, through a personal connection to "art, art, art," perhaps the finest private art collection in America. Harry particularly liked Chinese porcelain and Japanese tea bowls, which he had begun acquiring before their marriage. Over time the couple filled their three-story mansion on Fifth Avenue with these purchases as well as paintings by Rembrandt, Goya, El Greco, Manet, Corot, Courbet, Degas, and others, artists then little known in the United States.

Their trips to Europe, adventurous treks involving difficult roads and difficult bargaining to "bag their game," involved all three: "Miss Cassatt was ever ready to recommend, Mr. Havemeyer to buy, and I to find a place for the pictures in our gallery," as Havemeyer wrote though she also exercised her own judgment about the paintings that they bought (*Sixteen to Sixty*

195). Their search for paintings by El Greco, then viewed by many English critics as too eccentric and extreme, took them to Spain: "My Greco cost me a little over two hundred and fifty dollars, and I carried it in my arms, frame and all, to the hotel to show it to Mr. Havemeyer." Together wife and husband chose *View of Toledo*, which they thought resembled the actual city view and thus found less expressionistic than did later critics. With these purchases on display in their home and with other enthusiasts following their lead, they were able, as she wrote, "to open the market for Grecos" (*Sixteen to Sixty* 135). Having caused the popularity of El Greco's work to increase, they later had to negotiate for four years to obtain his *Portrait of a Cardinal.*

While her husband participated with her in the purchasing, it was Louisine Havemeyer who created their home as an exclusive private gallery for friends and family. She chose to work with Louis Comfort Tiffany and Samuel Colman to create this elegant showplace for their varied and important collections. In the terminology of the aesthetic movement of the late nineteenth century, hers was an "artistic house," carefully created for the best of people (Dodge 21). Such a home might employ an array of materials and features: oak-lined interiors, wallpaper, the drapery of theatre, ceramics from the Orient and Europe, Turkish rugs, marble or medal clocks, highly decorated lamps, historical furniture, Japanese artifacts and especially fans, stained glass, and decorated screens. It could include watercolors and prints, but the most prized item of serious art was the oil painting. To create these treasure hoards, homeowners relied on agents and generally repeated the same, rather conservative choices in oil paintings: nymphs and gypsies in woodland settings; prime moments of military history; portraits of Catholic clergy; Moorish and Spanish scenes; Arab horsemen (Introduction 25). While Havemeyer was heavily involved in creating the *de rigueur* private artistic space, her tastes differed greatly from those of many other wealthy New Yorkers.

As they entered the Havemeyers' unique home, the few chosen guests came through double doors inset with glass to a large entrance hall, its floor made of a million and a half stones laid to imitate the mosaic flooring in Byzantine chapels of Ravenna. This hall also featured a fountain flowing into a basin filled with ferns and orchids and beyond it a marble staircase. Up these impressive steps, the picture gallery featured a perforated metal flying staircase, hanging from the ceiling by chains, which led to a balcony. On both levels of this large gallery, display cases featured porcelain and glass pieces, and paintings filled the spaces between these cases. Then, the second large display room, the library, featured carved wood walls and moldings with carved furniture reiterating the varied stains and patterns. A pebble-and-glass chandelier, installed in the Byzantian tile ceiling, provided the lighting for this room that housed the family's Rembrandts along with other paintings. While Havemeyer joined with Tiffany and Colman to decide on these ceilings, floors, staircases, and furnishings, Havemeyer decided on where and how to display the works of art, the best combination of porcelains, bronzes, potteries, and glassware to coordinate well with the paintings. She experimented with an array of colors and fabrics, eschewing the dull red velvet favored by many galleries (Weitzenhoffer, *The Creation* 147–51).

At the end of 1907, Louisine Havemeyer's full life of collecting and decorating suddenly came to an end. In December of that year, her husband died suddenly of kidney failure. Two days later, her mother died. She was then suddenly embroiled in federal suits against the American Sugar Refining Company, the government claiming that the company, by tampering with weighing scales, had avoided paying duty on 41,000 tons of sugar (Weitzenhoffer, *The Havemeyers* 186). In 1908, while she was battling in court and withstanding harsh press coverage of the suits and her company, her twin grandchildren died.

In 1908, Havemeyer entered a period of depression that led to a suicide attempt, her collecting days seemingly over without her husband and her life seeming to have little other purpose with her children grown. At that time, "feeling little interest in art," she refused two El Grecos for which the couple had been bargaining: she did not buy any more pictures for several years (*Sixteen to Sixty* 8). To help her mother, her daughter Electra organized a trip to Europe in February of 1909. Havemeyer was at her most unstable on the voyage and attempted to throw herself overboard. Electra became engaged to James Watson Webb in the fall, but this happy family event did not seem to resuscitate her mother.

Both Electra and Mary Cassatt felt that Havemeyer needed a new passion, something that would restore meaning to her life. Cassatt wrote to Havemeyer on December 8, 1909, envisioning for her friend a new involvement in the world: "Go in for the Suffrage, that means great things for the future." Cassatt herself was a strong advocate of women's rights, an "ardant suffragist" who believed that only women could bring peace to the world, and she thought that the suffrage effort could help her friend restart her life (Weitzenhoffer, *The Havemeyers* 195). She again wrote in August of 1914, with war looming, that Havemeyer should "work for suffrage, for it is the women who will decide the question of life or death for a nation" (*Sixteen to Sixty* 279).

As Cassatt suggested, Havemeyer began to see in the suffrage campaign a means of starting again, of forming new interests and creating a new purpose, though she came to this involvement in small steps. She first joined the Women's Political Union (WPU) in New York City, intending that a membership and little else would engage her sufficiently in the cause. Founded by Harriot Stanton Blatch in 1907 to advocate for civil and political equality, this organization had 19,000 members of diverse backgrounds a year later, including factory, laundry, and garment workers from the Lower East Side along with members of the upper class (Dodge 51). Through this group, Blatch organized and led suffrage parades in New York and lobbied for a state constitutional amendment to give women the vote.

As soon as Havemeyer began attending meetings, Blatch realized that this influential and wealthy New Yorker could support reform efforts through her own funds and her influence. Blatch immediately encouraged Havemeyer to take on the active role that Cassatt had urged. When Blatch came to the mansion to discuss the cause, she saw the collection that had been viewed only by the select few, and she recognized that it could become a powerful part of the suffrage effort. She suggested to Havemeyer that this art be made available not just to family and friends, but to a much larger audience and for a political cause — to associate new ideas in art with new ideas in politics and to symbolize equity and unity, in that this most wealthy of women would be inviting others to share in her possessions and her political goals. After talking with Blatch several times, Havemeyer decided to create her first public exhibition, with an entrance fee going to the suffrage campaign, moving her private love, her exclusively shown collection, into a public space and for a public cause.

On April 12, 1912, *Loan Exhibition of Paintings by El Greco and Goya* opened at the M. Knoedler and Company Gallery on Fifth Avenue as a fundraiser for the suffrage campaign, the gallery seeking a future relationship with Havemeyer and thus willing to host this political event. The nineteen-day show featured her El Greco portraits, including the *Portrait of a Cardinal* and *The Duchess of Alba*, as well as *View of Toledo*. From among her Goyas, she picked highly artful portraits of women, such as *Majas on a Balcony* and *Portrait of Queen Maria Luisa of Parma* ("Art for Woman's Suffrage"). Though she was proud of this effort for suffrage, she regretted the dark red backgrounds against which her pictures were hung: Goya's *Princess de la Paz*, for example, "the dainty royal lady," seemed "faded and pale like a drooping flower" against this color (*Sixteen to Sixty* 177). Having to accept the museum's backgrounds, she put her own efforts into the entrance: she decorated it to attract visitors, using colored draperies and glass as she had done in her home.

This exhibit was well received in the press and made money for the cause. The anti-suffrage *New York Times* even featured it in four different articles. One of them enjoyed a joke at the suffragists' expense: it spoke of El Greco's *Portrait of a Cardinal* as "fierce of face and gray of beard, looking through his horn-rimmed spectacles with such vitality and energy of character that the most militant and courageous suffragist must instinctively quail before that glance" ("Art for Woman's Suffrage"). But another, much longer, article admitted, concerning Goya and El Greco, that "there is little chance outside of Spain to study them in the various stages and phases of their development" and that this exhibit gave viewers that opportunity. In this piece, the *Times* focused on the painters' lives, their methods, individual paintings, and their influence in the history of portraiture ("Art at Home"). Another article listed the suffragists serving as hosts and giving talks in conjunction with the exhibit ("Art Exhibit for Suffrage: Paintings"). Because Havemeyer had loaned the paintings anonymously, not yet feeling ready for a completely public role in activism, the *Times* articles did not mention her involvement.

Although the exhibit had been a success, loaning paintings would not create a new life for Havemeyer — it could not occupy the days and months ahead. After the exhibit, she became increasingly involved with the WPU, working on a state referendum for suffrage, beginning to use her own name and participate in a more public way. By May of 1913, she marched in a suffrage parade up Fifth Avenue, much to the dismay of her children who thought such involvements inappropriate and dangerous. Regardless of their preferences, as she recalled in a two-part article in *Scribner's Magazine* in 1922, Havemeyer began developing from a participant behind the scenes to one of the WPU's most visible members, one of the most accomplished campaigners for the vote. While participating in marches, Havemeyer also became a regular worker at The Shop, a huge space on Fifth Avenue that suffragists decorated and used for meetings. Drawing on her artistic background from creating her own home, she decorated The Shop's large Fifth Avenue window as "a little theatre where the history of suffrage was illustrated with dolls," and created a patriotic display around an eagle, "a huge bronze, too heavy to lift" ("The Suffrage Torch" 530).

In The Shop, at "very brilliant meetings," Blatch talked Havemeyer into a next step into activism: public speaking (Havemeyer, "The Suffrage Torch" 531). Havemeyer began slowly, answering anti-suffrage criticisms, prevailing clichés like a woman's place being only in the home, at the end of talks given by others. She next repeated speeches of early suffrage activists. She then began giving her own talks, at rallies on the streets as well as in the headquarters, bringing her grandson on stage as she argued that women should not have to wait until his generation grew up to begin to vote. As Havemeyer wrote in a two-part article about her involvement in the campaign, "It was Mrs. Blatch who insisted that I could speak; that I must speak; and then saw to it that I did speak. I think I spoke just to please her." With this encouragement, she soon realized that "one can learn to speak" ("The Suffrage Torch" 528).

In April 1915, the year of a New York state suffrage vote, Havemeyer prepared another art exhibit for suffrage. For a *Loan Exhibition of Masterpieces by Old and Modern Painters*, again at Knoedler's, she exhibited works by Degas and Cassatt as well as older paintings ("Exhibition for"). For this exhibit, Blatch and Havemeyer planned for the combination of paintings, of the best older combined with the best newer artists, to symbolize the best traditions of social thought that would soon include the extension of the franchise (Rabinow 89).

While Havemeyer wanted to incorporate older painters and accepted tradition, as though these great artists were casting a vote for suffrage, she decided that the modern should outnumber the ancient, as new ideas of the electorate and democracy should overwhelm any other governmental tradition that had previously existed. The Old Masters included Dutch artists Holbein, Rembrandt, Rubens, and Vermeer. The exhibit also featured a photograph of Cassatt and a portrait of Degas, along with nineteen of Cassatt's and twenty-seven of Degas' works, twenty-two of this total coming from Havemeyer's collection. The old masters appeared in two small rooms, followed by the Degas and Cassatts in one large room, to symbolize an opening up of modern possibilities of talent and equality. This time Havemeyer planned for the placement of each piece — and for the colors of the backgrounds.

Although Havemeyer made the selections, they were vetted through a Committee of Ladies, well-known New Yorkers who added respectability to the undertaking. Though Havemeyer could have supplied the entire exhibit by herself from her collection, she thought that a committee of selectors and a group of providers created a sense of common purpose. Havemeyer owned six of the eighteen old masters in the exhibit, with others being loaned by New York collectors sympathetic to the cause, a highly publicized partnership ("Art Exhibit for Suffrage: A Rubens").

For this exhibit, Blatch felt that a public introduction would allow these themes of tradition and change to be tantamount in the viewers' minds — and this time Havemeyer was willing to be the featured speaker. Her remarks allowed the WPU to shift the price from one dollar to five and to earn additional money by selling the speech text. Royal Cortissoz, an art critic at the

New York Tribune, helped Havemeyer plan her remarks, but she didn't read the formal, historical speech that they had written together. Instead she decided to shift to a more anecdotal presentation, telling stories about Degas and Cassatt and then comparing the older and modern schools while advocating the forward thinking of universal suffrage. "I was very much frightened at this venture into a field of oratory different from anything I had ever attempted before," she wrote afterwards. "It was very easy to talk about the emancipation of women, but art was a very different and difficult subject" ("The Suffrage Torch" 529). The *New York Times'* review of her talk spoke of her specific anecdotes that brought viewers closer to the paintings. Her entertaining and elucidating remarks, quoted in the newspaper at length, "quite refuted the impression held in many quarters that a collector is only superficially acquainted with the art he collects," a judgment separating her from so many of the aesthetic movement's wealthy collectors and furthering the positive public image of this suffragist ("'Art and Artists'"). The exhibit, advertised and enriched by her talk, was a critical and financial success.

When four states, including New York, voted against suffrage amendments in the fall of 1915, thus rebuffing so many arguments and so much hard work, Blatch's group joined with the NWP to work for a national amendment. Havemeyer recognized that her target was no longer one state's legislators but Wilson and his party, both completely opposed to this extension of the franchise: "Those were the days," she wrote, "when a little band of women had to fight single-handedly an administration and a political organization armed cap-a-pie against them." But she felt buoyed by the leadership now not just of Blatch but of Alice Paul, "a remarkable young woman of Quaker descent, inheriting the valiant, stern determination of her sect and gifted with a wonderfully keen political instinct" ("The Prison Special" 661).

In support of this new, larger cause, Paul and Blatch asked Havemeyer to go on a ten-day speaking tour in upstate New York. She took her landaulet car, with a convertible top folding over the rear seats, which she called the Jewel Box. The car allowed her to be comfortable and independent of railroad timetables; she could open the top and stand on it, and thus use it as an exotic stage from which to speak outdoors.

On this speaking tour, Havemeyer honed her rhetorical skills and her control of visual symbols. In earlier talks in New York City, she had witnessed the powerful visual effect of bringing her grandson out on stage as an example of a younger generation on whom suffrage should not have to wait. In Long Island, she was given "the celebrated Liberty Torch, as great a piece of campaign publicity work as Mrs. Blatch ever did," a large torch meant to link women with the American Revolution and with American patriotism ("The Suffrage Torch" 532). In the western part of the state, using a lunch wagon as a speaker's stand, she greeted male workers at noon as she "lifted the torch as high as I could and for once I did not have to think—the words came to me as if by inspiration.... I could not utter them fast enough; I feared the moments would pass before I had told those men all I wanted them to hear." Then that night in Beeman, New York, she spoke at a street meeting: "I began with a few boys and ended with a big crowd" ("The Suffrage Torch" 534). As she held the torch up, she said that it was like the one held in the outstretched hand of the Statue of Liberty, which also stood for freedom, what American women were seeking. For ten days across the state, she averaged seven speeches a day. In all of these sites, women asked to hold the torch along with her and thus be part of an American call for liberty.

The positive publicity within the state stirred Blatch and Havemeyer to consider greater possibilities for the torch, especially since they had begun working for a federal amendment. They made plans to transfer it from the New York to the New Jersey branch of the WPU, in the middle of the Hudson River, with the respected and well-known Havemeyer making the connection. She was a bit dizzy out in the heat, with delays occurring because the New Jersey group had not secured a license needed to receive the torch. Though exhausted when the time for the exchange finally came, Havemeyer got up and made her speech: "I blessed the father of the great river, and the brave men of the Empire State who were to give us our freedom in the coming elections, and I confided the sacred token of liberty, the beloved torch, to our sisters in the neighboring State." With cameras recording the event for the newspapers, as Havemeyer wrote, "the threatened fiasco ended in a glorious finale" ("The Suffrage Torch" 535–36).

Having fully witnessed the power of the visual symbol, Havemeyer went on to design her own prop, using the latest of modern technology. This was a ship of state, resembling the *Mayflower*, which she brought out and lit at the end of speeches, an event that people waited for, the electric lighting controllable with a button at the key moment in a speech when she was ready for it. She varied the large, hand-held ship's import for different occasions. She lit it, for example, as she spoke about the woman who was the first settler to leave the *Mayflower* at Plymouth Rock, claiming the land as America for both women and men. She lit it as she described America's democracy through a story: both men and women had bought tickets to get on a boat that ultimately only men had been allowed to board; simple justice dictated that both sexes should gain equal access. She lit it as she told a story concerning a woman who paid her taxes and participated in her town but could not truly board an American ship of state. As she said of such stories and the ship's power to illuminate their meaning, "that illustration never failed me" ("The Suffrage Torch" 539).

To extend Havemeyer's authority as an American patriot emphasizing women's rights as a key part of democracy, in 1917 Blatch encouraged her to take an active role not just in suffrage work but in war work, thus melding suffrage with other patriotic choices for women. Havemeyer soon became a "seasoned campaigner" for the war effort as well, speaking for Liberty Loans, food conservation, and relief efforts along with the suffrage that could extend women's contributions to their nation ("The Suffrage Torch" 528). During these speeches, she asked speakers to help her in a "jam campaign," sending jam and other staples to wounded soldiers at the front. While speaking on the solidly wholesome topic of jam, she also lobbied for the Army Nurses Corps to secure the military ranks available to women in the Canadian and Australian armies — and for suffrage.

As Havemeyer became increasingly involved in public speaking for the war and for women's rights, she began to return to art collecting in Europe, where she found more competition for the work of her cherished painters than earlier, partly from her having advocated for them in the United States. As she put it, "I regained my courage and was once more buying pictures" (*Sixteen to Sixty* 199).

With such a reputation as a speaker, a collector, and a patriot, Havemeyer could make a further contribution beyond exhibits and talks on jam: by entering prison and joining those who planned to tour the nation, speaking about her experience. Alice Paul asked her on February 9, 1919, on the night before a Senate vote on suffrage, to come to the large demonstration in Lafayette Square in which suffragists burned the president in effigy. As Havemeyer recalled, though she had told Paul that she didn't want to participate, "Nevertheless, when Miss Paul called me up from Washington and asked me to take part in the demonstration, and to bring my 'grip' in case we should have to go to prison, I did just as she requested, for how could I do less with such examples before me! I asked the family if they needed me, and told them I was going to Washington for a few days" ("The Prison Special" 663).

As soon as Havemeyer arrived, Paul asked her to lead the group and hold a flag, a choice she found quite daunting as the suffragists amassed to begin their march: "All were greeting me and I was trying to look unconcerned, but I assure you I don't think I ever had such a struggle for poise in my life." But once she saw the effigy, held by Sue Shelton White, a prop like those she had used before, and was told that she should speak for freedom as she had done before, she felt more confident in starting out: "I stepped out and I instantly felt as placid and calm as if I were going out to play croquet on a summer afternoon" ("The Prison Special" 664). She turned down Pennsylvania Avenue into a dense crowd, which seemed to part before her, and then headed resolutely to the White House where the marchers placed their effigy and urn.

Each time that the women tried to light the fire on which the effigy would burn, rows of police with fire extinguishers came up to put it out. Lucy Burns asked Havemeyer to join in the attempt so that she would go to jail even though the officer by her side, Captain Flathers, did not want to arrest her: "Poor old Flathers! He almost wrung his hands, and implored Lucy Burns to call me off, but I knowing I *had* to qualify for speaker for the Prison Special, kept on throwing bundle after bundle toward the urn" ("The Prison Special" 666).

Havemeyer was arrested with thirty-nine other women and taken to the station house, the press focusing especially on her arrest. The *New York Times* article on the arrests entitled "Suffragists Burn Wilson in Effigy; Many Locked Up," had as a shocking subheading "Mrs. Havemeyer Arrested." She went with the others to the old abandoned jail, "discarded ten years before," as she wrote, as unfit to hold a human being" ("The Prison Special" 667–70).

In this horrible jail space, however, Havemeyer suddenly felt a new sense of resolution and strength, a power that she had not expected:

> I entered with the other prisoners, and as the great double doors rolled with a rusty, clanking sound and closed behind me, there came over me a feeling which made me plant my feet together and stiffen up as if it were not I but the reincarnation of those heroic women who could rise to sublime heights of sacrifice and daring. I would have dared anything. My very heart stood still for an instant, and then bounded beneath my ribs and crackled as the sparks of indignation snapped within. Where was my Uncle Sam? Where was the liberty my fathers fought for? Where the democracy our boys were fighting for?

She recognized the seriousness of place and situation, "for prison and a hunger strike are still formidable to the oldest and most hardened campaigner." But, in this harsh space, she felt herself "plant my feet together and stiffen up," and she became aware of her own courage and willingness to sacrifice for freedom: "I was fairly lost in admiration of the possibilities that I knew were within me" ("The Prison Special" 670).

As Havemeyer considered her new level of strength and commitment to justice, she compared herself specifically to other heroic women: "I understood what nerved the hand of Judith, what enabled Jael calmly to drive a nail through Sisera's wretched head, or the courage of Corday to spill the blood of a French tyrant." As she reflected on these biblical and historical stories of women with the courage to kill men who had instigated tyrannical reigns of terror, she considered herself within their tradition yet with a much easier sacrifice to make. She felt further buoyed by realizing that John Bunyon, Galileo, and Martin Luther had gone to prison for their beliefs, but her ultimate inspiration came from Joan of Arc: "the brave girl who feared not prison, the leader of armies in the mighty assaults and attacks that level all obstacles and make you victorious over your foes" ("The Prison Special" 670–74).

For Havemeyer, the worst reality was that she had to call upon this tradition of courage and sacrifice to oppose her own American government. For peacefully protesting against it, an absolute right in a democracy, she had been incarcerated in a cell located below ground level, cold and damp, with the windows all black, with dirty straw beds and with gas vapors escaping from sewers. She had to hunger strike to insist on political prisoner rights, which ironically failed to exist in American prisons. While she suffered these dangers and indignities in the United States, a country then acclaiming itself as democracy's champion in a world war, German women were voting. In fact, as she knew, women were voting in every nation in Europe, except for Spain and France, while American women went to jail for deigning to ask for the right: "The women of America were to languish in a dirty, discarded prison, because they dared to ask for *their* democracy, while our President was hawking democracy abroad like a belated edition of an evening paper" ("The Prison Special" 671).

While Havemeyer found herself changed by the experience and proud of her commitment to real democracy, her children were not so moved, their shock and dismay over a well-publicized prison sentence resembling that of many suffragist families. When the news reached New York, her family reacted harshly, her daughter telling her on the telephone that Havemeyer's children and grandchildren were mortified over this scandalous act and that it was making Havemeyer's sister ill. She and Alice Paul agreed that Havemeyer should return to New York immediately, and that she could still qualify to go on the Prison Special because she had spent time in jail: "I promised, if I could prop up the family tree and put a little life into it, I should be ready to go the following Sunday, and then I returned to New York" ("The Prison Special" 673).

The next week, "with only the qualified consent of the 'family tree,' which by this time had stiffened up a little from its storm-and-stress experiences," Havemeyer returned to Washington to board the Prison Special.

At their stops, she generally spoke first, lending respectability and her well-honed speaking skills to the effort. In Chattanooga where the crowd was small, she said that there were more people in the audience than had signed the Declaration of Independence and by supporting woman suffrage they could matter as much. For large crowds, as in New Orleans' City Park, she spoke as loudly as possible, about the democracy American troops were fighting for, until "the crowd grew beyond the possibility of hearing us." In Boston, she entered the auditorium along with women who had been jailed and injured that February of 1919 for protesting the president when he returned from peace talks in Europe, and she spoke of the original colonists' belief in freedom as well as the courage of those women who continued that American tradition. The tour ended at Carnegie Hall where Havemeyer and the others addressed a standing room only crowd, emphasizing the need for all Americans, recent immigrants seeking freedom as well as those from families that arrived in earlier centuries, to fully participate in government.

After the experience of suffrage, with the clarity of purpose and strength that it gave her, Havemeyer continued with collecting art in Europe, but she also decided on a much larger audience for her paintings, not just her children to whom she had initially willed her collection. Instead, she sought a larger educational purpose for them, to open Americans to new creative possibilities. Throughout the 1920s, she investigated the various museums that might make her artworks public, providing the largest possible audience for her beloved Degas, Manets, and other acquisitions that could acquaint Americans with vibrant, challenging artists and aesthetic theories. She believed that she could thus involve a large group in re-examining artistic and cultural traditions, extending to them a form of creative education that could enrich their lives and make them more open-minded and valuable citizens of a democracy, goals that her suffrage speeches and imprisonment had also served.

When she died in 1929, the headlines of the obituary essay in the *New York Times* labeled her as "Art Patron," "Widow of Former President of American Refining Co."—as well as "Militant Suffragist"—and the text featured the terms of her new will: she had left the vast majority of her paintings to the Metropolitan Museum of Art, with which she had entered into long negotiations ("Mrs. Havemeyer, Art Patron, Dies"; "The Exhibition of"). Codicils in the will required her children to turn over five-sevenths of the collection to the museum in the next five years and encouraged them to donate others that had already been given to them. She gave 142 paintings, then worth three and a half million dollars, and her children added another 111, the total including a large assortment by Rembrandt, Degas, Cassatt,

Manet, Monet, Pissarro and other painters that she had helped to introduce to Americans in the suffrage exhibits, along with prints, ceramics, armor, textiles, and bronzes. The entire bequest included two thousand works that enriched nearly every segment of the museum's collections but created the contemporary art wings. This was, as the *New York Times* declared, "one of the most magnificent gifts of works of art ever made to a museum by a single individual," a bequest that "transformed the collections of the Metropolitan Museum" ("Havemeyer Art Gift"; Tinterow 3). Frank Jewett Mather, art critic, wrote in 1930 that the gift "doubles the prestige of the Metropolitan Museum in painting" (452). Of art of the second half of the nineteenth century, the Havemeyer paintings at the Metropolitan are considered as second only to the collection at the Musee d'Orsay (Tinterow 3). The family also donated paintings to the National Gallery in Washington, the Getty, the Brooklyn Museum, and other sites.

Ultimately, Louisine Havemeyer built not a private collection but a national treasure, available to generations. As she attested, suffrage brought her back, gave her the strength through which to continue her collecting. But it also imbued in her a responsibility for the future of her nation, not just her family. It taught her that she could make a difference in American life, that in a democracy she could be fully involved with other citizens and transform their lives. Suffrage made her a dynamic public speaker and public figure, and it taught her that she could create great changes whether they were initially approved by her own family and social circle or not. Meetings and exhibits and ultimately public speaking, jail, and a national tour were good for Havemeyer and tremendously good for the nation.

Rhoda Kellogg (1898–1987)

Like Louisine Havemeyer, Rhoda Kellogg found the suffrage campaign to be a transforming experience, one that also led her to making an impact on the art world that she had not envisioned before. Much younger than Havemeyer at the time of her suffrage involvement, Kellogg gained a new independence and sense of creativity from it that helped to shape an entire career. For Kellogg, as her journal notes record, the jail term — that she had not sought — did not re-open the world for her but opened it: to the power of examining accepted traditions from a posture of independence and strength. Like Louisine Havemeyer, she began to realize through the suffrage campaign that she had the possibility and even the duty to help change the world that she found.

From a conservative family in Minneapolis, Kellogg entered the University of Minnesota in 1916 and planned to attend for a year or two before starting a short career as a teacher, as could still be done at the elementary level without a complete college education. She planned, after a few years, to leave this career for marriage and family.

But Kellogg believed in a woman's right to vote, and she thus joined the Equal Suffrage Association at her university. In 1875, Minnesota had given women the "school vote," the ability to vote in school board elections. As women sought full suffrage in 1916 and 1917, they were led by Clara Ueland, a devoted supporter of the arts, who had been involved with the suffrage movement from the time of the 1901 convention of NAWSA in Minneapolis. In 1913, Ueland founded the Equal Suffrage Club of Minneapolis, a group that immediately formed a university division, involved in a six-year effort, leading to the granting of presidential suffrage, but not full suffrage, in 1919 (Stuhler). That long campaign, which Kellogg participated in for three years, taught her the frustrations of a state-by-state approach and thus led her to the NWP, as she began to view a federal amendment as necessary for securing full suffrage.

At the urging of fellow students, Kellogg went to Washington in January 1919 to observe the exploits of NWP activists. When she came to the capital, as her journal notes attest, she had no plans to picket or to enter prison herself but instead to attend as a sympathizer (Pruitt, "Sarah Tarleton Colvin" 106). The group particularly wanted to be in Washington to see the watchfires against Wilson and the Congress — as well as the national monuments.

But that January, though Kellogg did not seek it, prison found her. Along with her friends from Minnesota, she went into a courtroom where prisoners from that day's picketing entered to receive their sentences. With other supporters, she applauded these women as they mounted the witness stand, a seemingly safe choice, but for this act the judge, attempting to gain control over a large crowd, gave Kellogg and a few others a sentence of a day in jail.

Though she just stayed in jail for just twenty-four hours, Kellogg found this experience almost unbelievable, that as an American citizen she could not even place her hands together in an American courtroom, that she was completely vulnerable to arrest even when she had not picketed and had not participated in the watchfire: the judge didn't even know that she had been present at the fire. The experience was even more shocking for her because she had not prepared for it. As she walked in the line to the prison van and expressed this exasperation to those walking near her, as her journal notes attest, the other women found her naïve. "You are not really an American citizen," she later recalled that they told her. "You cannot vote. You have no recourse, no power, no reason to assume equality when you have no rights" (Journal Notes).

For Kellogg, a college association led without much planning to Washington, and Washington led without any intention to jail, but jail itself led to a mighty change, to an awakening concerning a lack of rights but also the courage and unity with which these women were acting and with which important changes could occur. As her journal notes indicate, one day in jail awakened Kellogg to what women had endured during sentences of six and seven months, what they were willing to undertake to secure their rights — and what any woman might have to undergo without political power in the United States. That same month, before she returned to school, she participated in a watchfire demonstration for which she was sentenced to another five days in District Jail, where she hunger-struck with the others, this time choosing to embrace both radical behavior and its consequences as a woman seeking equality (Pruitt, "Bertha Berglin Moller" 137).

Kellogg may seem like a representative of the ineffective first wave because after women achieved the vote she did not go forward into a political life. But she was completely changed by the event, and her early interest, of a career working with children, afterwards led her to the choice of not just teaching for a short period before marriage but of becoming a lifelong educator and leader who altered American thinking about children's education and creativity.

After she returned to Minneapolis, Kellogg went on to a level of education that she had not intended to pursue before, but one that she felt would be necessary for a long-term career and leadership role: she graduated from the University of Minnesota and then secured graduate training in education at Columbia University. Instead of remaining in her home state, she next moved to San Francisco, the site of an education reform movement of which she felt able to be a part, just as she had ultimately embraced suffrage activism in Washington.

Before Kellogg moved there, California had been a prime site for the charity kindergarten movement, often called the Kindergarten Crusade, which involved a commitment to the philosophy and practices of Friedrich Fröebel, a German teacher and scholar who advocated early education for all children through an active learning style, with activities carefully designed to lead to critical thinking for citizenship (Bhavnagri and Krolikowski). In the late nineteenth century, kindergarten pioneers, who included philanthropists, university presidents, and kindergarten teachers, sought to "save the children" from the vice and hopelessness confronting them in the slums (Ross). They believed that the Froebelian approach would help these children become upstanding adults who would fully participate in democracy. "The more kindergartens the fewer prisons" was a common saying of this group (Riis 181). Kate Douglas Wiggin started the first free kindergarten in San Francisco, the Silver Street Free Kindergarten, in 1878. With her sister in the 1880s she also established a training school for kindergarten teachers, especially to provide instruction for teaching the children of Chinese immigrants (Vandewalker 66–68).

At the beginning of the twentieth century, with Chinese immigration having ended in 1882 and the first advocates having begun to retire, reform-driven schools were closing or shrinking. But Kellogg's interest in San Francisco did not just concern what had happened there. As someone who had advocated for a federal amendment for suffrage, she was interested in building a commitment to education that was national and ongoing, not a thing of one decade or one state.

Along with teachers of an earlier generation, she began the Golden Gate Kindergarten Association, a group that met to consider teaching techniques and that lobbied for funding for educational facilities, for kindergarten and for the less accepted concept of nursery school for younger children. She also helped to found the Golden Gate Kindergarten, a school intended as an educational model. She served as its executive director until 1970 and afterwards as a member of its board of directors. Throughout her career, while she administered a preschool association, she taught new teachers through the University of California Extension Division; gave speeches around the world at conferences, schools, and universities; wrote books on education; and advocated in Sacramento and Washington for early education. As she had learned in the suffrage campaign, she could alter inadequate institutions through her own commitment and her involvement in strong groups that might begin on the local level but could make a much wider impact ("Rhoda Kellogg").

In her books, she espoused the theories of early education that informed her own teaching of children, parents, and teachers. She felt that early education began in the home. In *Babies Need Fathers, Too* in 1953, as in her talks and pamphlets, she espoused a view of wives and husbands as responsible in a democracy to respond to the dictates of their own consciences, a code also inherent in the suffrage campaign:

> Today there is no final source of authority to which most American individuals can turn except the voice of one's one conscience; for this idea that conscience is superior to external authority is inherent in our democratic way of life. It

applies to women as well as men. An individual's inner voice is well set before marriage; therefore a woman cannot comply with her husband's conscience if it violates her own [14].

As she critiqued the current system and spoke for independent thinking, she always argued that change was needed to help men as well as women achieve greater happiness in their home lives and thus become better parents. In speeches and in *Babies Need Fathers, Too,* she asserted that men could become uneasy strangers in their own homes, taking a passive role in raising children and withdrawing from their families because of a culturally determined lack of emotional involvement. But, Kellogg argued, "children want more than 'fathers by marriage'; they want fathers who are as close and real as mothers are" (19). And both women and men can enjoy their family life if they move beyond the roles prescribed for them. To apply the "self-appraisal, self-discipline, and self-denial" needed for change improves a man's personality and character as well as the lives of his children and the quality of his marriage (236). She ended with the following coda, which she often used in speeches: "What the world needs is more men who enjoy being fathers, for babies need fathers, too" (256).

In *Babies Need Fathers, Too,* as in her many speeches about parenting, Kellogg followed her general remarks with a guide on thumb sucking, weaning, bed wetting, and toilet training, making the assumption that men would be involved in all parenting work. She also strove to address the needs of both genders of children, beginning with linguistic parity. In this book, she says that she will be calling the child "he" because there is no better choice in English for communication; she admits the annoyance factor of "his/her" or "(s)he." But she recognizes that the simpler choice of using "only the masculine pronouns seems to produce the effect of over-emphasis on the male child." And she asked, "Is it not a comment on the relationship between the sexes that no words exist in the English language for solving this problem of more exact communication?" (11).

While focusing on active parenting, Kellogg wrote extensively and advocated for the early education for children of all classes that could prepare them for participation in democracy — not just for poor immigrants or rich children in a few cities, but for all American children. She claimed that all children required a place where their needs could be met first: "to be respected, loved, wisely guided and controlled" (9). In talks, in pamphlets, and in her influential *Nursery School Guide*, she disassociated the new nursery schools from an older style that lacked an educational commitment. She argued that many nursery schools for both rich and poor had ill-informed teachers; well-written guides and short training programs could teach them the basics of child development and educational methods so they could set up active classrooms based on experiential learning.

As a suffrage activist, she had learned that the government could value women when they were needed, as during wartime, but then deny their rights otherwise. Such temporary value and attention, she recognized, could also be ceded to children. In Kellogg's analysis, the history of state-sponsored nursery schools mirrored the needs of the state. Some federal and factory nurseries offered care during World War I so that mothers could work, but closed subsequently. Then, beginning in 1933 and 1934, WPA schools provided employment as well as a place for poor and abandoned children. When that funding ended at the beginning of the 1940s, 50,000 children had to immediately leave 1500 schools. Then in November 1942, in response to the need for women in the wartime work force, the federal government funded Lanham Schools, but then closed them in February 1946; at their peak they educated 15,310 children in 369 schools in California alone, one of which Kellogg supervised in Vallejo, California. Through the years, Kellogg argued both in Sacramento and in Washington that the needs of the youngest citizens should not be controlled by the vicissitudes of the economy or of warfare, but should be recognized in every generation, an argument that came to fruition, at least for the poorest of children, in Head Start legislation in 1965, which paid for eight-week summer programs for disadvantaged children beginning that year. Although Kellogg praised this legislation as "the salvation of children ... condemned to school failure" and worked hard to enact it, she felt that classes might begin before Head Start's designated age of three and that classes combining students of different economic groups would be better for all involved ("Montessori Today").

Though Kellogg devoted much of her time to helping parents, teaching, administering schools, and lobbying for school legislation, she is best known for her extensive study of children's art. Beginning in 1953, she collected art each week from nursery and elementary school teachers in San Francisco, as she wrote in the early 1970s: "My study of children's art began more than 20 years ago, primarily out of a desire to understand very young children, my favourite people" (*The Crucial Years* 1). In 1960 and 1961, she added additional pieces during an around-the-world lecture tour, finally creating a collection of two million pieces. This work resulted in a series of research studies, such as *What Children Scribble and Why* (1955), *The Psychology of Children's Art* (1967), *Analyzing Children's Art* (1969), and *Children's Drawings/Children's Minds* (1979). By examining the products of the youngest group that could hold a crayon, she identified art as a natural instinct and pleasure, following the same developmental patterns around the globe, a key means of symbol making and self-expression even for the youngest of artists. In this extended research, Kellogg was reexamining traditions and reorienting evaluations of cultural worth, as she did in her participation in the suffrage campaign.

In her work, Kellogg created a new perspective on child development and on inappropriate controls on the child, her goal to reform education and thus extend possibilities for human creativity. Art begins, Kellogg maintained in several books, in twenty basic scribbles, such as vertical, horizontal, diagonal, circular, curving, waving, and zig-zag lines. Beginning with these lines and with dots, Kellogg explained, children move through various artistic stages: placement, shape, design, pictorial. Even in their earliest drawings children carefully place their pictures on the page, at the bottom or top, on the diagonal, or in the entire space; by age three drawings have borders and particular shapes, including crosses, circles, rectangles, triangles, and ovals. They then make combines of two shapes and aggregates of more than two.

As children work through these stages, Kellogg asserted, they are not trying to create pictorials but instead to exercise their own imaginations and develop symbol systems. Children naturally will move toward making some pictorials, she concluded by studying varied student groups, but not at the rate sought by many parents and teachers, and they would continue with more abstract or symbolic depictions if allowed to do so. Stick figures to represent men and other such pictorials come only with adult comments and instruction and thus are not what she calls "self-taught child art" (*The Psychology of Children's Art* 17). "The stenciled minds of well-meaning adults" thus make art less the children's own, more a matter of outside judgment that is often negative; and by applying these judgments, teachers and parents may arrest artistic development ("Understanding Children's Art" 73). Throughout her books, Kellogg argued that allowing children to draw, without adult commentary, will help to "recapture the un-adult-erated aesthetic vision of the child" (*The Crucial Years*, Conclusion, np). Such an approach can lead children to continue their own artistic development and prepare them for reading, writing, and critical thinking since the language arts also involve a "symbolic language" ("Understanding Children's Art" 74) .

With careful study of art and human history, Kellogg asserted, educators and parents would come to see not just the natural development possible through art but also the connection to the most powerful forms of creativity. *The Crucial Years* and her other books, for example, note that children as young as three make mandalas, designs based on a crossed circle, for which Freud and Jung claimed great human and psychological significance. Jung saw such circular images as "movement towards psychological growth, expressing the idea of a safe refuge, inner reconciliation and wholeness," the spontaneous expression of the unconscious (99). In these shapes and in freely drawn lines, adults can thus observe a symbolic and spontaneous expression worthy of study in itself, for both the understanding of human development and the appreciation of meaningful human expression: "Children's art is to be seen as aesthetic composition if it is to be understood" (*Children's Drawings/Children's Minds* 1).

As she investigated creativity, Kellogg moved her research beyond the United States. After collecting samples from around the world, she concluded that early creativity was a human trait, identical for children in all countries (*What Children Scribble and Why* 1). In the introduction to *The Psychology of Children's Art*, she discusses the similarities of houses and trees, for example, in the pictorial stage even though the children lived in very different places. Recognition of these shared stages reveals the universality of children's artistic impulses and thus of creative thinking.

In this discussion of children's art, Kellogg was an innovator and an educational leader whose influence remains significant. In *Draw Me a Picture: The Meaning of Children's Drawings and Play from the Perspective of Analytical Psychology* (2007), psychologist Theresa Foks-Appelman wrote that psychological research on children's drawing began with Kellogg and still relies on her collection (29). In *Art Heals: How Creativity Cures the Soul* (2004), therapist Shaun Mcniff described Kellogg as "the pioneering researcher in children's art" (261). In *Growing Artists: Teaching Art of Young Children* (1997), educator Joan Bouza Koster argued that Kellogg instigated the study of children's art that has occurred in the last sixty years. In *The Handbook of Research and Policy in Art Education* (2004), researchers Elliot W. Eisner and Michael D. Day discussed Kellogg's as the first influential discussion of children's scribbling and shapes. In *History of Psychology* (2003), historian David Hothersall referred to her as "a distinguished contemporary developmental psychologist," influential for her advocacy of early education and for her extended study of children's art (435).

Throughout her long and important career, as she taught generations of researchers and teachers about children's education and children's art, Kellogg never forgot the lessons of her trip to Washington and her two jail sentences, that being a bystander to life was not necessarily what she wanted, that she could assume the strength to stand up and challenge entrenched viewpoints, about women or about men or about children. After her suffrage imprisonment, she left home to serve a larger purpose, to create reform through education. She was willing to fight against accepted truths by relying on herself and joining with others to make voices heard that were being ignored, to secure better educational opportunities, to change attitudes and lives. She was willing and able to forge ahead, beyond accepted facts and traditions, and thus create a new understanding of human creativity and the best means of nurturing it.

Betsy Reyneau (1888–1964)

Like Havemeyer and Kellogg, other women who went to prison for suffrage would improve their nation through art. Having learned to question their president and stand up to oppression, they were willing to go beyond institutional judgments of worthy and unworthy, sanctioned and unsanctioned. Betsy Reyneau was one such woman. She became not a collector of art or an art educator but an artist, one informed by the values of social justice and of individual and group strength learned through suffrage.

Like other women, Reyneau came to the suffrage campaign for renewal, as a site for expressing her own needs and frustrations, not just gaining the right to vote. Betsy Graves Reyneau, from Battle Creek, Michigan, spent much of her early life in Detroit with her grandfather, Benjamin Graves, chief justice of the Michigan Supreme Court from 1868 to 1883. Reyneau wanted to be a painter, a choice that her father discouraged as inappropriate for a woman, not at all conducive to a home and family. As the *New York Times* later attested, she "bore the opposition met more often by artists of an earlier generation and ran away from home to make her own way in the art world" ("Betsy G. Reyneau Exhibits"). She left Michigan for Cincinnati where she studied with Frank Duveneck, who had come there from Munich in 1904 to head the Art Academy and taught Reyneau a realistic style of portrait painting. From Cincinnati she went on to Boston and the Boston Museum School, having broken off her relationship with her father to do so. As Bessie Bowen Graves, she studied there from 1909 to 1914, with a break in 1912, a long stay at an art school at that time. Though she did not pursue a degree, she took a variety of classes, including advanced painting, life modeling and portraiture, and classical art (Murphy). In 1915, she married Paul Reyneau, an engineer who received his training at Cornell, and they returned to Detroit, where she continued to paint while also starting a home. She did not use her full name but instead signed her initials on her work; some subjects did not know her gender until they called to offer her a commission. On the basis of work seen in private homes, officers of the Circuit Court of Detroit asked her to do a portrait of Benjamin Graves: they did not know that they were dealing with a woman artist or indeed with his granddaughter. Her own father was asked to do the dedication; he did not know who the painter was because he was not in touch with her ("Betsy G. Reyneau Exhibits"). Although Reyneau was working professionally after she returned to Detroit, she felt controlled by the negative judgments, like those of her own father, and the limited artistic opportunities of her hometown. Her plans for an artistic career stymied, she felt drawn to the suffrage movement as a site in which women could make a difference and work for the equality that she had been seeking in art.

While she turned to suffrage to seek involvement and change, Reyneau soon recognized the frustrations of state campaigns. At a state constitutional convention held by the Michigan legislature in 1908, woman's suffrage was defeated 57 to 38, but women who paid taxes were given the right to vote on local bonding and tax issues. In 1912, Governor Charles Osborn urged the legislature to put the suffrage question before the electorate in November. With Clara Arthur of Detroit leading the campaign, the proposal appeared to be winning until the last moments of vote counting, the loss thus occurring under suspicious circumstances. In 1913, a state suffrage proposal was again put on the ballot and again defeated (Harper et al., vol. 6, 303–12).

In 1915, when Reyneau returned to the state, she learned about all the suffragists' efforts and their repeated lack of success. That year, she joined in the state campaign, which would finally succeed at least partially when women gained the right to vote in presidential elections in 1917, but the reversals and huge outlay of time and money made Reyneau turn her attention toward a federal amendment. When the NWP made the call for pickets to come to Washington during the difficult days of the summer of 1917, those who went from Michigan included Betsy Reyneau.

On July 14, Bastille Day, Reyneau was one of sixteen women who went out with banners reading "Liberty, Equality, Fraternity, July 14, 1789." On July 17, at their trial, the government went further than before—by meting out sentences of sixty days to Reyneau and the other fifteen pickets. Press releases and other publicity about these sentences caught the nation's attention: papers across Michigan carried the story of Reyneau and featured the connection to her grandfather ("Prison Lulls 'Suffs'"). Several subsequent articles, like one on the next day, reported on frightening but inspiring news from Reyneau in prison: "Detroit suffragettes have heard no word from Mrs. Reyneau since she and the others started serving their 60-day terms but a message is expected by Friday. Mrs. Reyneau has wired to her husband, Paul Reyneau, that she is determined not to pay her fine but to fight for the principle involved. He upholds her in her stand" ("Mrs. Whittemore," "'Suffs' Resume").

Faced with the public outrage caused by this sentence, the government's resolve lasted only three days: Wilson chose to pardon the women, as his wife Edith Bolling Wilson attested, so that they would not become martyrs to the cause (138). Subsequent articles, like those in the *Detroit Free Press*, told of these women's return to the line after their release and the president's desire not to further incite response by again jailing them.

Having withstood both arrests and pardons, these women, Reyneau among them, resumed their picketing on July 23, carrying the "battle-scarred banner" bearing Inez Milholland's last words—"Mr. President, how long must women wait for liberty?"—that they held on Bastille Day and again in court when they were sentenced. On that day, Reyneau was again accompanied by Doris Stevens, Anne Martin, and others, including Eunice Dana Brannan with whom she was becoming close friends ("Militants to Picket"). Arrests were not forthcoming.

This sacrifice, of picketing, accepting jail terms, and then returning to the line, seemed to have an effect in Michigan as throughout the nation. In 1918, with little further work required of state organizations, Michigan voters approved a state constitutional amendment granting full suffrage to Michigan women. The strength of these pickets' commitment, their courage and sacrifice, had redounded in Reyneau's home state, the combination of state and federal efforts finally affecting legislators.

But the effect of this picketing and jail was as great for Reyneau herself as it was for her state and nation. For after the fight for suffrage, she decided that she would return to her earlier goals and establish a life beyond Detroit. She had proved that she could go to Washington; she could picket; and she could survive a jail sentence—she could also pursue a career as a painter that could make a difference to herself and her nation.

After the suffrage campaign, like so many other participants, Reyneau felt strong enough to work towards larger goals. She moved to New York and opened her own studio at 31 W. 46th Street. One of her great supporters in New York was Eunice Brannan, who commissioned a portrait and encouraged her friends to do so also. In December 1922, Reyneau had an exhibition at the Art Centre on 56th Street. One of the strongest portraits in her exhibit was the one of her grandfather, the story of which Brannan and Reyneau sent to the *New York Times*, which covered the exhibit at length. Of this portrait, the reviewer commented positively and specifically: "The head and softly painted figured silk of the gown stand out sharply against a background of vivid red" ("Betsy G. Reyneau Exhibits"). The exhibit also contained her portrait of Brannan, several portraits of children, and a commissioned portrait of Sam Hume, director of the San Francisco Theatre, whom she had known in Detroit ("Art in the Current Exhibitions").

Reyneau moved to Europe in 1927 and stayed for twelve years where she wrote magazine articles and perfected her drawing technique through work for *The Bookman*, a prestigious book-review monthly published in London from 1891 to 1934, for which she made the detailed etchings of readers and books that appeared at the ends of essays while also helping to select the portraits of artists and their homes placed throughout each issue. In London, she also became engrossed with war preparations and opened her home to Jews seeking refuge. The rise of fascism, in London as well as on the continent, ultimately caused her to return to the United States.

When she began living in the States again, Reyneau witnessed a type of fascism existing here in the lack of civil rights for African Americans, and she sought to make a positive impact that could move her beyond a career and into a social calling — by helping to change that situation of the Other through art. Like suffragists during World War I, she felt that America needed to extend equality to all citizens if it were to function as a beacon of democracy. Her art could educate Americans about a citizen group that should be respected in the armed forces and in the United States.

While she was in Florida in 1942, Reyneau did a portrait of Edward Lee, a young garden worker, a project that sparked her interest in celebrating un-celebrated lives, in bringing the neglected forward, as she had done through the suffrage campaign. As she sought to increase the knowledge of and respect for a poorly treated American group, she decided to look for a second subject that would matter politically, especially during wartime. She thus went to the flight training program at the Tuskegee Army Air Field to depict an airman, one of the million African Americans then serving in the armed forces. When she arrived in April of 1942, however, classes were temporarily not in session: the first aviation cadet class had completed its nine-month training course in March. But she found there another subject who would be the impetus for her work during the next twelve years: George Washington Carver ("Breaking Racial Barriers").

There at Tuskegee, with a fine American before her, Reyneau decided that Americans needed greater awareness of the contributions of African Americans in a variety of fields, not just those temporarily involved in warfare. Soon after Carver received his master's degree from Iowa State University in 1896, he had accepted an offer from Booker T. Washington of a post at Tuskegee, which Washington had founded in 1881. Carver spent nearly forty years there conducting research and teaching agricultural methods.

When Reyneau approached him, he was not interested in having his portrait made, declaring himself too old at seventy-eight for such a project. He had refused other artists who had asked to paint him. But he liked Reyneau's portrait of Edward Lee, of which she reported that he said, "you paint the souls of people," and he liked her suggestion that she paint him in his laboratory, at work on his plants. With his consent, she painted the last picture of him before his death three months later and the only known portrait of him painted during sittings instead of from photographs. In the picture he is shown wearing a laboratory apron and examining a red and white amaryllis, a hybrid that he developed as part of a lifelong hobby (Schatzki).

A few months after Carver's death, the Tuskegee Institute displayed the portrait, but for Reyneau such a tribute was too limited, like suffragists simply speaking just to like-minded groups or working for change just in their own hometowns and states. She sought a larger audience, of black and white Americans, who could learn about Carver's contributions and those of his race.

From Tuskegee, she thus went to Washington and the Smithsonian, which then had no portraits of African Americans in any of its galleries. She knew that Congress had granted the Interior Department the right to purchase Carver's birthplace and make it a national monument. With the sense of timing that she shared with Alice Paul, she recognized that she had a perfect opportunity to make a difference in race relations, by interesting the Smithsonian first in this portrait and then in a series of portraits of African American heroes. In 1943 her Carver portrait appeared on the cover of a pamphlet used by the Smithsonian to seek funds for the national monument. The Smithsonian also agreed to take the painting into its collection, the first portrait of an African American in any national collection (Fleming 14).

As Reyneau described her larger purpose, exhibitors at the Smithsonian put her in touch with the Harmon Foundation. Like Paul, she knew that she would need support to accomplish the goals she had in mind. She had begun these portraits to comment on American democracy and to change minds and lives. A gardener in Florida led her to airmen at Tuskegee and then to Carver; with a group allegiance at the Harmon Foundation, like a dedicated suffragist working with others in the NWP, she could move to a larger plan for change ("Breaking Racial Barriers").

Real estate speculator William Harmon (1862–1928), whose father was a lieutenant in the Tenth Colored Cavalry in Oklahoma after the Civil War, started the Harmon Foundation in 1922 and came regularly to the aid of African American artists. In 1925, the foundation instituted the Harmon Awards to grant assistance especially to unknown artists and sponsored exhibitions from 1926 through 1934 to showcase the work of award recipients. Harmon died in 1928; Mary Beattie Brady directed the foundation from 1928 to 1967 to continue the ideals of self-help and equality. Like Harmon, Brady had goals of equality and integration, of using art to help African Americans secure a better place in society (Fine 88; Scott and Rutkoff 251–52).

After Reyneau met with Brady, together they made a plan for an exhibit, *Portraits of Outstanding Americans of Negro Origin*, that would be the foundation's most successful project. They planned to pick a group of stellar figures from education, art, music, business, science, armed services, law, and government to fulfill a particular political goal: of increasing the position of African Americans by recognizing their accomplishments as Americans. Just as Reyneau had stood up for the Other through her involvement in suffrage, attempting to increase the status of women in American society, so she did here through her involvement in art.

Together Brady and Reyneau decided to involve an African American artist in the project to split the work on the pieces and provide an important symbolic union. Some artists were not interested in the restrictive form here, of art controlled by a clearly stated social cause. Both Brady and Reyneau were happy when Laura Wheeling Waring decided to join them. After graduating in 1914 from the Pennsylvania Academy of Fine Arts, Waring had studied portraiture in Paris. In 1927 she had exhibited her work in the country's first African American art exhibit, sponsored by the Harmon Foundation. She was the only woman to have received the highest Harmon award, her work exhibited by the Harmon Foundation as well as the Pennsylvania Academy of Fine Arts, the Corcoran Gallery, the Brooklyn Museum, and the Smithsonian. When Waring joined in this effort, she used her artistic connections to solicit sittings by well-known artists and writers, such as Marian Anderson and W.E.B. Du Bois (Ploski and Kaiser 720).

In planning this exhibit, Brady, Waring, and Reyneau solicited the help of Alain Locke, who throughout his career promoted African American artists, writers, and musicians, encouraging them to depict African and African American subjects. Locke edited the March 1925 issue of the periodical *Survey Graphic*, a special issue called "Harlem: Mecca of the New Negro," which helped educate black and white readers about the flourishing culture in Harlem. Later that year, he expanded the issue into *The New Negro*, an anthology of African American fiction, poetry, drama, and essays. Like Reyneau, Locke believed that the American view of itself as a bastion of democracy must be reviewed in the light of its record with citizens deemed as Other. In "Color: Unfinished Business of Democracy," a special issue of

Survey Graphic in November of 1942, he contrasted institutionalized racial discrimination in the United States with the Allies' avowed democratic war aims. Locke's cultural critique impressed Reyneau, and so Brady wrote to Locke in 1943 that the project needed his input: "I think Mrs. Reyneau would be very glad to have you talk over with her the people who should be considered for the portraits for this exhibit" (Fleming 19). Locke gave suggestions for subjects to include and helped make connections with them, his goal to make the exhibit uplifting and influential.

The exhibit opened at the Smithsonian on May 2, 1944, and generated the type of response that Reyneau, Waring, Locke, and Brady wanted. At the opening ceremony, with Eleanor Roosevelt there, Vice President Henry Wallace officially presented the portrait of Carver to the Smithsonian. In her syndicated "My Day" column on May 4, Roosevelt commented, "This portrait will be added to the national collection of fine arts and will permanently hang in the Smithsonian," and she praised the overall exhibit.

Then, after the successful opening, the Smithsonian decided on a national tour to sites where both black and white Americans could see the paintings. Reyneau toured with social activist Bella Taylor McKnight, then director of the Cleveland branch of the NAACP, since Laura Waring was ill. Waring died in 1948.

When the exhibit, generally a combination of some Reyneau and Waring originals and some reproductions of them, came to a town, it appeared at an integrated library, school, church, art gallery, or meeting hall. Opening ceremonies generally involved the mayor and other dignitaries, often little accustomed to celebrating African American culture. After these festivities, visitors could attend lectures concerning the portraits and their subjects. In her talks, Reyneau spoke out forcefully against racial injustice and fascism and the lack of knowledge concerning African American contributions to American life. She used personal recollections in her talks, including anecdotes about the suffrage campaign, to describe injustice. She then segued to her interest in African American achievements in World War II and to the purposes of the exhibit. McKnight then further discussed the subjects of the portraits, the two believing that their joint physical presence provided a visual symbol of equality and unity (Fleming 24).

Prompted by press releases, newspapers across the country tied the exhibit to the furthering of race relations and of the position of African Americans in the United States. This tone was set by the *New York Times*, which wrote of the paintings at the opening exhibit: "The members of this little gallery, which could be much enlarged, may be taken to indicate in some degree the various achievements of a gifted people" ("Portrait"). When in 1945 the exhibit came to the Brooklyn Museum along with an a group of paintings by African American artists, the *Times* commented, "Exhibitions such as those now being held in the Brooklyn Museum are illuminating in themselves. They should be instrumental, besides, in helping to break down prejudice, disruptive of the ideals of democracy, wherever it may exist" ("Negro Art Show").

When the show began touring, it contained sixteen paintings by Reyneau and seven by Waring. Two others that Waring had painted prior to the commission were added later; her paintings included those of Marian Anderson, W.E.B. Du Bois, Jessie Fauset, and James Weldon Johnson. To increase interest as the tour continued, Reyneau kept adding additional works. Of the final total of fifty, the rest, forty-one, were hers. When she received her commission from the Smithsonian, she went directly to Howard University to begin her work. There she had completed, in five months, portraits of educators Charles Hamilton Houston, Mordecai W. Johnson, and Alain Locke, among others. The portrait of educator Mary McLeod Bethune took Reyneau the longest to paint as she sought to capture Bethune's "vibrant personality." Her painting of statesman Dr. Ralph Bunche also took several weeks during which time, Reyneau said, she was "constantly tripping over diplomats."

By the time she completed her total of forty-one, Reyneau's portraits included African American men of many different accomplishments: Thurgood Marshall; Alain Locke; Joe Louis; Lester Blackwell Granger, social scientist and executive director of the National Urban League; William Henry Hastie, attorney, judge, and dean of law at Howard University; Charles Spurgeon Johnson, the first black president of Fisk University; Theodore K. Lawless, physician and researcher, the first to use radium to treat cancer; Asa Philip Randolph, labor organizer and civil rights leader; Paul Robeson, appearing in his costume as Othello; Walter Francis White, head of the NAACP; and Charles Drew, surgeon.

Through her portraits, Reyneau also brought to national attention many African American women: Jane Matilda Bolin, the first black woman to receive a law degree from Yale University and the first black woman judge; Anna Arnold Hedgeman, lecturer, activist, and sociologist; Edith Spurlock Sampson, a judge and delegate to the United Nations; and Helen Adele Johnson Whiting, a state supervisor of rural education in Georgia, who wrote children's books on black folklore. One of her most exciting opportunities was the chance to paint Mary Church Terrell, a fellow suffrage picket. A graduate from Oberlin College in 1884, Terrell became the first president of the National Association of Colored Women and by the early 1900s was deeply immersed in a host of efforts to combat racial discrimination. Included in her activities was her involvement in founding of the NAACP and in picketing for suffrage. This portrait is the one that Reyneau kept after the exhibit ended.

Reyneau carefully picked the props for each portrait, emphasizing the professionalism of the subject through books, stethoscopes, and other accoutrements of their careers, as she had done with George Washington Carver and his amaryllis plant. As the *New York Times* review of the exhibit commented, "In some instances the treatment is especially ingenious, involving appropriate symbolism in the background" (Jewell). In Reyneau's portrait, Harlem Renaissance painter Aaron Douglas stands in front of *Song of the Towers*, the last in a series of four murals, *Aspects of Negro Life*, that he completed in 1934 under the sponsorship of the Works Progress Administration to trace African Americans' history, the towers here being the skyscrapers of the industrialized, urban North to which black Southerners were migrating. Her portrait of Ralph Johnson Bunche, a diplomat from the State Department who took a leadership role in intelligence efforts during World War II, presents him as composed and reflective in front of maps of the world. In her portrait, surgeon Charles Drew, a Howard researcher who had resigned from his position of director of the American Red Cross blood bank during World War II when the organization began separating blood by race of donor, held a test tube in his hand (Schatzki). In painting Mary McLeod Bethune, an influential educator, Reyneau included a picture of Faith Hall, the first major building erected at Bethune's normal-industrial school that opened in 1904 in Daytona Beach, Florida; in the foreground, the forward-thinking Bethune has her hand on a globe. In her portrait of Marian Anderson, one that she did not need to do since Waring had painted the singer, Reyneau had a specific scene in mind. While Waring painted her in a long red dress preparing to sing in a concert hall, Reyneau chose the coat that she wore for her concert on Easter Sunday 1939 at the Lincoln Memorial after the Daughters of the American Revolution refused permission for her to sing to an integrated audience in their Constitution Hall. Reyneau held the painting and submitted it to the National Portrait Gallery after the traveling exhibit ended; she had not wanted it to replace Waring's on the tour. Although most of Reyneau's paintings had props of professional life and specific triumphant moments, with Martin Luther King, in an often reproduced portrait, she made another choice, showing him looking forward, grasping his own hands, in a business suit with handkerchief, in stark black and white: an eternal figure, no accoutrements needed.

As the exhibit went on, Reyneau added some paintings because their debut could be the occasion for separate ceremonies and celebrations. Like suffragists planning specific events for the pickets, as on July 14 of 1917, Reyneau knew that continued drama could mean continued news value. She unveiled her portrait of Mary Lee Mills, a lieutenant commander who had worked in health clinics and nursing schools around the world and was then heading the navy's public health services for the near east, in January 1953 during a meeting of the advisory council of the American Nurses Association in New York. At this meeting Betsy Reyneau discussed her artwork and Mary Beattie Brady spoke of "the outstanding action of the American Nurses Association in taking the lead in wiping out color lines": the ANA had been one of the first all-white professional organizations to invite members of a separate black organization to meet together and then amalgamate ("Nurse Portrait Unveiled").

When Reyneau painted William Ayers Campbell, the first black pilot to drop a bomb in fighting over Sicily, this portrait also responded to specific events. A September 1943 *Time* article questioned the need for training and employing African American pilots when these servicemen were much better suited to mechanical jobs: "No theater commander wants them in considerable numbers; the high command has trouble finding combat jobs for them. There is no lack of work to be done by Negroes as labor and engineering troops — the Army's dirty work" ("Training: Experiment Proved?" 68). In response, a hearing was convened before the House Armed Services Committee to determine whether the Tuskegee Airmen experiment should be allowed to continue. When Reyneau painted Campbell as hero in early 1944, she was making a statement of support. She at first entitled the painting *The Aviator* to create a symbolic portrait of participation and heroism in war. After the portrait's first appearance in the exhibit, with the pilots still under attack, it appeared with Reyneau's own inspiring note:

> Capt. William Ayers Campbell of the Ninety-ninth Pursuit Squadron was the first Negro pilot to drop a bomb. He fought at Pantelleria, Sicily, Salerno, Anzio. He flew as much as twelve hours a day during the critical days when it seemed as if the troops at Salerno would be pushed back into the sea. They were saved from complete disaster by the air umbrella of the planes. He was sent home having completed his mission, but asked to be sent back immediately as he wished to fight as long as a white or black flier still faced the enemy. I painted him at the Tuskegee Air Base, on his short furlough. He is now at the European front again [Fleming 50].

The continuing enlargement of the exhibit gave Reyneau the opportunity to create other portraits of the war heroes who had interested her on her initial visit to Tuskegee and to associate these individuals with perseverance and strength. One of these heroes was Hugh Nathaniel Mulzac, the first African American merchant marine naval officer to command an integrated crew during wartime. As her written narrative that accompanied the portrait stressed, he had earned his captain's rating in the Merchant Marine in 1920, but racial prejudice had denied him the right to command a ship. He sailed instead as a mate, working his way up through the ranks to chief cook. Later the Navy offered Mulzac command of a ship with an all-black crew. He refused, declaring that "under no circumstances will I command a Jim Crow vessel." During World War II, his demand for an integrated crew was finally met as he took command of the S.S. *Booker T. Washington*. The ship, where Reyneau painted Mulzac, made twenty-two round-trip voyages in five years and carried 18,000 troops to Europe and the Pacific ("Breaking Racial Barriers").

Although Brady and the Harmon Foundation approved Reyneau's support of Campbell and Mulzac, they ultimately opposed her judgments about Paul Robeson. Reyneau's 1944 portrait of Robeson portrays him in one of his greatest roles, as Othello; during the sittings, Reyneau had the opportunity to talk with Robeson about politics and their shared dedication to righting social wrongs, a commitment to activism that shaped his career as an artist as it did her own. Following his first trip to Russia in late 1934, Robeson became fluent in Russian, studied Russian history, and wrote numerous articles demonstrating his deeply held beliefs that the United States should seek peace and understanding with Soviet Russia. On October 7, 1946, in California, he testified before the Fact-Finding Committee on Un-American Activities, the Tenney Committee, that he was not a Communist Party member despite his unwavering support of socialism. But because of the controversy surrounding him, as a supporter of Russia, of civil rights for African Americans, and of labor unions, Robeson's recordings and films lost mainstream distribution, and he rarely performed publicly. In 1950 the State Department denied Robeson a passport and issued a stop notice at all ports, effectively confining him to the United States. When the Harmon exhibit arrived in Boston later that year, the mayor ordered Robeson's portrait barred from the show. In response to public pressure there and elsewhere, the Harmon Foundation removed the Robeson portrait from the exhibit, Mary Brady commenting, "I hope the time will come when it will be practical to again emphasize Mr. Robeson's achievements as a singer and an actor." The decision was indeed Brady's: as a social activist who had opposed her government in the suffrage campaign, Reyneau did not agree with this choice since she viewed Robeson as an artist and critic playing a key role in a democracy, much like herself (Stewart; "Breaking Racial Barriers").

The exhibit toured the country for ten years, discontinuing when *Brown v. Topeka Board of Education*, for which portrait subject Thurgood Marshall was the lead attorney, offered a reason for its no longer being needed although by then audiences had dwindled. In 1967, the Harmon Foundation gave forty-one of the original fifty portraits in the exhibition to the National Portrait Gallery, a group of works gathered again for a 1997 exhibit there ("Breaking Racial Barriers").

After the tour ended, Reyneau worked on the museum placement of other portraits. She felt that her activism, her commitment of her own time and talents, working as an individual and within a group, had made a difference in American life. She had gained in suffrage the strength to overcome adversaries and press forward toward the goal of justice: she ultimately would exhibit that strength as an artist as well as a suffragist.

Havemeyer, Kellogg, and Reyneau were changed by the suffrage campaign. They did not enter politics after the vote was gained, but they had other designs on their time, designs that the suffrage experience helped them to envision and enact. They did enter the larger political arena as determined women who thought of themselves as fully capable of changing American definitions: of who could make valuable art and what subject it might concern. As they advocated for an understanding of modern artists, of African American artists and subjects, and of children as artists, they did so confidently: with hard work, they could change the categories of acceptable and unacceptable, of respected and not respected — just as women had done in seeking the vote.

3

Not to Simply Teach, but to Transform Education

As artists, art collectors, and art scholars, suffragists influenced their nation in the years after they achieved the vote. In the larger field of education, similarly, they created an immense sense of change but perhaps not in traditionally noticed categories. In the twentieth century, women dominated elementary and high school teaching in the United States and gained a lesser place in university teaching. In 1910, 80 percent of teachers below the university level were women, with numbers higher for elementary than for high school. This percentage held steady in 1920 and 1930 and in the second half of the century though it decreased somewhat during the Depression years, to 74 percent (Bank et al. 662; Cott, *The Grounding of* 218). Given the growth in the number of normal schools, seminaries, and women's colleges, women's participation in college teaching advanced sharply at the beginning of the century, to 30 percent of the total in the 1910s, but decreased afterwards as more students entered co-educational state schools where male teachers dominated until the 1960s and 1970s (Cott, *The Grounding of* 218–19).

After the suffrage campaign, many suffrage supporters taught at all levels, as part of these enlarging percentages of participation, though at institutions rarely within their control. For women who were fully involved in the campaign, however, remaining within accepted roles as educators would not always be enough. They viewed themselves as having the right to learn and teach outside of accepted categories, to work together, emphasizing the knowledge that could prepare women for professional careers and for self-actualization. They viewed education as a lifelong activity, especially necessary for adults who might be unable to engage in traditional schooling. As they initiated reform, they sought new levels of access for those who were generally barred from American institutions, new types of curricula, and new approaches to professional training. Women like Agnes Chase, Alma

Lutz, and Helen Keller had through the suffrage campaign energized their own lives, and they took from it a model of adult education, especially of women but of men also, with a far-reaching effect.

(Mary) Agnes Chase (1869–1963)

After the campaign ended, some women returned to their first goals, of traditional careers, but they did so imbued with new standards of activism and group responsibility, standards that would have a substantial professional impact. Mary Agnes Chase devoted her life to the study of grasses, working to expand existing knowledge about the plant that "holds the soil" and provides "the principle food of animals that furnish meat and milk" as well as "all our breadstuffs, wheat, corn, oats, rye, barley, and rice" (*First Book of Grasses* 115–17). As a botanist, author, and agrostologist—a specialist in grasses—she ultimately traveled the world to collect and catalogue more than 10,000 species of grasses, many of which she discovered. In the early part of her career, she dealt with gender discrimination, which brought her to the suffrage campaign. Afterwards, she no longer depended on male mentors, as she had before, but instead became a mentor herself—to women and men from the United States and elsewhere. Suffrage did not lead her into a political career; it served instead as a means for seeking professional opportunity and justice for herself and others, a model for professional activism.

Chase was born Mary Agnes Meara on April 20, 1869, in rural eastern Illinois, Iroquois County, a child who lacked opportunities. Her father, an Irish railroad blacksmith, died when she was two. Her mother then moved her five young children to Chicago where they lived with the maternal grandmother and both women worked to support them. After Chase finished grammar school, all they could afford for her, she began working as a clerk to help support the family. As she told an interviewer when the University of Illinois gave her an honorary doctorate at age eighty-nine, "Girls didn't get to go to college when I was young. I had to just pick up my education as I went along" ("Mrs. Agnes Chase").

A scholarly child, Chase soon found a job suitable to her meticulous, single-minded nature: working as a proofreader and typesetter at a small magazine for country schoolteachers, the *School Herald*. This job led to her meeting William Ingraham Chase, the magazine's thirty-four-year-old editor. In January of 1888, the couple was married. At that time, William Chase was already ill with tuberculosis and he died within the year, leaving the nineteen-year-old Chase a widow saddled with his large debts from his pub-

Mary Agnes Chase joined the Department of Agriculture in 1903 as a botanical illustrator, and eventually became principal botanist in charge of systematic agrostology at the Division of Plants, United States Museum. After Chase was arrested in Lafayette Square and refused to accept bail, she demanded political prisoner status, instigated a hunger strike, and was force-fed. The photographer here is unidentified. Photograph (from ca. 1960) is held by Smithsonian Institution, copied here from Wikimedia Commons.

lication. To support herself and pay his creditors, she worked as a proofreader on the *Inter Ocean* newspaper, where she learned a crisp style that later served her well in science writing, and she moonlighted at a general store owned by her brother-in-law.

At the store she struck up a strong friendship with her nephew, Virginius Chase, and discovered that she shared the boy's interest in plant identification. Chase became increasingly fascinated by botany and read voraciously on the subject. She went out into rural areas around Chicago whenever she could, keeping notebooks in which she sketched plants and wrote about what she observed. As she could afford to, she also enrolled in extension courses in botany at the University of Chicago and the Lewis Institute. Both boy and woman were especially inspired by the plant-collecting exhibit at the 1893 Columbian Exposition in Chicago (Bonta, *Women in the Field* 130–33).

As she sought to turn her interest into a career, Chase had help from a series of male mentors. Working in the fields around Chicago, she met the Rev. Ellsworth Jerome Hill, an amateur student of spore-reproducing plants, retired from the ministry and lacking the funds to hire someone to make drawings of the new species, especially of mosses, that he was discovering. They made an agreement: she illustrated his papers; he taught her more about botany and allowed her to experiment with his compound microscope.

As their work progressed, Hill suggested that Chase meet with Charles Frederick Millspaugh, director of Chicago's Field Museum of Natural History. In 1901 Millspaugh offered Chase a part-time job as an illustrator for two museum publications, *Plantae Utowanae* and *Plantae Yucatanae*. Because the drawings required the rendering of minute details, at this job she increased her skills with the microscope, obtaining a level of knowledge that she parlayed into a full-time position, as a meat inspector for a Chicago stockyard, a job offering the increased pay that she and her mother needed.

Since Chase sought a future in botany not in stockyards, with Hill's encouragement in 1903 she applied for a position as a botanical illustrator at the U.S. Department of Agriculture (USDA) Bureau of Plant Sciences, located in Washington, D.C. Awarded the job, Chase set about providing botanical illustrations for the bureau's many publications and took advantage of her position to spend much of her free time at the USDA's herbarium. (Bonta, *American Women Afield* 126).

At the USDA, Chase had found a job with one of the few scientific institutes open to women, though only to make illustrations, certainly not to participate in scientific analysis and classification, work for which she was deemed unsuited by gender and inadequate academic certification. Beginning in the nineteenth century, women had been employed at collecting and drawing plants since, as a *Science* article from 1887 attested, this sort of scientific activity was commonly judged as not "a manly study; that it is merely one of the ornamental branches [of science], suitable enough for young ladies and effeminate youths, but not adapted for able-bodied and vigorous-brained young men who wish to make the best use of their powers" (J.F.A. Adams 116; Rossiter 61–64). As historian Sally G. Kohlstedt notes in "Women in the History of Science," however, by the first decades of the twentieth century even this limited method of entering into a scientific career was becoming less common as universities set up graduate programs, professional societies, and hiring requirements that omitted women.

At the USDA, Chase fortunately met another powerful male mentor and collaborator, Albert Spear Hitchcock, who did not subscribe to traditional limitations for women. In 1907 she went to work as Hitchcock's scientific assistant in his study of agrostology. She published her first scientific paper in 1906. Hitchcock advanced her to the position of scientific assistant in systematic agrostology that year and assistant botanist in 1909 as together they developed a research program to collect, describe, identify, and classify the grasses of the Americas. Beginning in 1905, Chase began traveling across the United States doing research for the USDA, work resulting in a book coauthored with Hitchcock, *The North American Species of Panicum* (1910).

As an agrostologist working for the federal government, Chase became involved in industrial as well as academic research. While Chase and Hitchcock specialized in species found in the wild, they also catalogued and studied commercially developed strains. They thus ensured that newly introduced commercial grasses and other forage plants were not marketed using fraudulent claims. They also made recommendations regarding feed grass for livestock. With their work on wild and commercial strains growing, Chase served as assistant custodian of the grass herbarium, which had been transferred from the USDA to the Smithsonian.

Although Chase had advanced well into a career with the help of male mentors, in 1911 she had the professional experience that made all too clear to her the real status of women in the American scientific community. Chase wanted to go to Panama in 1911 and 1912 to participate in a major survey of the region being completed alongside work on the Panama Canal, a project involving many of the best North American scientists. These experts set up the Barro Colorado Island Biological Laboratory where they collected and analyzed data while also collaborating on grant applications and publications. Women scientists could not spend the night and needed a pass to be there during the day: with permission, they could come by boat from the mainland only if they returned the same evening. David Fairchild, the well-connected son-in-law of a laboratory benefactor, described the men's priorities in 1924 when a dormitory for women was being considered (and turned down): "Let us keep a place where real research men can find quiet, keen intellectual stimulation, freedom from any outside distractions" (Henson, "Invading Arcadia" 586). On the island, women were not the only excluded group: no Latin American scientist of either gender could work at the facilities. Thus both groups, Latin American men and all women scholars, lost the chance for field work and membership in an intellectual community. When Albert Hitchcock asked the Smithsonian to intervene for Chase, and even informed Frederick W. True, assistant secretary of the Smithsonian, that she would provide her own funding, True turned them down, writing that "I doubt the advisability of engaging the services of a woman for the purpose" (Henson, "Invading Arcadia" 580). Like Fairchild, True felt that women would distract men, and he additionally argued that Chase might be endangered in Panama even though many North American women were living in the Canal Zone.

When Chase learned in early 1913 about Alice Paul's attempts at organizing a group to work for a federal suffrage amendment, she decided to get involved. She marched in the pre-inaugural parade in March of 1913, with a group of other women scientists. She also began attending meetings where activists were planning a boycott of Democrats and a new women's party, joining not for a future in politics but for increased respect and professional opportunity.

As the route toward suffrage grew more difficult, Chase did not shirk from her commitment: she stood on the picket line in 1917 even after Wilson declared war. Then on August 6, 1918, Inez Milholland's birthday, she was jailed for ten days for a rally in Lafayette Square, organized to oppose Wilson's refusal to keep the Congress for an extra session to bring the federal amendment to a vote ("Suffrage Demonstration"). After Chase was arrested and refused to accept bail, she was held in the abandoned and dangerous jail where she demanded political prisoner status, instigated a hunger strike, and was force-fed. For this jailing, the USDA threatened her with dismissal "for conduct unbecoming a government employee," but Hitchcock helped her to keep her job (Henson, "Invading Arcadia" 594).

After seeing the difficult fight undertaken by women for the basic privilege of voting and recognizing the continuing inequities in science, Chase's view of her own career changed drastically: she no longer thought it enough to secure her own mentors and improve her own job status. As historian Pamela Henson has written, Chase was afterwards able "to forge a highly productive style of relationship with her Latin American colleagues": she did so and reached out to women scholars from the United States as well through the influence of her experiences with suffrage (Henson, "Invading Arcadia" 594).

After women achieved the vote, Chase began applying the bravery, commitment, and physical strength required to picket and hunger strike to her own career. With little funding and no field-study base, she began traveling alone to Latin America, staying, for example, in Brazil for eight months in October of 1924. Since she had no assistants or guides, she forged relationships with locals, especially women missionaries stationed there, who welcomed her into their homes and helped her to travel. Little grass collecting had been done in the Amazon and other parts of Brazil; some areas had never been fully explored. In November, with two women missionaries, she visited the Paulo Afonso Falls, a series of rapids and cataracts in northeastern Brazil on the São Francisco River, as she wrote, a region "difficult of access until recently and not heretofore visited by a botanist" ("Eastern Brazil" 387). She spent December in the savannas and marshes to the north. In January, she did collecting on Itatiaia Mountain, one of the highest points in Brazil. Then from early February to the end of May, she was in the state of Minas Geraes, where the high hills and large, brushy campos created yet other types of vegetation and other traveling difficulties ("Botanical Expedition"). These trips resulted in the largest collection of Brazilian grasses ever assembled, with much analysis to come from it (Bonta, *Women in the Field* 141).

As Chase worked in Brazil, she collaborated with local scientists, getting them to venture out from their museums on collecting trips and to set up facilities in which they could house their own findings, relying on the confidence gained through her suffrage experiences to help her colleagues endure the physical risks that these trips entailed. The physical challenge of plant collecting, in fact, had caused *Science* magazine to overturn nineteenth-century judgments and consider it as properly a purview of men: "The botanical student must be a walker; and his frequent tramps harden his muscles, and strengthen his frame. He must strike off across the fields, penetrate the woods to their secret depths, scramble through swamps, and climb the hills" (J.F.A. Adams 117). But, contrary to the *Science* article's preferences, this adventurous "he" in Brazil was Chase and her associates. From the United States, Chase had been providing Dona Maria Bandeira, who worked on mosses at the Jardim Botanico in Rio de Janeiro, with advice and encouragement. In Brazil, they traveled together — by train, truck, bus, and car, with roads and no roads — and climbed one of the two highest peaks of Mount Itatiaia, descending with skirts full of specimens. Chase recorded the arduous route they followed, their attention always on collecting: "The trail was difficult, up over stones and through deep mud or across streams. It was necessarily slow going so I did not have to give much attention to the horse, but could keep my eyes on the forested slopes above and below, with their palms, tree ferns and great masses of hanging bamboo, and on the trail border were *Panicum*, *Ichnanthus*, and a silvery *Paspulum* promising rich collecting on the way back." As the two women climbed Mount Italiaia, they went straight up: "Above Italiaia Alta the peak, called Agulhas Negras (the black needles), rises abruptly, composed below of steep, bare granite cliffs deeply furrowed vertically. We climbed up the furrows on all fours and crossed from one series to another over steep slopes covered with a low bamboo (*Chusquea pinifolia*) most convenient to cling to. At the top of these furrowed cliffs is a great overhanging rock that seemed to stop all progress, but the way led through a crevice to one side and over and between boulders wedged in the crevice. The worst place was like a chimney flue, which we ascended with the help of a rope" ("Eastern Brazil" 393–94).

Besides offering challenging field experience and advice to young local scientists, Chase also brought with her American women who sought entrance into the scientific community. In 1929, when she returned to Brazil for another eight months, she collaborated with Ynes Mexia of the University of California at Berkeley. Originally a social worker, Mexia had started taking botany classes at the university at age fifty-one. Though they often clashed, Mexia finding Chase too dogged in her daily work schedule, Chase offered her a chance for professional work that she would not otherwise have had. Together they climbed the eastern side of Pontao Crystal peak, the site of a virgin rainforest, in difficult rainy weather, collecting all the way (Bonta, *American Women Afield* 126, 136–37).

While training individuals in the field, Chase helped Latin American governments to set up and improve their own facilities, a difficult political choice for an American scientist, one encouraging competition with the powerful Smithsonian. In 1940, for example, Chase was invited by the Ministry of Agriculture in Venezuela to develop a plan for research and range management of native grasses. At age seventy-one, she traveled through the country, forming a collection with Henri Pittier, who had worked for the USDA and was then director of the Servicio Botanico of the Venezuelan Agricultural Ministry. Chase urged the ministry to train its own specialists, instead of turning specimens over to the Smithsonian or to American scientists, and offered to take Zoraida Luces with her to Washington to study for a year in the National Herbarium, after which Luces was appointed a botanist at the Venezuelan Agricultural Ministry. For the rest of Chase's life, she and Luces corresponded, with Luces using the salutation, "My dear Grandma" (Henson, "Invading Arcadia" 597). In 1959, as Luces de Febres, she translated Chase's popular *First Book of Grasses* into Spanish.

With other young scientists as with Zoraida Luces, Chase took the step of offering training in Washington and even allowing them to board at her home. Luces was, in fact, one of dozens of young Latin American naturalists who stayed there, at the home they called Casa Contenta, and who studied in Chase's laboratory, where their mentor was, as Henson has written, "trying to open the doors for them that Chase had earlier found closed" ("Invading Arcadia" 598).

Along with helping scientists from Latin America, Chase sought to work with other American women scientists who might find themselves outside of the regular paths of career development. Wherever she went, she wrote about her findings to Alice Eastwood, curator at the California Herbarium, a Canadian who like Chase had come into the career without a formal education in science. In this correspondence, they discussed the specifics of their work. Even at ages eighty and ninety, Eastwood the older of the two, they were still working and still writing to each other, discussing their calling as it stretched well beyond formal retirement (Bonta, *American Women Afield* 86; Abir-Am and Outram 84–85). With Eastwood as with so many other scientists, as an article in the journal *Taxon* describes Chase, she was always ready to drop what she was doing "to identify a grass that has stumped the beginner or lesser worker and to explain the intricacies of the systematics of the enormous and difficult family Gramineae. This help to her colleagues will be, in the long run, not the least of her contributions to the science of systematic botany" (Fosberg and Swallen 145).

As Chase served as mentor and colleague, she thrived in her own career. In early 1936, she was promoted to senior botanist in charge of systematic agrostology at the USDA's Bureau of Plant Industry, taking over the role of her mentor, Hitchcock, who died in 1935. Her duties also expanded when, in 1937, she was appointed custodian of the Grass Herbarium. Although she retired from her position at the USDA in April 1939, she continued working long hours as a herbarium research associate and retained her custodial duties at the herbarium under the title of honorary custodian until near her death. According to *The Magnificent Foragers: Smithsonian Explorations in the Natural Sciences*, Chase was "custodian of the largest collection of grasses in the world ... the legendary figure in Botany ... the dean of American agrostologists and came to know more about grass than any person alive" (Sherwood 24–25). She discovered over 500 species of plants. Her frequent publications of professional papers and books, aimed at the professional scientist and at the amateur botanist, further extended her reputation and influence. She received an honorary doctorate from the University of Illinois at age eighty-nine and a certificate of merit at the fiftieth anniversary of the founding of the Botanical Society of America in 1956, as "one of the world's outstanding agrostologists and preeminent among American students in this field." At her death in 1963, the *New York Times* described her as "dean of the world's experts on grasses" ("Mrs. Agnes Chase"). Her awards came for her own research and publications but also for her aid to young scholars and to independent scholarship in many countries.

After her suffrage experience, Chase worked diligently to extend her profession and to involve others in it. As Henson noted, "She brought her personal egalitarian values to her scientific work and professional interactions. The obstacles she encountered forced her to take a different path that had positive effects on her scientific work and relationships with Latin American colleagues" (Henson, "Invading Arcadia" 600). In 1917, through suffrage, she developed an understanding of her career, as not just involving individual, but instead group achievement, as appropriately incorporating the work of those who might be judged as outsiders by American scientists: those who weren't Americans, lacked the accepted education, or weren't men. After her time in prison, she took on more physical difficulty and began redefining the scientific community. "She was the hub of the network, its creator, and the source of its continuing energy," wrote Pamela Henson. In these choices, as a "charismatic leader," she was still a suffragist ("'What Holds the Earth Together'" 451–53).

Alma Lutz (1871–1974)

While Agnes Chase helped scientists judged as Other to enter the profession, suffragists also engaged in changing the educational opportunities for the next generations by enlarging the materials that would be judged as worthy of study. In 1969, Gerda Lerner wrote that "the striking fact about the historiography of women is the general neglect of the subject by historians ("New Approaches" 231). Like Germaine Greer and other writers of the period, she argued that no generation before her own had seriously studied women's history and taught it to students: women's studies, she asserted, was then developing on university campuses solely as a priority of the second wave, a field ignored by scholars and universities in previous decades, the current accomplishment thus unprecedented. The Web site for the San Diego State University Women's Studies Department, formed in 1970, reiterates her arguments: it states that this oldest official program in the United States stemmed from "the social and political activism of feminists in the 1960s" ("History of"). In the 1970s, following the example of San Diego State and Richmond College of the City University of New York (now the College of Staten Island), many universities and colleges created departments and programs in women's studies. Funding from the National Endowment for the Humanities and from private foundations, especially the Ford Foundation, enhanced the standing of women's studies in the academy. The National Women's Studies Association, established in 1977, provided a forum for scholarship, program development, and political activism. The association's Web site now lists over 900 programs in American universities. Though these courses and this historical scholarship certainly flourished in the 1970s, it was another second-wave assertion to claim that neither had existed before.

Women' studies, in fact, had been engendered by the efforts of the much maligned women of the first wave, among them suffragist Alma Lutz.

Lutz was brought up in North Dakota, attended the Emma Willard School in Troy, New York, and then went to Vassar, where she graduated in 1912, imbued with the choice of activism. In January of her freshman year, she saw Anna Howard Shaw speak on the need for college students to take the suffrage campaign seriously and become involved (H.S. Howard). In March of her freshman year, she saw Inez Milholland, then a senior, at talks during which she advocated the militant approach favored by English suffragettes and criticized American women who were worried that participation in aggressive political acts would made them no longer ladies ("Vassar Girl Suffragette"). Although the Vassar president, James Monroe Taylor, hoped that Milholland's graduation in 1909 would end the campus suffrage movement, parades and meetings continued, as the *New York Times* prophesied that they would in "Vassar Students Are Now Radical." With Milholland as the "idol of the whole undergraduate body," this *Times* article argued, Vassar had become not "one of the most conservative of the women's colleges" but instead "a hotbed of Socialism and other radical ideas," a shocking development that the *Times* thought would only continue and worsen. Indeed, students began participating in shirtwaist strikes and they continued with suffrage activism, choices for which they had the encouragement not of the college president but of some teachers, including historian Lucy Salmon, a member of the National College Equal Suffrage League and the advisory council of the CU. She led an ongoing suffrage movement at Vassar, despite the disapproval of the trustees and of President Taylor, who believed that the school's mission should be classical education and not social reform.

When Lutz was in school, teachers like Salmon were not only engaging in activism but they were also changing historical study, incorporating women's daily lives as well as battles and elections into their classes. Lucy Salmon rejected the traditional method of teaching history that emphasized memorizing and recalling facts about prominent figures and events. As a member of the new social history school, she believed that such methods ignored key aspects of the past. Salmon encouraged scholarly independence by training her students, like Alma Lutz, to compare and criticize several interpretations before formulating their own conclusions and to consult primary source material in addition to secondary scholarship about an array of historical documents and objects used by women and men (Crocco and Davis 60). In addition to scholarly documents, Salmon's students analyzed kitchen appliances, architecture, *Life Magazine* advertisements, and even the

Vassar College catalogue for their historical and social significance. In her teaching of American history, course units covered women's lives from the colonies forward.

Salmon was a prolific writer as well as an innovative teacher, producing over a dozen books and over a hundred essays and lectures focused on actual American lives. Her *Domestic Service*, based on questionnaires that she distributed to domestic servants and their employers, was the first scholarly study of the subject. Her articles also concerned artifacts, such as family cookbooks, and spatial configurations, such as those on an American Main Street (Adams and Smith). As Salmon wrote in 1926 in "Research for Women," advocating a wider range of historical research, "the mental eye may easily discover worldwide, time-old records in the humble everyday concerns of common human affairs" (177). Her *Why Is History Rewritten?*, published in 1929, claimed as an answer to her titular question that the focus, methodologies, and audiences of historical writing had been expanded by new historians. Additionally she recognized the impact of the researcher—"History whether designated as old or new takes on somewhat of the coloring of the historian himself"—and that history would thus be changed when the historian in question was actually not "himself" (201).

Like Lucy Salmon, her student Alma Lutz became a suffrage activist during her years at Vassar. When she graduated in 1912, she returned to North Dakota and there began working within a state suffrage campaign to continue the activism begun in college. North Dakota had given women the right to vote on school issues in 1883, but the state legislature refused to grant a further extension of the franchise until 1917, after a long and hard fight, and then presidential suffrage only. A separate and again difficult fight went on in South Dakota that led to women gaining full suffrage that same year, the differences created by the preferences of individual groups of male legislators and voters.

In 1918, Lutz moved to Boston to attend the Boston University School of Business Administration. In a new state, she again witnessed the frustrations of state campaigns. In 1915, a state referendum to give Massachusetts women the vote had failed at the polls. During that campaign, state organizations of women opposed to suffrage, like the powerful Massachusetts Association Opposed to the Further Extension of Suffrage to Women, founded in 1882, had worked assiduously to keep the legislation from passing.

While Lutz was living in Boston, unable to find the employment that her education should have led her to and increasingly frustrated with the vagaries of state campaigns, she became involved with the NWP—to achieve the vote through a federal amendment and to secure new opportunities. Her friend Mary Ritter Beard, who had protested for suffrage in England with the Pankhursts while her husband, Charles, studied history at Oxford, had joined the CU at the request of Alice Paul and Lucy Burns. Beard became an executive member of the CU board and editor of the *Suffragist.* As an important contributor to the CU, Beard involved Lutz in helping to plan strategy and organize demonstrations.

Although Mary Beard and Alma Lutz became activists together, their views of the picketing were not the same. Beard objected to this technique, as well as to participating in war work to win the vote, as she wrote in a letter to NWP advisory council chair Elizabeth Rogers on November 17, 1917: "I can't fight the battle the picketing way any more than I can use war work as a cudgel even to win" (Beard and Cott 97–98). She asked to be removed from the advisory council in that letter to Rogers: she objected to the war but also to opposing the president during wartime. Alma Lutz, however, disagreed with Beard: Lutz felt that the militants were doing what had to be done to protest against a president who spoke about democracy but refused to enact it; picketing for her was patriotic, certainly not disrespectful or traitorous. She went to Washington to participate in the White House picketing, and protested in Boston on February 24, 1919, Presidents' Day, when Wilson returned from Europe as the great spokesman for democracy. During the ceremonies celebrating his return, Lutz and the other women who unfurled banners for suffrage were arrested for speaking on Boston Common without a permit ("Reminding the President"). When on March 9, 1919, Prison Special travelers participated in a meeting with the women who had been jailed, Lutz joined them on the podium. Soon afterwards, she began writing for the NWP journal, as the *Suffragist* and then *Equal Rights*, an involvement that continued to the 1940s.

When the suffrage movement ended, Lutz wanted to use the increase in opportunity that the vote signaled to expand the study of women's history, building on what she had experienced with Lucy Salmon as a student at Vassar. She could extend her suffrage activism both by writing and by participating in curricular reform, introducing other women to her heroes, creating a space for more stories about women in American history, expanding the territory of what mattered, as had Salmon. In her career as a historian, her friend Mary Beard would seek to stress only women's positive contributions in history, so that they would not find themselves belittled by negative depictions. In her books *On Understanding Women* (1931) and *Woman as a Force in History: A Study of Traditions and Realities* (1946) as well as other publications, Beard contended that the proper study of women's "long history," from the beginning of human life to the present, would reveal that women had played a key role in all civilizations (Cott, "Putting Women" 31). She emphasized that women's contributions, different from men's, had not been sufficiently noted by historians. Careful study would reveal that their history was not primarily one of political or sexual oppression, and thus to concentrate on discrimination denigrated what women had achieved (Lane 68). But Lutz wanted a fuller and more nuanced picture to emerge, of glorious acts and great difficulties. Though both friends began to extend their activism through historical research and publication, they did so with different goals.

Grounded in the sacrifices of the suffrage movement and determined to look carefully at key moments in which American women fought oppression, Lutz's first books concerned suffragists: *Created Equal: A Biography of Elizabeth Cady Stanton* (1940) and *Challenging Years: The Memoirs of Harriot Stanton Blatch* (1940). She also published *Susan B. Anthony: Rebel, Crusader, Humanitarian* in 1959.

Before Lutz published her *Created Equal*, essays about Stanton had appeared in Willis John Abbot's *Notable Women in History* (1913); further evaluation of her impact had also occurred in Allan Seager's *They Worked for a Better World* (1939), containing portraits of American reformers. Family members published *Elizabeth Cady Stanton as Revealed in Her Letters, Diary, and Reminiscences* in 1922; Stanton had written her own account, *Eighty Years and More*, in 1898. But here was the first biography of Stanton, certainly complimentary but also a well-researched and evaluative book of 345 pages, covering Stanton's life and influence, drawing on her manuscripts and letters, speeches and articles, with a full bibliography on the person and times. Lutz wrote it not as a friend but as a researcher and professional writer creating a serious portrait of an American. Lutz saw her book as significant to both women and men, as she wrote in the foreword: "Every woman who cherishes freedom owes a debt of gratitude to Elizabeth Cady Stanton. Every man who recognizes that the unhampered co-operation of men and women is necessary for the building of a better civilization will admire her determination to gain a fuller, freer life for women" (vii).

Throughout the book, Lutz ties this study to a consideration of the times in which Stanton lived, creating a frank discussion of gender discrimination of the type that many history courses, and Mary Beard, tended to avoid. As she wrote, "Elizabeth Cady Stanton lived in an era when the law cast the shadow of a 'defect of sex' over women, and not only was this 'defect of sex' reflected in the laws relating to women's property, their children, their work, and their marriage, but in the traditions which had grown up regarding their mental ability and their place in society" (vii). Fighting within this climate,

Stanton had the satisfaction of seeing only four states — Wyoming, Colorado, Idaho, and Utah — enfranchise women: she never felt satisfied by the meager returns on her efforts. Lutz says of Stanton, "How she would have rejoiced in the militant campaigns of Emmeline Pankhurst and Alice Paul, and of her own daughter, Harriot Stanton Blatch!" (317). Lutz anticipates more heroes spurring on women, a chain of effort reaching from Stanton, to Paul and Blatch, and to her readers, an argument that would occur in later women's studies' texts and courses, as women leaders suggested possibilities for the students' own lives.

As Lutz began acquainting younger readers with the previously undocumented lives of women who preceded them, she also became a co-writer for the biography of Harriot Stanton Blatch, forging a type of collaboration that would later be common in women's studies. In 1939, Blatch suffered a fractured hip and moved to a nursing home in Greenwich, Connecticut. Vassar College encouraged Lutz to help finish the book, with Blatch's permission and help, so that it could be among their seventy-fifth anniversary publications. Lutz finished the project by expanding Blatch's manuscript of the first two parts, of which there would be five, from notes and from written records of Blatch's work and thought, creating a first-person narrative throughout. As she honed the personal sense of Blatch's voice, she also carefully studied the political situation of the time and how it impacted American women, employing the social history approach that tied her work to Lucy Salmon's as well as to later women's studies texts (Du Bois 269).

In her books, Lutz also covered less well-known women whose impact on American history deserved attention. She wrote a book about Emma Willard, for example, who founded the Troy Female Seminary in 1821 as well as the high school that Lutz had attended, with a guiding purpose to "free women from the ignorance to which they had been bound by custom and narrow scriptural interpretation." Willard's Plan for Improving Female Education, submitted to the New York legislature in 1819, as well as her seminary helped to create a space for other women's seminaries and later for their college education. Willard is thus, for Lutz, a "national figure," whose work is "still being carried forward to-day." Again, as with her other subjects, Lutz extends the influence and thus her own audience to men: "Not only women, but men and the whole Nation have reaped the benefits of the intelligent useful womanhood developed under her plan of education" (preface, np).

In writing about Willard, Lutz shows her own openness, necessary to later women's studies, to honoring various forms of activism and achievement. She makes it clear, for example, that Willard did not advocate suffrage although she worked her entire life to improve the status of women:

> To be sure, Mrs. Willard did not give her support to the work of Lucretia Mott, Susan B. Anthony, or Elizabeth Cady Stanton. She had had no sympathy with earlier feminists, such as Frances Wright. Yet, she herself was continually stepping out of the so-called sphere of woman, and had struggled all her life to widen that sphere for other women. It is difficult to see just where she drew the line, except that she felt that education rather than agitation would solve woman's problem. One cannot imagine Emma Willard with her interest in history and politics, refusing the ballot if it were offered her. Still the ballot seemed unimportant to her in comparison with the value of education for women" [238].

Like women's studies scholars of later generations, Lutz also wrote books about groups of women who were less well known but whose lives involved them in key historical moments. In 1945, she published an anthology of letters that women wrote during World War II, entitled *With Love, Jane: Letters from American Women on the War Fronts*. She dedicated the book in the preface "to the young women whose letters make up this book and to all the gallant women who have served and are serving our country overseas" (np). The book included letters from army nurses on the front line, from WACs, and from women working abroad for the USO — not letters written to soldiers, but those from women writing home. Each entry begins with a biographical paragraph on what the woman did before the war and the job she did during it. The inclusion of several letters from each woman brings readers into the details of their war work. Lutz's epilogue discusses women's roles in all American wars beginning with the American Revolution. Although she concludes that in World War II "women have proved once again their value to their country and their high patriotism," she also through her headnotes and letters stresses the difficulties with which they struggled, not only those created by war but also by societal judgments of them (199).

While chronicling the lives of women against the backdrop of American values and history, Lutz also included African American women in this picture, helping to right another wrong of much historical study, as women's studies scholars of later generations would also attempt to do. In *Crusade for Freedom: Women of the Antislavery Movement* (1968), she again grounded her project in research, as she stated in the acknowledgments where she included a long list of libraries and archives that had provided materials for the study. Her preface states her argument for women's inclusion in the history of abolition. "Women made an outstanding contribution to the abolition of Negro slavery," she writes, but in histories of the movement their important contributions had been overlooked." While she considers with more detail the contributions of Elizabeth Cady Stanton and other white activists with whom she was familiar through the suffrage movement, she also attempted to chronicle the substantial contributions made by African American activists such as Sojourner Truth.

Throughout her writing career, Alma Lutz attempted to involve her readers in the lives of women like Susan B. Anthony who were being granted some level of respect, women like Frances Willard who were being written out of American history, religious leaders like Mary Baker Eddy who were being ignored by academic scholars, and abolitionists like Sojourner Truth whose contributions had been given very little attention. She also concerned herself with women who served their country in wartime. As she wrote these histories and corresponded with other scholars, she was creating the space of women's studies, recognizing what women had achieved while also analyzing the times in which they lived.

As Lutz extended her career as a historian of women, making a place for others to follow, she also began working with college teachers on the curriculum in literature, economics, and other fields, most substantially in history, creating the interdisciplinary class materials that would become women's studies.

As Lutz began to work on expanding the curriculum, especially in history departments, she felt that the women teachers who might be altering their syllabi would need a supportive group from within which to work. Along with Jeannette Nichols of Swarthmore and Mary Beard, she arranged for a group of about twenty women historians from New England and New York to meet in the Connecticut countryside in 1930 and constitute themselves as the Lakeville History Group, soon to be renamed the Berkshire Conference of Women Historians. They decided to initiate this conference and communications between meetings "for the dual purposes of bolstering their status as academic practitioners and promoting women as worthy historical subjects" (Kerber 11; Des Jardins 217). The immediate impetus for the format of the spring weekend came in response to a week-long retreat for male historians led by J. Franklin Jameson when he was the executive secretary of the American Historical Association. Whereas the men's group collapsed when Jameson died, the women's weekends have continued to the present, evolving into two overlapping groups, the Berkshire Conference of Women Historians and the Berkshire Conference on the History of Women.

At the annual conventions and at smaller meetings among these teachers of women's history, Lutz acquainted other professionals with the research that she was doing for her books, with her methods and primary sources, and encouraged them to work on the many historical subjects that deserved scholarly attention. At these meetings, the speeches that she gave included "Women's Role in American History, 1800–1860," "Women Were There: The

Unsung Warriors of 1861," and "The Learned Lady: The Story of Hannah Adams (1755–1831)." Lutz also brought and shared her collection of primary materials on historical figures such as Abigail Adams, Clara Barton, Alice Stone Blackwell, Louisa May Alcott, Amelia Earhart, and Helen Keller as well as documents concerning social history and the lives of various groups, especially colonial women, western pioneer women, and working women, such as the Lowell Mill workers. She also shared her own bibliographies of the women's history materials available in the libraries at Smith, Vassar, Radcliffe, and other schools (Berkshire Conference).

While attending the conventions, conducting her own research, and collecting research materials, Lutz communicated with teachers across the country, acquainting them with work done by other teachers and helping them accumulate source materials and devise new research methods. Her copies of these letters, included in her papers housed at Vassar, reveal the variety of courses about women across the country. Her correspondents from both women's and co-educational schools included Blanche Hinman Dow, of Cottey College, in Nevada, Missouri, who taught courses on women's history beginning in the late 1940s and continuing after she became president of the college in 1949. Eunice Hilton, from the home economics department at Syracuse University, wrote to Lutz concerning Sociology 153 and 154, a six-hour sequence entitled The Status and Responsibilities of Women in the Modern World, which began at Syracuse University in 1942. Hilton wrote that the course's teachers included Marguerite Fisher and Erna Bowes of the political science department. Suffrage activist Betty Gram Swing, as the letters attest, taught women's history at Syracuse. Beginning in the 1920s, other letters note, Goucher College's Department of History began offering The Woman's Movement in the United States, the description in the college catalog in 1935 being, "History of the struggle for equal educational, political, legal, industrial, and professional rights for American women. Comparison with similar movements in other parts of the world. Lectures, supplemented by reference reading, especially the biographies of women leaders." Goucher professor Mary Wilhelmine Williams wrote to Lutz in 1935 that this offering was "a little more popular than the average college course, I think" (Women's History Courses). Lutz also worked not just on new classes about women but also on the inclusion of more materials concerning women in established courses about history and other subjects. She credited Arthur Schlesinger of Harvard for bringing research about women into his courses at Harvard and she sought more such courses, as she wrote in the *Vassar Alumnae Magazine*, especially at women's colleges: "The whole background of women's history should be an essential part of every woman's education"

("To the Vassar Alumnae Magazine"). As she discussed at Berkshire Conferences in sessions in which she debated with Mary Ritter Beard, she wanted these courses to concentrate both on oppression and achievement.

As a Vassar alumna, Lutz especially worked to foster educational reform at her own alma mater. As president of Vassar from 1915 to 1946, Henry Noble McCracken was open to changes in teaching and learning, to fostering the active classroom and connections to current life that President James Monroe Taylor had guarded against when Lutz was a student (Bruno and Daniels 59). Vassar historian Evalyn Clark, a founding member of the Berkshire Conference, emphasized, as she told an interviewer, "the development of critical, informed thinking and independent judgment," close attention to an array of sources and openness to whatever the facts might mean. During the 1940s, in her course Contemporary European History, 1870 to the Present, Clark expected students to grapple with the meaning of World War II, working from contemporary *New York Times'* accounts of both battles and the homefront back to the causes of war. Her course entitled European Thought and Culture since 1750 included not just theory but social history, involving the cultural mores governing the behavior of women as well as men.

Other teachers influenced by the Berkshire Conference started innovative courses at Vassar. In classes on American and Russian history from the 1930s to the 1950s, professors like J.B. Ross and Lucy E. Textor involved students in women's achievements as well as men's and in social and cultural history as well as political and military facts. In the English department, Helen Lockwood's Public Discussion engaged students in current issues and their impact on both genders. In 1937, along with Genevieve Lamson of the geography department, Lockwood opened a Social Museum in Blodgett Hall that concerned current social history, especially from a women's perspective. At the opening of the museum, Eleanor Roosevelt spoke on women and housing, in connection with a Conference on Housing being held in Poughkeepsie (Bruno and Daniels 72).

Evidence that these efforts were being recognized by the profession came in an invitation by the American Historical Association in 1940 for a panel entitled Some Aspects of the History of Women. Mary Beard refused the offer to chair, but Mildred Thompson, then a Vassar dean and history professor, and a member of the Berkshire Conference, accepted. Jeannette Nichols of Swarthmore gave a paper on "The Nurture of Feminism in the United States" and Lillian Fisher of the Oklahoma College for Women spoke on the Mexican Revolution and the status of women, while Lutz served as a respondent along with Vera Brown Holmes of Smith (Beard and Cott 221).

As Alma Lutz worked on establishing the Berkshire Conference and expanding its impact and as she communicated with teachers around the country about new courses and course units, she also participated in the formation of archives for housing primary materials about women, an extension of the type of collection that she had been making to conduct her own research and sharing with others. In August of 1943, Radcliffe College received from alumna and suffragist Maud Wood Park her collection of books, papers, and memorabilia on women reformers. Alma Lutz was immediately put on an advisory committee for the new collection and helped transform one woman's papers into the major research collection on women in the United States (*Fortieth Anniversary* 4). Along with Park's friend and classmate Inez Haynes Irwin, who had been an active member of the NWP and wrote *The Story of Alice Paul and the Woman's Party* in 1921, Lutz worked to insure that NWP as well as NAWSA was well-represented there, angering Carrie Chapman Catt who placed her own collection in the Library of Congress, despite pleas from Radcliffe that she place her papers there (Des Jardins 203).

To honor Harvard University historian Arthur M. Schlesinger and his wife, Elizabeth Bancroft Schlesinger, who helped expand the collection, the archive was renamed the Schlesinger Library in 1965. When a new women's movement developed in the 1960s and 1970s, the library grew rapidly, with special collections on suffrage, feminism, religion and missionaries, politics and law, professions, the labor movement, medicine and reproductive issues, organizations and their leaders, the arts, social work, and Radcliffe College. Support from the Rockefeller Foundation in 1976 also made possible the Black Women Oral History Project, autobiographical interviews with more than fifty women (Howells 133; *Elizabeth Schlesinger* 1, 6, 11; *Fortieth Anniversary*).

In her writing, Lutz helped to form the space of women's studies as she documented women's participation in the suffrage campaign, world war, abolition, and religion while also researching the lives of individuals; in her involvement in curricular reform and library development, she helped to foster the serious study of women's lives at American universities. Certainly modern women's studies programs grew out of the women's movement of the 1970s, but these scholars were not undoing decades of inaction. Women had been researching their history and teaching it — in classrooms, at conferences, and in libraries — from the suffrage decade onward. Alma Lutz was a leader of that movement, a member of that first wave who insisted as soon as the suffrage campaign ended on further changing the status of women in American life through education.

Helen Keller (1880–1968)

Throughout her life, Alma Lutz worked to educate women concerning their history and their possibilities, to help them create their own sense of self-respect and to re-orient the values of their society. She realized that a more inclusionary form of education, involving the study of human lives as well as the traditionally valued facts, could be transformative: this sense of purpose, grounded in historical research and analysis, arose for her from the suffrage campaign. Similarly, Helen Keller, another strong suffrage advocate, sought to eradicate a narrow academic perspective — that only some citizens deserved education and respect and that only the traditional curriculum had value. Like Agnes Chase and Alma Lutz, she wanted to create entirely new categories and purposes of education, involving training for adults beyond established curricular boundaries, and she possessed the determination and courage to do so.

After studying with Annie Sullivan at home, Keller went to the Perkins Institution, where she learned the manual alphabet, and then worked with Sarah Fulton, principal of the Horace Mann School for the Deaf in Boston, to learn to speak. News of her accomplishments in 1890 and 1891 made her a celebrity, with stories regularly appearing in the *New York Times* about her, featuring headlines such as "A Phenomenal Child: Acquirements of Little Deaf, Dumb, and Blind Helen Keller" and "Wonders of Patient Teaching: How Helen Keller, without Sight or Hearing, Learned to Speak." She enrolled in Radcliffe in 1900 as a phenomenon, with funds supplied by a campaign that Mark Twain initiated; headlines like the *New York Times*' "The Blind Deaf-Mute Passes the Examination and Is Admitted" stressed her "remarkable" accomplishment ("Helen Keller at Radcliffe"). And indeed the way was difficult: no college texts were in Braille; Annie Sullivan had to finger-spell most written materials as well as class lectures; Keller had little opportunity to communicate with other students or with her teachers. But what she found most distressing was the traditional curriculum, provided by Harvard professors long before reformer Arthur Schlesinger joined the faculty in 1924, that made little reference to societal conditions about which she wanted to learn (Nielsen and Kaye 16–17). Though the *New York Times* judged college classes as a surprising finish to a young disabled woman's education, Keller sought not finishing or art appreciation but the tools with which to evaluate and alter the culture that confined her.

Like many other young women at the beginning of the twentieth century, Keller intended to secure a college degree and then become useful in society. She thought that the college-educated woman should be able to lead progressive reform: "By throwing herself into college affairs," as Keller described the college woman, "she acquired the habit of rendering intelligent and efficient service to others; so that when she graduates, she becomes a practical force in the world, and a responsible member of society" ("An Apology" 92). As Keller wrote about a new level of political involvement that college graduates sought, she claimed that the woman's role as social reformer had evolved from the home and from housekeeping outward: "Woman's place is still the household. But the household is more spacious than in times gone by" ("The Modern Woman" 76).

In 1913, Helen Keller began corresponding with Alice Paul and Lucy Burns and then joined with them to help form the Congressional Union. She participated in parades and rallies, including the pre-inaugural parade in March of 1913, at which the crowds of people and horses made it impossible for her to give her speech after the march. Afterwards, she traveled around the country giving speeches on suffrage as a right of the dispossessed. Photograph dated ca. 1905, photographer Edmonston, Washington, D.C. Photograph from National Woman's Party Records. Source: Library of Congress Manuscript Division.

But though in her generation many women sought civic involvement, Keller believed that they were being kept from engaging fully and making the impact of which they were capable. She noted in 1905, in the *Ladies' Home Journal*, "the avenues of usefulness open to me were not many." As she wrote about her own restrictions, she stressed not her blindness or deafness, but her gender, as her biographers Kim E. Nielsen and Harvey J. Kaye commented: "In her political writings from 1900 to the mid–1920s, the limitation she acknowledged was that of being female — the *gendered* body" (44). Discussing her reluctance to comment on the conditions of poverty that lead to blindness, Keller wrote about the difficulty that any woman would encounter in public speaking: "Moreover, the subject was one of which a young woman might be supposed to be ignorant, and upon which, certainly, she would not be expected to speak with authority. It is always painful to set one's self against tradition, especially against the conventions and prejudices that hedge about womanhood." Keller viewed this denial of women's abilities, and thus of their need for advanced education, as similar to the public judgment of her as a person who was deaf and blind: "The argument brought against me, that no deaf-blind person had ever gone to college, was precisely the kind of argument brought a generation ago against any woman's going to college. True, there had been seminaries and academies for girls, but no colleges of a university standard; and the so-called universities for men showed stern oaken doors to all women" ("An Apology" 87).

For Keller, the desire to seek change, to use her education for activism, came not just from a vague desire for a meaningful contribution but also from her commitment to socialism. In speeches that she gave after graduating from college, she declared that "poverty is abominable, unnecessary, a disgrace to our civilization." And endemic poverty, she argued, inexorably derived from capitalism: "The land, the machinery, the means of life, belong to the few, while the many are born and live with nothing that they can call their own except their hands and their brains.... The rich are willing to do everything for the poor but to get off their backs." The capitalist system, which denies to workers the rights of human beings, she considered to be "fundamentally wrong, radically unjust and cruel" ("Blind Leaders" 232).

Keller shocked Americans when the news of her allegiance to socialism became publicly known. In November of 1912 in the New York *Call*, she wrote that "for several months my name and Socialism have appeared often together in the newspapers. A friend tells me that I have shared the front pages with baseball, Mr. Roosevelt, and the New York police scandal." Reporters assumed that the poor blind girl who had been lauded in the *New York Times*, even though by then she had graduated from college, was being manipulated by those around her, particularly Annie Sullivan Macy and her husband, claims that Keller rejected: "Mr. Macy may be an enthusiastic Marxist propagandist, though I am sorry to say he has not shown much enthusiasm in propagating his Marxism through my fingers. Mrs. Macy is not a Marxist, not a Socialist." Her wide reading of socialist writers, she insisted, was her own choice, not evidence of "the exploitation of poor Helen Keller" ("How I Became a Socialist" 18, 23).

Though Keller realized that neither blind nor sighted women were encouraged to critique their country's political and economic status quo, in her analysis they were most needed to do so because the capitalist system, in which they had no voice, was especially destructive for them. As non-citizens, without the right to vote, they had to seek practical education, not just housekeeping skills or acquaintance with the liberal arts, and fight to find their own means of solving their problems within an exploitative system: "We must know why a woman who owns property has no voice in selecting the men who make laws that affect her property. We must know why a woman who earns wages has nothing to say about the choices of the men who make laws that govern her wages. We must know why a hundred and fifty of our sisters were killed in New York in a shirt-waist factory fire the other day, and nobody to blame" ("The Modern Woman" 43). In a society unwilling to treat and pay its workers fairly, she recognized, those with the least power met the worst fate: "Women and children are bound to machines in unclean workrooms to eke out the small earnings of the men.... And what about the dignity of womanhood? Only a small part of the millions of workingwomen receive enough pay to maintain a decent home and give their children proper care and education" ("Blind Leaders" 234). To make a difference, as she recognized, she needed a type of practical, political education that she had not received at Radcliffe: "I shall study the economic questions relating to woman and do my best to further her advancement" ("My Future as I See It"). In this "crippling" system that must be reformed, as she wrote, "the laws made by men rule the minds as well as the bodies of women"; women had to develop and use their own minds, studying not just art and literature but economics and social trends, to secure reform ("Why Men Need Woman Suffrage" 66).

As Keller considered the discrimination with which women had to cope, she was drawn to suffrage as a source of greater power, recognizing that the lack of even basic voting rights meant that women had no control at all: "What dignity do women have as citizens when they may not even elect those who shall decide for them vital questions affecting food, clothing, shelter, education?" ("Blind Leaders" 234). As a social critic and socialist, she connected woman suffrage to securing rights for the dispossessed: "I do not believe that the present government has any intention of giving women a part in national politics, or doing justice to Ireland, or the workmen of England. So long as the franchise is denied to a large number of those who serve and benefit the public, so long as those who vote are at the beck and call of party machines, the people are not free, and the day of woman's freedom seems still to be in the far future" ("Letter to an English Woman-Suffragist" 115–16). She thus argued that "the enfranchisement of women is a part of a vast movement to enfranchise all mankind," to end what she viewed as a sham democracy, actually run "for the richest, for the corporations, the bankers, the land speculators, and for the exploiters of labor" ("Letter to an English Woman-Suffragist" 117–18).

For Keller, as for so many women, the suffrage campaign thus involved larger goals, not just securing the vote, but greater social change. In August of 1944, in fact, she told the *New York Times* that she was voting for the first time to support Roosevelt, so certainly achievement of the franchise had not been her primary goal ("Jo Davidson"). To secure the larger changes that she sought through the suffrage campaign, she became as involved as she could, even though Annie Sullivan did not agree with her about women's voting as she did not about socialism.

Like Louisine Havemeyer coming into this activism in stages, Keller began by lending her name and writing to the cause. In 1911, in "A Letter to an English Woman-Suffragist," printed in the *Manchester Advertiser* and then in the *Call*, she declared herself "indignant" at the imprisonment and forced feeding of British suffragettes. In 1913 in an article in the *New York Times*, she labeled herself a militant suffragist and urged American women to follow the lead of the Pankhursts: "They would get the ballot much faster if they did. They cannot hope to get anything unless they are ready to fight and suffer for it." And in that article she again made her larger goals clear: "But I am a militant suffragette because I believe that suffrage will lead to Socialism, and to me Socialism is the ideal cause" ("Helen Keller a Militant").

In 1913, Keller took the further activist steps of corresponding with Alice Paul and Lucy Burns and then joining with them to help form the Congressional Union. She participated in parades and rallies, including the pre-inaugural parade in March of 1913, at which the crowds of people and horses made it impossible for her to give a speech after the march, which planners had intended to feature between the parade and a tableau on liberty on the Treasury Building steps (Burrell 31). Afterwards, she traveled around the country giving speeches on suffrage as a right of the dispossessed. In Tennessee, for example, in the fall of 1913, over 4,000 people attended her talks in both Knoxville and Memphis, spurred by an interest in her education and speaking skills as well as the amendment, a much larger crowd than either suffragists or anti-suffragists had secured in the state before (*Committee on Woman Suffrage* 196). In 1915, she undertook an extensive tour of the West, speaking on suffrage as well as other reforms necessary for social justice ("Welcome Dr. Shaw"). At San Francisco's Panama Pacific International Exposition that year, the CU sponsored a booth, seeking an event that would garner huge crowds and positive sentiment, a choice that Alice Paul later remembered as "one of the very big things that we did" (Fry, "Conversations"). After Keller spoke there, on a special Helen Keller Day on which both she and Annie Sullivan received awards as teachers, she left a large signed photograph that hung in the booth for the rest of the fair (Lash 418–19).

Besides participating with other suffragists in parades, meetings, and a world's fair, Keller also joined the CU advisory council, women whose prestigious names appeared on the left-hand side of CU stationery, a strong visual symbol of support that ultimately took up two columns and left little room for writing ("New Members of the Advisory Council"). In 1916, Keller involved herself further, in the effort to form a separate party, the National Woman's Party. At the first party conference, in Chicago on June 5 through 7, 1916, shortly before the Republican and Progressive conventions in that city, speakers included Keller as well as Lucy Salmon, Crystal Eastman, Mary Ritter Beard, Inez Milholland, Charlotte Perkins Gilman, Alice Chipman Dewey (John Dewey's wife and first principal of the Laboratory School at the University of Chicago), and Florence Kelley (founder of the National Consumer's League and advocate of minimum wage and child labor laws). At the Republican convention, which Keller also attended as a special correspondent for the *Call*, Hughes endorsed a national amendment but did not place it on the Republican platform (Lash 432–33). That month in the *Call*, Keller spoke for the power of the NWP in representing the half of the population that the established parties continued to deny: "The Woman's Party means more than votes for women. It is the symbol of our solidarity. It stands for the best national efforts of American women. It embodies the aspirations of millions of intelligent women — women who think and have enlightened opinions. It focuses our struggle for independence" ("The New Woman's Party" 87). Though she supported the NWP, she did not participate in the 1916 boycott because Wilson was promising to keep the United States out of war, especially an essential promise for the well-being of workers, Keller believed, who sought greater safety and power internationally.

In 1917 and 1918, Helen Keller attended advisory council meetings for the NWP, supporting the decision to picket although, with picketing and jail a difficult physical risk for her, she did not participate. As her biographer Joseph Lash has written, concerning labor strikes also, "blindness and deafness kept her off the picket line" (387). In July 1916 when the Cloakmakers' Union went on strike in New York, she told the *New York Times* that "I am with the cloak strikers, heart and soul. If it were possible I should come to New York to help them with my voice, too" ("Settlement Near"). In December 1919, when women in New York, members of the American

Woman's Emergency Committee, picketed on Wall Street in protest against the government policy of refusing clearance papers for ships bound to Russia, Keller worked on the planning committee, along with Harriot Stanton Blatch ("To Picket Wall Street"). As with suffrage picketing also, she was deemed one of the group though she did not stand on the line.

As Keller worked for suffrage, she also became further involved with the rights of labor and especially with the International Workers of the World (IWW), seeing in both the ability to change American social structure (Einhorn 30). In 1913, when the Socialist Party expelled leading IWW member Bill Haywood from its executive committee for being too radical, Keller led a campaign to get him reinstated. When in 1915, Joe Hill, a leading IWW organizer, was accused of murder, Keller joined the campaign for his release. She again shocked the establishment in 1916 by declaring in the *New York Tribune* that she was not only advocating for the fair treatment of these labor leaders but she had joined the IWW. She told the interviewer that "I became an IWW member because I found out that the Socialist Party was too slow. It is sinking into the political bog.... The true task is to unite and organize all workers on an economic basis. It is the workers themselves who must secure freedom for themselves" (Bindley).

Immediately after women achieved the right to vote, Keller continued her social activism primarily by advocating for the education and rights of people who were blind or visually impaired. As a biographer wrote, with woman suffrage achieved, "Helen Keller entered the 1920s seeking a meaningful public life" and assuming that she had the wherewithal to achieve it by working with state organizations as well as the American Federation for the Blind, founded in 1921 (Nielsen and Kaye 47). Regardless of the preferences of the groups with which she cooperated, Keller was not interested in simply raising money for supporting the indigent blind, but in helping blind adults to participate fully in their society, with equal rights and employment, goals that she had also sought for women through the suffrage campaign. In many speeches and articles, she sought support from charitable organizations, states, and the federal government for establishing help that would move blind adults to productive lives: "They do not want to be fed and clothed and housed by other people. They want to work and support themselves." Such opportunities could alleviate the tendency toward idleness, "the cruelest, least bearable misery that can be laid upon the human heart" ("Our Duties to the Blind" 127–29). By the end of 1924, she had lectured to over 250,000 people at 249 meetings in 123 cities, speaking of the best means by which people who were blind or visually impaired could achieve independence and a meaningful work life, the same goals she had set for herself when she entered college and that she sought to achieve for women through the suffrage campaign (Lash 524–29; 530–31; Keller, *Midstream* 232). As suffragists had done, she also lobbied political leaders, more fully in the 1930s and 1940s, for fund-raising for educational institutions, for Braille books, and for job training.

Just as women attempted to carefully study voting history, party structures, and media power as they worked toward the vote, Keller strove to understand the causes of blindness, no longer for her a "misfortune beyond human control" as she had earlier judged it (Bindley). In her article "Preventable Blindness" in the *Ladies Home Journal* and her speeches, she discussed infantile ophthalmia, an eye disease acquired at birth that could be cured with an eye wash and drops. She also described industrial accidents, the awful realities of the capitalistic profit system that robbed adult workers of their sight: "gas, steam, deadly vapors, white lead, phosphorus, chlorine from the bleaching-room" (234). And she recognized that poor women who turned without other choices to prostitution could be similarly afflicted: "I found that poverty drove women to a life of shame that ended in blindness" (Bindley). She continually advocated for changes in medical care and industry to change lives, especially of the poor, altering the American pattern of illness and destitution.

While attempting to impact medicine and industry to lower the rate of blindness, she also sought to change childhoods and adult lives. She repeatedly argued that many people expect those who are blind to be either dull and solitary souls or special "poets, musicians and thinkers," both mistaken opinions, like views of women as either needy dependents or moral beacons. Instead, she wrote, people who are blind are "ordinary, industrious, self-respecting citizens," with an array of human weaknesses and strengths. Children who are blind, like all others in Keller's analysis, need physical activity as they grow up. She advocated for schools for the blind to move out of the restrictive grounds of cities and into sites with yards and playgrounds where children can build their bodies. They then need a complete education but especially training for an occupation, which she advocated for all women and men, with the expectation that the blind would become self-supporting, as she argued that they were expected to do in Europe ("What Might Be Done" 9260).

Through the Perkins Institution, as well as many other organizations, Keller advocated for programs for adults, involving sheltered workshops as well as training and support. In Massachusetts, the Commission on the Blind opened a shop selling handicrafts, including curtains, pillows, linen suits, and rugs — for their value not just as charity ("The Heaviest Burden" 216).

Women and men who were blind, she argued, could also work as piano tuners, shampooers, masseurs, typewriters, store clerks, farm hands, chair-makers, singers, and church organists. She advocated segregated work opportunities where necessary, a stance that would seem limiting to some later critics (Nielsen and Kaye 29–30).

Within this country and internationally, Keller continued to take risks and speak out for people who were blind, just as she participated in parades, meetings, and fairs and wrote articles about suffrage. Like suffragists lobbying for the amendment, she also worked vociferously for legal change. She supported the Social Security Act in 1935, and lobbied especially for an amendment to it that expanded vocational training for blind people. In 1944, she urged expansion of the Social Security Act to support "the particular needs of the poorer blind." Her testimony before the House Labor Committee highlighted the circumstances of "the deaf-blind" and of racial minorities, as "the hardest pressed and least cared-for" among her "blind fellows." In 1934, she rebuked Hitler and Mussolini and voiced her fear of Nazi intentions for Jews and for people with disabilities. When the United States government refused entrance to "defectives" targeted by the Nazis, she condemned this decision to *New York Times* interviewers ("Helen Keller Hits"; "Helen Keller, Back"). During the war, she spent much of her time visiting with soldiers who came home disabled, the "hundreds and hundreds confined to their beds" (Keller, "An Epic of Courage"). She lobbied the federal government and private foundations to extend the care of soldiers while also working on the protective measures that the army could employ to help blind people in England during air raids. On international trips, before and after the war, she focused on the needs of people who were blind and raised money for them, in places where people with disabilities might have few rights and few advocates. She traveled to Japan before the war and afterwards, through the auspices of the Foundation for the Overseas Blind, and went in 1946 to Europe where so many people were displaced and without services, bringing with her funds that she had raised at home. As the *New York Times* noted in 1955 of this continuing travel, she had "a quality of courage that enables a few gifted and benign souls to overcome their own handicaps and to give themselves to humanity and for humanity" ("Courage"). After the war, in the United States, she also urged the continued employment of adults who were blind at jobs they had been allowed to do during wartime as well as training for those who had been disabled in battle ("Work for Blind Urged").

Keller had to soften her politics sometimes to reflect the public image that foundations and the public wanted, to be the kindly blind woman without a radical agenda, but she was never willing to do so absolutely. For she felt that soliciting funds for educational opportunities was a radical act, not just a kindness to a repressed group, not just a chance for philanthropists to write a check and feel better about themselves without changing economic realities. As she sought funds for books, schools, and job training, she viewed herself as providing people with handicaps the tools by which to control their own lives, what women sought for themselves through suffrage. Like Alice Paul, she sought real change and thus, even as an avid fundraiser, she spoke against philanthropy as a simple offer of support: "I regard philanthropy as a tragic apology for wrong conditions under which human beings live, losing their sight or hearing or becoming impoverished, and I do not conceal this awkward position from anybody" (Letter to Nella Braddy Henney) She was not embracing "antiradicalism," as a biographer posits, as she turned her attention to the needs of people who were blind: working for a specific group could change American society, she believed, as women also sought to do through suffrage (Nielsen and Kaye 49).

She recognized that she faced an array of compromises to continue her work because of what the country wanted her to be, as she commented in 1924: "So long as I confine my activities to social service and the blind, they compliment me extravagantly, calling me 'archpriestess of the sightless,' 'wonder woman' and 'a modern miracle.' But when it comes to a discussion of poverty, and I maintain that it is the result of wrong economics — that the industrial system under which we live is at the root of much of the physical deafness and blindness in the world — that is a different matter! ... I do not mind having my ideas attacked and my aims opposed and ridiculed, but it is not fair fighting or good argument to find that 'Helen Keller's mistakes spring out of the limitations of her development'" ("To Senator Robert M. La Follette" 113). Though she made compromises, she always viewed her goal as radical, as a reorientation of who would be educated, how, and why.

Like many other suffragists working in the field of education, Helen Keller viewed her advocacy of people who were blind as transformative. She didn't seek to just join in earlier efforts, but instead to work towards self-respect and independence for the blind, values from the suffrage campaign that meant much more than the vote. As the *New York Times* commented in 1955 concerning her unflagging efforts around the world, in a sentence that also described her suffrage efforts, "With her goes a love of democracy and of freedom" ("Courage"). Keller, Chase, Lutz, and many other women went forward after the suffrage campaign to question traditional education and change it — by encouraging women and men to educate themselves throughout adulthood, to question received truths, and to reach for goals that might seem unattainable. They felt that education should be extended to those considered less worthy, whether they were Latin Americans, the blind, or women, and they created models to increase access to information and opportunity, drawing on the lessons of the suffrage movement.

4

Influence Through a Writing Career

As we saw in the last chapter, many suffragists committed themselves to changing education, especially of those deemed as Other. Their choices, made through individual and group effort, often outside of regular sources of funding and support, were political though perhaps not narrowly defined as such. As suffragists worked to re-form the boundaries of art and education, they also expanded their impact through writing. Like their suffrage colleagues, these activists did not simply desire to partake in what had gone before; they sought to change accepted notions of professional writing as well as governmental and societal conventions, as they had in seeking suffrage. They acquainted readers with the realities faced by various groups of people treated as Other, both in the United States and abroad, tying American to international politics as they introduced their readers to new combinations of genres, involving a personal tone, description, detailed scenes, frank discussion, and argumentation. The suffrage experience opened this group, as with art professionals and education reformers, to their own strengths — and to the power of the stories that they could tell. The writing and editing of these women, such as Alice Gram Robinson, Louise Bryant, Helena Hill Weed, Beatrice Kinkead, and Martha Foley, would not just reiterate older themes and styles; it would take them, along with their readers, into new territories of genre and political persuasion.

Alice M. Gram Robinson (1896–1984)

Like many other women, Alice M. Gram Robinson viewed the suffrage campaign as a beginning, not just to voting but to writing and editing. It spurred her to devote a career to insuring that a greater amount of political information, concerning all sides of issues that might not be fully covered in other venues, be made available to Americans, both women and men, so that they could contribute to their democracy as active citizens.

Robinson was born in Omaha, Nebraska, but grew up in Oregon and entered the University of Oregon in 1914. There she became involved with the College Equal Suffrage League, and she traveled with the group to Washington for the picketing in the fall of 1917, during her senior year. When the group set out to the White House after Alice Paul was given a seven-month sentence on November 10, 1917, Robinson was arrested along with forty other women from sixteen states, including her sister Betty Gram, who later taught women's history at Syracuse, Lucy Burns, and Dorothy Day. Though they were detained overnight, these protestors were then released because government officials realized that they were creating martyrs and very negative publicity. Although detention was meant to chasten these women, an ongoing government assumption, they immediately returned to the picket line. To help with the effort, Robinson left college and remained in the capital, where she would live until a year before her death in 1984 ("Publisher, Writer").

Like so many other women involved in the suffrage campaign, Robinson immediately went on to a close examination of other issues that involved misuse of governmental power — and to professional writing. She wanted to study pending legislation and enable other citizens to do so as independent judges. Before the suffrage campaign ended, she became an assistant in the press department of the NWP, sending articles about women's issues to an array of newspapers and magazines. She co-founded the Women's National Press Club in 1919 with Helena Hill Weed, an organization needed because women couldn't join the National Press Club, which had been co-founded in 1908 by Norborne T.N. Robinson, the man she would marry ("Publisher, Writer").

Robinson wanted, however, to reach a larger audience than the NWP publications, to bring more people into the key issues of government. Thus, after the amendment passed, she founded a publication, the *Congressional Digest*, that presented opposing views on controversial national questions, which she planned and edited at first primarily by herself, with her suffrage colleagues, such as poet Velma Hitchcock, offering support and becoming her first subscribers. She solicited articles defending and critiquing bills, written by both legislators and organizations involved, and presented them along with her own essays on the legislation's history. With information appearing in a succinct two-column pro and con format, as the publication's Web site attests today, if a woman "became enthused about some new Federal proposal, she could consult the opposite page and soon find out its shortcomings," thus learning to question her own assumptions and gaining a thorough, objective training in government. From her journal's beginning in 1921, as a publication intended primarily for new women voters, Robinson built an ever enlarging pro-and-con monthly of which she served as publisher and president until she retired in 1983. As the Web site states, the publication's audience began as new women voters but came to include "students, educators, libraries, opinion leaders, policy-makers, foreign leaders and individuals," a powerful grouping with none situated as Other, none preferred or viewed as more important, all rightly involved in their democracy (*Congressional Digest*).

From the beginning, Robinson gave attention to bills that specifically affected women and their children as well as to other legislation. She thus encouraged interest in bills that might not have been given thorough consideration in other magazines or in newspapers. Her first item in her first issue, in October 1921, with pro and con considered, was the Sheppard-Towner Maternity Bill, which provided matching funds to states for prenatal and children's health centers, legislation introduced in the House of Representatives in 1919 by Jeannette Rankin. In that first year, Robinson also considered bills concerning health and education, lynching, and naturalization. In subsequent years, her pattern of writing about an array of bills continued. In 1922 and 1923, she wrote about the Cable Act, called the Married Women's Independent Nationality Act, and the Child Labor Amendment as well as the Tariff Act; in 1923 and 1924, the Equal Rights Amendment and the Sterling-Reed Education Bill as well as Philippine independence; in 1927, topics included a Uniform Marriage and Divorce Law as well as capital punishment and copyright revision. In the 1930s, she continued with legislation concerning women that might not be given much attention in newspapers: an entire issue concerned Equal Nationality Rights for Women; in 1931, she featured the New Maternity and Infancy Bill and federal birth control legislation. Through that decade she also tried to explain other new legislation occurring through the New Deal. In 1933, for example, her subjects included currency expansion, suspension of anti-trust laws, and the National Industrial Recovery Act. Throughout the 1930s and World War II, as her audience grew to include men as well as women, she was assuming that all voters needed to know about the bills that most obviously concerned women, but she expected for both women and men, as citizens, to be interested in the array of issues that affected the nation.

The Congressional Digest Corporation (CDC) today continues that tradition of thorough attention to an array of issues under the direction of Page Robinson Thomas, Robinson's granddaughter, and her husband, R.

Griffith Thomas. The CDC's main publishing division is now Pro & Con Publishers, covering Congress and the Supreme Court as well as the United Nations and other international tribunals. Once a month, the 36-page flagship publication, still called *Congressional Digest*, highlights competing views on current affairs — subjects recently like civil liberties, the Iraq War, and media shield laws. The company now also sponsors *International Debates, Supreme Court Debates,* and *Pro & Con Online.* As the creator of this publishing enterprise, which still involves citizens with legislation and legislators, Robinson spent her career, made aware through suffrage of the power of the individual in creating change and the need for all citizens to engage in their democracy.

On the afternoon of February 9, 1919, Louise Bryant was one of a column of thirty-six suffragists, led by Louisine Havemeyer, who left the NWP headquarters and marched to the White House, where they burned Wilson in effigy. In front of the judge, when the group sought political prisoner status, Bryant spoke for them, citing her experiences in Russia as she discussed the difficulties that political protestors could encounter in prison and their need for special protections, thus comparing America's judicial system to Russia's. Photograph by Mark Morosse of items at Yale University Library, copied here from Wikimedia Commons.

Louise Bryant (1885–1936)

In biographies and histories, Louise Bryant is often referred to as the wife of John Reed. The first biography concerning her, Barbara Gelb's *So Short a Time*, from 1973, covered only the years that she spent with him. In the second one, Virginia Gardner's '*Friend and Lover': The Life of Louise Bryant*, from 1982, the identifying phrase in the title and thus the positioning of her came from a quotation from Reed. The film *Reds* from 1981 also cast her as existing within his influence. And though Leslie Fishbein's *The Rebels in Bohemia: The Radicals of* The Masses, *1911–1917*, from 1982, featured a picture of her with Reed on the cover, Bryant's name appears on only two pages of the book. As her third biographer Mary Dearborn commented in *Queen of Bohemia: The Life of Louise Bryant* from 1996, "her place has been obscured by a pattern of trivializing and minimalizing," with so many writers considering her as only existing within Reed's orbit, but still this book focused on the king along with his queen (307).

Bryant spent four years of her life with Reed and frequently worked with him during that time, but she was not simply his reflection, and her politics and writing deserve separate attention. After her early involvement with the suffrage campaign, more crucial to her than her later trip to jail for picketing, she went to Russia from whence she wrote two important books that, along with her daily journalism for Hearst newspapers, had an impact on American views of Russia as well as on nonfiction. Armed through suffrage and her travel with a growing independence of thought and writing style, she increasingly chose a "personalized, participatory style" to acquaint readers with Russian women and men at a most controversial juncture in history (Dearborn 68). Like so many other suffragists, Bryant found that the campaign opened her up to American political realities and to a life of activist involvement in political journalism.

Like other young women who became involved in the campaign, Bryant was searching for a means of making her own mark after getting an education but finding no meaningful means of using it. She was born in December of 1885, as Anna Louise Mohan. Her father was a journalist and an alcoholic who often disappeared and left her mother to fend for the family. In 1885 Bryant's mother moved to Reno and sought a divorce. Her mother then married Sheridan Bryant, a train conductor on the Southern Pacific who brought them stability and security. Louise went from University High School in Reno to the newly created University of Nebraska, serving as a staff member of the *Student Record.* She transferred in 1906 to the University of Oregon in Eugene, where her brother and sister lived. There she came under the influence of English teacher Herbert Crombie Howe, a socialist and agnostic whose lectures against the notion of original sin and in advocacy of the most daring of authors, such as Ibsen and Zola, left many parents furious and many students, like Louise Bryant, fascinated (Greene). She left the university during the spring semester of 1908, taught school for two months, and then went to San Francisco to secure a writing job, which as a woman she could not do. Then she went on to Portland where again she could not find work at a newspaper. After a short time teaching school, she secured a position on a weekly tabloid, the *Spectator.* She rose there to society editor, her assignments involving parties and weddings, the news judged as fit for a woman to cover, not to the position of news reporter that she had sought for herself. She married John Trullinger, a dentist, in 1909, and continued to seek a reporting job at one of Portland's four dailies (Dearborn 24).

As was true of many other women, Bryant found the clear moral imperative of suffrage appealing; the campaign offered greater meaning than a conventional marriage and a restrictive job. In Portland, she met suffrage activist Sara Bard Field, and through this friendship, which lasted the rest of her life, became involved in the local campaign (Field). This work for suffrage in Oregon, beginning in 1912, signaled a breaking away, a chance to make a political difference, to have a public voice. Field invited her to join the College Equal Suffrage League, formed by Emma Wold, under the tutelage of Oregon's leading suffragist, Abigail Scott Duniway. As the league's paid state organizer, Field devoted herself to suffrage work. Without pay, Bryant joined Field on her state tours, helping to plan meetings and pass out literature for the cause (Dearborn 27; Hamburger 230–31).

Like Louisine Havemeyer and other suffragists, Bryant came under the tutelage of effective organizers and speakers as she engaged in the campaign. Field was especially well known for her effectiveness in addressing hostile crowds. Bryant served as one of her warm-up speakers at first — billed as Mrs. P.A. Trullinger, a society editor, the wife of a dentist, thus bringing an establishment air to the proceedings to which she added her own growing ability at public speaking and her flair for dramatic dress. In June of 1912, the *Oregonian* reported on a suffrage float in a Flag Day parade with "eight pretty maidens" gracing it, and Bryant was one (Munk). She went to Astoria, Oregon, on the next day, the beginning of a full-state tour during which she sometimes appeared as the main speaker. These efforts paid off in Oregon: woman's suffrage became law there in the fall of 1912. As Bryant worked successfully for the vote, with approval seemingly coming quickly though suffrage had taken years of dogged work to achieve, she saw herself as involved in a campaign that mattered, in which individuals and a dedicated group were able to make a difference. According to her biographer Mary V. Dearborn, surveying decades of risk and activism, this first involvement in suffrage represented "perhaps the most firmly held political conviction of her life" (29).

As Dearborn and other biographers emphasize, Bryant met Jack Reed when he came home to Portland in the summer of 1914 for a visit. By January of 1916, after he had visited again, she left for New York and a whirl of activity there, seeking out a newly opening world of possibilities. Sara Bard Field, in New York after a well-publicized cross-country car trip for the CU and the federal amendment, took Bryant to a meeting of Heterodoxy, a club for unorthodox and radically thinking women, where she met suffrage and women's rights activists such as Crystal Eastman, Charlotte Perkins Gilman, and Zona Gale.

In 1915, she continued her writing interests on the stage along with a group of friends at Provincetown, Massachusetts, who had begun putting on plays at the home of theatre enthusiast Hutchins Hapgood. Susan Glaspell was there writing and acting, as were George Cram ("Jig") Cook, John Reed, Neith Boyce, and Mary Heaton Vorse. On Hapgood's veranda overlooking the harbor, they first performed Boyce's one act *Constancy*, a spoof of the romance between wealthy art patron Mabel Dodge and Jack Reed; the actors then moved to the living room and the audience to the veranda, for a performance of *Suppressed Desires*, by Susan Glaspell and Jig Cook. The next summer, 1916, witnessed the arrival of a young playwright, Eugene O'Neill. His one-act play *Bound East for Cardiff*, which takes place mid-ocean, impressed the group with its raw realism when produced on Lewis Wharf, reaching about one hundred feet into Provincetown harbor, where throughout the performance incoming waves flooded underneath the audience's feet.

Another play that summer was Bryant's *The Game: a Morality Play*, in which she may have been reiterating, with mythic characters, her own decision to choose Reed and New York and leave her husband. Here the characters Life and Death play dice for the right to dominate the Youth (a poet) and Girl (a dancer), who have left home together for the love of art. The male Death and the Youth repeat clichés about women that Bryant knew well and had combated through the suffrage campaign. When the female Life requests a favor, Death says, "A favor. A favor. Now isn't that just like a woman? I never saw one yet who was willing to abide by the results of a fair game" (29). When Life asks to change the fate of Youth and Girl, Death comments that "the universe would be in a wild state of disorder if the women had any say!" (30). When Life asks Youth whether Girl understands him, Youth replies that "women do not have to understand. They must be fragrant and beautiful — like flowers" (33). While the play reviews judgments of women that Bryant knew all too well, it also reveals her understanding of the self-proclaimed male artist and revolutionary, of a man like Reed. Here Death tells the Girl about the Youth's egotism: "It is not you he loves, but your dancing of his songs. He is a Poet — therefore he loves only himself" (38). But even though the Girl, like Bryant herself, understands the drawbacks of her partner, she chooses Youth when Life saves them both, blithely declaring, "how brave — how strong — how beautiful is my lover!" (40).

While Bryant wrote for the theatre about gender and love, she also pursued other forms of professional writing. In the summer of 1916, for example, she wrote many poems, which *The Masses* published. In fact, she sent six poems to editor Floyd Dell who wrote to her: "These poems hit me hard. I think they are almost terribly beautiful — like Greek fragments. They go in the next issue unless something extraordinary happens to stop them" (Gardner 33). One of them, "From the Tower," describes the dangers of the large industrial cities into which Americans, and Louise herself, had moved and which might nourish or destroy them.

> The city is a great grey dragon
> Reaching out with its long claws
> And clutching the water.
> Winding its sprawling body
> Over the land,
> Lashing the purple hills with its tail.

That summer her essay on the Irish Easter Rebellion, called "The Poets' Revolution," also appeared in *The Masses*. Here she analyzed the war craze into which Americans had been led: "We saw a carefully fostered Pro-Ally feeling growing up in this country, fed on such sentimental lies as England's motherly feeling for small nations like Belgium and Serbia, her overwhelming love for America." For Bryant, the possibility of alliance in a world war with an aggressive colonizer such as England necessitated a careful examination of that country's record and purposes that Americans seemed loath to undertake: "The public seemed so hopelessly deluded by all this that they forget India, they forgot South Africa and they even forgot Ireland."

Though Bryant had gotten to New York and had begun a more serious writing career than in Portland, writing about politics as well as love, *The Masses* did not offer her the activist opportunity that she sought. At this male-dominated radical magazine, many of her efforts were belittled, her achievements already being attributed to her associations with Reed and O'Neill. As Dorothy Day, who was an assistant to Floyd Dell, later told an interviewer, "The *Masses* people didn't like Louise. I think it was jealousy. She had no right to have brains and be so pretty. They were constantly minimizing her" (Gardner 16). Regardless of this critique, Bryant wanted more than to write about revolution from afar, to publish a few poems, or to participate in a small theatre involving mostly friends. Like Agnes Chase, she had taken aggressive steps to launch a career but was finding the paths to full participation closed to her.

Having involved herself first in suffrage and then in the opportunities and restrictions of New York writing, Bryant sought to further develop her skills in a center of revolution — to chronicle the possibility for change through a radical extension of rights to the disenfranchised. She secured press credentials with the Bell Syndicate, a competitor to United Press, and sailed to Europe on June 9, 1917, taking her first tentative steps as a war correspondent. Her story about the trip over to Bordeaux, a difficult voyage during wartime, appeared in the New York *American*, indicating "her growing flair for description" (Dearborn 68). Eight days out her ship was attacked by a German submarine, as she described vividly in the *American*: "Bells jangled violently, the ship trembled with all the engines could bear, and we began to zig-zag, lurching heavily, to outwit the monster trying to get us broadside on. I stumbled down to my room, and just as I reached the door, our ship opened fire from her after gun" ("Woman Tells").

Once she arrived in France, she went immediately to join army troops, reaching the front lines in early July, as the only journalist there. Her pieces included one on the American Ambulance Corps, in which she wrote especially about Jack Trenner, from Chicago, who had "left home for adventure but had found long, hard days of fear," on one of which, he said, he had "gotten lost from his unit, with no sense of where he was, night coming, and finally the sound of men marching nearby, luckily his own comrades whose voices he recognized" ("American Ambulance Corps"). She was here feeling her way journalistically, crafting a personal voice and bringing readers into the lives of those distant from them.

After Bryant came home in August, both she and John Reed left for Russia within days, on August 17. She had press credentials again from the Bell Syndicate as well as *Metropolitan* magazine. The February Revolution of 1917 had led to a provisional, non–Communist government under Alexander Kerensky, whose envoys NWP pickets had addressed in their banners of June 1917. In return for his pledge to continue the war, the United States had begun providing him with economic and technical support. The Russian army, however, proved to be no match for the German and Austro-Hungarian forces on the Eastern Front, the Russians being overwhelmingly defeated there on June 18. Even though Kerensky pledged to continue, the demoralized Russian army, plagued by mutinies and desertions, was severely weakened and the Eastern Front quickly collapsed (Fitzpatrick 44–67).

Bryant and Reid arrived before the October Revolution brought about a dramatic change in the social structure of Russia; Bryant and Reed took great risks to remain there so that they could report on this crisis and its aftermath. The Revolution took place in Petrograd on October 24–25 when revolutionaries entered the Winter Palace where ministers were in hiding. When delegates from other parties tried to reach there to sacrifice themselves in fighting against a state movement to communism, Bryant and Reed were with them. As Cossack troops marched on Petrograd with Kerensky at their head, Bryant stood in the streets alone to watch them pass (*Six Red Months* 82–87). By October 31, Kerensky's troops were smashed, and he fled in disguise. Much heavier resistance occurred in Moscow, six days of intense fighting, leading to eight hundred dead, a site from which only the most courageous and determined journalists reported: Bryant and Reed went there on the first available train (Gardner 122).

After observing the violence of revolution, Bryant reported on the beginnings of a new government. Lenin came to the Congress of Soviets to plan for new Russian leadership in sessions that she attended. She carefully recorded the plans for free universal health care, universal literacy, and especially equal rights for women. She also attended meetings of war prisoners: "I was the only woman ever present" (*Six Red Months* 203).

While Bryant endeavored to be present for as much of the fighting and as many of the meetings as possible, she was also struggling to get interviews with the parties involved. After the October Revolution, Bryant and Reed interviewed Lenin, whom Bryant found less personable than Kerensky but a stunning intellect. She eventually interviewed both Trotsky and Lenin repeatedly and heard them speak countless times. On October 30 she won an audience with Trotsky and spoke with him for an hour (Dearborn 82). Bryant felt especially honored and lucky to have secured the audience because of the administrative schedule that Trotsky kept, as she described it: "For weeks Trotsky never left the building. He ate and slept and worked in his office on the third floor and strings of people came in every hour of the day to see him. All the leaders were frightfully overworked, they looked haggard and pale from loss of sleep" (*Six Red Months* 48).

Bryant left for home in January 1918, arriving in New York on February 18, where she plunged into writing about what she had seen and heard. She was not greeted warmly, by either friends or former employers, because of the changes brought on by America entering the war, freedom having lessened for revolutionaries in wartime.

When Bryant and Reed wrote about Russia, they created very different types of books. Reed focused on the history and speeches of leaders creating the new Russian government, the change from a tsarist regime to communism, a big picture of history made by great men. But Bryant's book *Six Red Months in Russia*, published in 1918, is where a reader could turn "for the texture of daily Russian life in the days of the revolution." As she gathered the material for her book, as biographer Mary V. Dearborn has written, "Louise discovered her vocation," of presenting political analysis while engaging readers, through dialogue, description, and action, in the lives of the people involved (86).

In this book, from the beginning, Bryant asks her readers to approach Russia with tolerance, with a clarity of judgment concerning equal rights that she associates with woman's suffrage, her own entrance into political awareness and activism. In asking readers to abandon their "all too obvious and objectionable prejudice against Russia," she specifically references woman's suffrage: "Socialism is here, whether we like it or not — just as woman suffrage is here — and it spreads with the years" (ix–x). In a section on revolutionary Angelica Balabanov, she examines arguments concerning whether women deserve the vote because they are different from or the same as men:

> She told me in Stockholm "Women have to go through such a tremendous struggle before they are free in their own minds that freedom is more precious to them than to men." I wish I could believe it, but I can never see any spiritual difference between men and women inside or outside of politics. They act and react very much alike; they certainly did in the Russian revolution. It is one of the best arguments I know in favour of equal suffrage [169–70].

The equality sought through suffrage in the United States, for Bryant necessary because of the equality and sameness of human beings and not because of their differences, mirrors the equality sought for all Russians through communism. Bryant also used suffrage as her comparison as she discussed differences separating various generations of revolutionaries, as she wrote about Katherine Breshkovsky, called Babushka: "And thus it was that Babushka, who stood so long for political revolution, balked at the logical next step, which is class struggle. It is a matter of age. If Julia Ward Howe were alive-an old woman of eighty-one could hardly expect her to picket for woman's suffrage in front of the White House, although in her youth she wrote the Battle Hymn of the Republic" (111–12).

Bryant thus asked readers to consider the Russian revolution and its aftermath with open minds, with the same respect for rights that she expected would lead American women to obtaining the vote. Although she asked readers to make comparisons, she also attempted to help them be well informed about the Russian situation and thus to remove the most deep-seated of their prejudices. Using a spelling then common, she wrote, "Our most deep-rooted prejudice against Lenine is that he is accused of being pro-German. I could never find evidence of that; I tried very hard. All I could find out about Lenine forced me to the opposite conclusion; to the conclusion that he plans the destruction of every great German institution, especially Prussian militarism.... And if it comes to a choice of accepting as allies one or the other of those two diametrically opposed forces, Prussianism or Socialism, in a fight for world freedom, we cannot hesitate to choose Socialism; and by that I do not mean we have to embrace it" (137).

For Bryant, an awareness of the path to revolution involved an understanding not only of Marxist principles, but also of the grinding nature of Russian poverty and the disenfranchisement of the masses that finally led them to revolution: her writing thus stressed cultural differences between the United States and Russia as well as similarities. In Russia, abject poverty, existing alongside the extreme privileges of a small upper class, she felt, more than war and more than any specific socialist principle, had led to revolution: "There was only food enough to last three days, there were no warm clothes at all and I passed window after window full of flowers, corsets, dog-collars and false hair" (37). The Bolsheviks, she argued, thus garnered their power from the desperate masses: "We must remember that in Russia 80 per cent of the people are proletariat or semi-proletariat. That is, they are either entirely without property or they have such small holdings that they are unable to exist from them" (54). Thus Americans should be willing to accept communism as an appropriate reform there, a reaction to a real situation, even though they might oppose it for the United States.

But her desire to foster understanding led not just to historical and economic analysis, but also to the further development of her own participatory style of nonfiction. She tried throughout the book to use specific description, characters, scenes, and dialogue to bring readers into this world with which they had no previous experience, as in this description of travel through Finland, which provides details about passengers on a train to depict the disruption and confusions of a country in rebellion:

> Next to my compartment was a General, super-refined, painfully neat, with waxed moustachios. There were several monarchists, a diplomatic courier, three aviators of uncertain political opinion and, further along, a number of political exiles who had been held up in Sweden for a month and were the last to return at the expense of the new government. Rough, almost ragged soldiers climbed aboard continually, looked us over and departed. Often they hesitated before the General's door and regarded him suspiciously, never at any time did they honour him with the slightest military courtesy. He sat rigid in his seat and stared back at them coldly. Every one was too agitated to be silent or even discreet. At every station we all dashed out to enquire the news and buy papers.
>
> At one place we were informed that the Cossacks were all with Korniloff as well as the artillery: the people were helpless. At this alarming news the monarchists began to assert themselves. They confided to me in just what manner they thought the revolutionary leaders ought to be publicly tortured and finally given death sentences.
>
> The next rumour had it that Kerensky had been murdered and all Russia was in a panic; in Petrograd the streets were running blood. The returning exiles looked pale and wretched. So this then was their joyful home-coming! They sighed but they were exceedingly brave. "Ah, well, we will fight it all over

> again!" they said with marvellous determination. I made no comments. I was conscious of an odd sense of loneliness; I was an alien in a strange land.
>
> At all the stations soldiers were gathered in little knots of six and seven; talking, arguing, gesticulating. Once a big, bewhiskered *mujik* thrust his head in at a car window, pointed menacingly at a well-dressed passenger and bellowed interrogatively, "*Burzhouee!* " (Bourgeoise). He looked very comical, yet no one laughed....
>
> We had become so excited we could scarcely keep our seats. We crowded into the narrow corridor, peering out at the desolate country, reading our papers and conjecturing.
>
> All this confusion seemed to whet our appetites. At Helsingfors we saw heaping dishes of food in the railway restaurant. A boy at the door explained the procedure: first we must buy little tickets and then we could eat as much as we pleased. To our astonishment the cashier refused the Russian money which we had so carefully obtained before leaving Sweden.
>
> "But this is ridiculous!" I told the cashier. "Finland is part of Russia! Why shouldn't you take this money?"
>
> Flames shot up in her eyes. "It will not long be a part of Russia!" she snapped. "Finland shall be a republic!" Here was a brand new situation. How fast they came now, these complications [27–29].

In a participatory style, she also takes readers to the Congress of Soviets where speakers, many of them peasants, come to the podium, creating a powerful rhetoric like what she had witnessed for suffrage:

> Often a peasant, who had never made a speech in his life, would give a long sustained talk of an hour's duration and keep the close attention of his audience. Not one speaker had stage fright. Few used notes and every man was a poet. They said the most beautiful and simple things; they knew in their innermost hearts what they wanted and how they wanted it [63].

In this scene, to describe the emotions and confusions among people who had not tried to govern themselves before, she turned to a pastiche of dialogue:

> Some events and some personalities stand out sharply from that long fortnight of oratory, when the representatives of over fifty races and 180 million of people spoke all that was in their hearts. I remember a tall, handsome Cossack, who stood before the assembly and, blushing with shame, cried out: "The Cossacks are tired of being *policemen!* Why must we forever settle the quarrels of others?"
>
> I remember the dark, striking Georgian who rebuked the speaker who preceded him because he desired national independence from Russia for his small nationality. "We seek no separate independence," he said, "when Russia is free, Georgia will also be free!"
>
> There was a gentle-looking peasant-soldier who gave solemn warning: "Mark this down well, the peasants will never lay down their arms until they receive their land!"

> And the nurse who came to describe conditions at the front, how she broke down and could only sob: "Oh, my poor soldiers!"
>
> There was a stern little delegate who arose and said: "I am from Lettgallia... "and who was interrupted by serious interrogations of "Where is that?" and "Is that in Russia?" [64].

As Bryant moved to the leaders, she tried to examine the complexities that lay behind oft-repeated American judgments of these revolutionaries. For example, she wrote of Trotsky, "No other man creates such an uproar, such hatred at the slightest utterance, uses such stinging words and yet underneath it all carries such a cool head," recognizing the stereotype of Trotsky as a hothead but then drawing attention, in this sentence and further paragraphs, to the intellect behind the constant action (67). She also tried to engage readers in her own judgment process and thus in the possible criteria by which they might judge for themselves:

> It is not easy to write fairly of Lenine, I confess that. For example, if a reporter were to interview two representative Russians, Lenine and Kerensky, he might easily throw all the weight of his argument in favour of Kerensky because he *liked* him best. Kerensky has "personality plus," as Edna Ferber would say; one cannot help but be charmed by his wit and his friendliness; he is a lawyer and a politician. On the other hand, Lenine is sheer intellect—he is absorbed, cold, unattractive, impatient at interruption. And yet here are the facts: Kerensky is spokesman for the defunct Provisional Government; he is discredited; he has no power in Russia. It would be as silly to try to re-establish him as if some outside force would try to place William Jennings Bryan in the White House and eject Wilson [137].

Along with details and discussion of the leaders, Bryant devoted attention, as in no other book, to the women involved in revolution, chapters drawing on interviews and other research. With powerful descriptive skills, she introduced readers to women who paid the cost of war and revolution in the loss of their sons, as witnessed specifically at a burial ground:

> Women all around began to sob and one quite near me tried to hurl herself after a coffin as it was being lowered. Her thin coating of civilisation dropped from her in a moment. She forgot the revolution, forgot the future of mankind, remembered only her lost one.
>
> With all her frenzied strength she fought against the friends who tried to restrain her. Crying out the name of the man in the coffin, she screamed, bit, scratched like a wounded wild thing until she was finally carried away moaning and half unconscious. Tears rolled down the faces of the big soldiers [190–91].

Bryant also wrote at length about the women involved in revolutionary leadership. She was impressed by the people's commissar for social welfare, Aleksandra Kollontai, a widely read scholar and expert linguist, who criticized the Bolsheviks for not fully including women, even those who had fought beside them, in their legislative plans. Through this portrait, Bryant stressed the disconnect between the communist rhetoric of equality and the actual treatment of women: Soviets were not making laws to create fuller political and economic participation of women, regardless of what they promised at their Congress meetings. Thus like Woodrow Wilson, the worldwide advocate for democracy, these revolutionaries seemingly did not have regard for the rights of half of their citizens.

As Bryant depicted Kollontai's efforts, as the only woman in the cabinet, to effect immediate reforms in marriage and divorce laws as well as maternal and infant care, she turned to a specific moment, presented along with the dialogue of the interview, to illustrate Kollontai's commitment to respecting and helping others:

> One day when I went to see Kollontai a long line of sweet-faced old people were standing outside her door. They had come as a delegation from one of the old people's homes. Kollontai explained their presence.
>
> "I have removed the people who used to be over them and turned their institutions into little republics. They come in every day now and express their gratitude. They elect their own officers and have their own political fights; choose their own menus — "
>
> I interrupted her. "What would that consist of in the present day?" I asked.
>
> Kollontai burst out laughing. "Surely," she said, "you must understand that there is a great deal of moral satisfaction in deciding whether you want thick cabbage soup or thin cabbage soup!"
>
> And this was the whole secret of Kollontai's success, that she allowed other people to make their own decisions [134].

Bryant was impressed with the specific steps that Kollontai was taking, many not popular with the Bolsheviks, whose high-flown rhetoric of equality, like that of Woodrow Wilson as well as the men at *The Masses*, often did not translate into real reforms for women.

With suffrage for American women still much a part of her thinking, after Bryant finished with *Six Red Months in Russia*, she decided to undertake the next difficult activist steps, of picketing and entering jail for the suffrage campaign. She was in Baltimore giving a speech entitled "The Truth About Russia" in February of 1919, newly famous and infamous for the book, when Clara Wold, her old friend from Portland and her neighbor in the Village, telegraphed her from Washington to tell her that she was needed there for suffrage and that the NWP would pay her way. On the afternoon of February 9, 1919, the eve of the last senatorial vote on suffrage in the Sixty-Fifth Congress, she arrived to be one of a column of thirty-six suffragists, led by Louisine Havemeyer, who left the NWP headquarters and marched to the

White House, where they burned Wilson in effigy (Havemeyer, "The Prison Special" 665). They were charged with "varied and sundry" offenses, like building fires after sundown or on the sidewalk, and twenty-six were sentenced to two to five days for setting fires. In front of the judge, when the group sought political prisoner status, Bryant spoke for them, citing her experiences in Russia as she discussed the difficulties that political protestors could encounter in prison and their need for special protections, thus comparing America's judicial system to Russia's. She repeated these arguments to the warden as she entered the prison and there chose to hunger strike when these men refused to meet with her ("The Demonstration of" 10).

Immediately after the picketing line and jail, Bryant continued with American political activism, accompanied by her suffrage group, ready to move beyond writing and beyond public speaking before sympathetic groups, instead entering more difficult public spaces to improve the status of the Soviets as she also sought to do for American women. Now fully engaged in American activism, she testified before the Senate's Overman Committee on Russia, mandated "to begin an investigation of Bolshevism and all other forms of anti–American radicalism in the United States," a group little interested in hearing from witnesses who asked to testify positively about the Bolsheviks (Dearborn 119). When these men refused to admit her, she burst into the room and demanded to speak. On February 20, the day on which she was finally allowed to testify, the gallery was packed with an audience of mixed sympathies, Bryant's suffrage friends there to support her in this next step for justice. The senators asked her about her NWP affiliation and she replied, "I do not know what that has to do with the truth about Russia ... I believe in equality." The senators delved into her past, even her marriage to Trullinger, but she again repeated that she was there to tell the truth about Russia. When asked about her circumstances in going there, she explained that she did not go in Russian employ but as a reporter. A committee member then responded with, "You didn't go for money, you went for love, hey?" a comment to which she didn't respond. When she finally forced these men to question her about circumstances in Russia, she said that the choice of government had to be the Russians' own, that they had the right to self-determination, even through violence, as had been necessary in other countries, including their own (Dearborn 123–24; Miller 64–65).

Buoyed by the support of her suffrage friends and her success at finally making a statement in the legislature about Russian realities, on the second day she critiqued the committee. She told the senators that they had treated her "like a traitor": witnesses against Russia, she pointed out, had been given adequate time to speak but she had been repeatedly cut off. Senator Overman then said, "You seem to want to make a martyr of yourself, when you have not been treated unfairly as far as I can see. You are a woman and do not know anything about the conduct of an examination such as we have in hand here. I am going to treat you fairly and treat you as a lady." Even after this castigation, or perhaps because of it, Bryant continued to upbraid the committee for its harsh and gendered mode of interviewing: "Even my morals have been suggested by Senator Nelson. He has given me regular lectures as to what I ought to think, and how I might, somehow, come out of this terrible slump I have gotten into" (Dearborn 125–26).

As an imprisoned suffragist and Russian sympathizer, Bryant went immediately from Washington to a full speaking tour, in demand as a speaker across the country. After the first stop in Detroit with a grand reception and articles in the papers, she went on to Chicago, Minneapolis, Seattle, Tacoma, Portland, and San Francisco, with additional cities added as she traveled. People had to be turned away in St. Paul and then in Minneapolis. In Salt Lake, Senator William H. King from the Overman Committee tried to have her arrested, but the mayor and the chief of police refused to do so (Dearborn 133). At these stops, she spoke against Allied intervention in Siberia; for the Seattle general strike as a native movement, not controlled by Russian Bolsheviks; for increased understanding among countries; and for woman suffrage. Like Louisine Havemeyer, she chose dramatic visual rhetoric to invigorate her speeches: she wore a long black cloak, lined in red; at the end of the talk, she threw it back and gave a dramatic twirl as she left the stage, as though she were wrapped in the red flag of Russia.

In July 1920, Bryant left for Russia again, traveling illegally as the wife of a Swedish businessman, to meet her husband and continue to combine activism with journalism. In Moscow she met again with both Lenin and Trotsky. After Reed died on October 17 of typhus, Bryant continued to work in Russia, as a correspondent for the International News Service. For eight months, she filed stories nearly every day, keeping a grueling schedule. She investigated the state of Lenin's health, explained internal and foreign policy, and covered the Kronshtadt rebellion in March. Undertaken first by sailors at the Gulf of Finland, this revolt soon also involved urban workers who went out on strikes primarily over the lack of food and shelter, problems that a new government had not solved, problems of poverty that Bryant still wrote about as central to Russian political change (Benvenuti 184–86).

In the early summer of 1921, Bryant went with a letter from Lenin to Bukhara, a perilous journey to a province where Bolsheviks had ousted the emir but local officials were attempting to achieve a democratic style of government that would allow private ownership of land and productive assets.

She continued traveling through the newly Soviet provinces of Central Asia, traveling nearly to India, through Muslim areas where treaties and revolts alternated, where local emirs were being ousted but an appropriate form of Soviet allegiance, as well as its effect on governmental, cultural, and religious practices, had not yet been determined. She reported from this volatile area as the only Western correspondent to do so in six years. In July of 1921 she came back to the United States where she lived for a year, continuing to write about the realities of "soviet union" for women and men and for residents of various areas and faiths. The first story in her sixteen-part series appeared on August 16 in the *New York American* and on the next day in the *San Francisco Examiner*. As she commonly did, she spoke frankly about conditions, her analyses backed up with descriptions and dialogue, her attention given to women and men, to officials and citizens.

In 1922, Bryant's assignments also took her to Rome, Paris, Athens, and Constantinople, where she interviewed important political figures to ensure that Americans had first-hand accounts of international politics and the effects of political change on women. She was the first reporter to gain an exclusive interview with Mussolini, who had come to power after his 1922 march on Rome, a piece appearing in Hearst papers in the third week of January 1923. She went on to Milan for family background that other reporters missed, much of it obtained in an interview with Madame Mussolini. In her feature article, she continued the suffrage theme as she quoted Mussolini's views of women, which she had pressed him to divulge: "Woman must think only of beauty and the home, and should not concern herself with politics" (Dearborn 210).

Bryant decided to return to Russia in 1922, with support from King Features, which supplied columns for Hearst newspapers, not to cable news stories but to draw on previous material and new interviews to create extended portraits of Russian leaders and citizens, published within Hearst papers and then in book form as *Mirrors of Moscow*. These long feature articles began appearing on June 4, 1922, advertised as pieces written by the "Famous American Newspaper Correspondent — Author of 'Six Red Months in Russia.'" Here she attempted through interviews to reveal the leaders of the revolution as actual people, she wrote, "as I know them in their homes, where the red glare does not penetrate and they live as other men" (xi).

Bryant used these extended articles, in their newspaper and book publication, to record women's need, even with suffrage, to work outside of regular politics. When she again wrote about Alexandra Kollontai, she stressed this leader's organization of women's congresses to engage urban and rural women in ongoing discussions of health care and civil rights. As Bryant reports Kollontai's remarks about women who came to the congress from harems in Turkestan, she returns her readers' attention to suffrage: "Everybody stares at them, they are a curiosity which gives the congresses a theatrical atmosphere. Yet all pioneering work is theatrical. It was distinctly theatrical when the audiences used to throw eggs at your pioneer suffragists.... How else would we get in touch with Mohammedan women except through women?" (121). Like American women, Bryant maintained, these Soviet women stood at the beginning of a long road leading to personal fulfillment and equal governmental involvement, with aid from a kind and dedicated leader like Kollontai essential and full progress not immediately to be attained: "But if her inspiration, which aims to lift women to the skies, lifts them only from their knees to their feet, there will be nothing to regret" (111).

In 1923, Bryant married William Bullitt, an assistant secretary of state under Wilson who had accompanied Lincoln Steffens on a mission to Russia to negotiate diplomatic relations with the Bolshevik regime and resigned when the president refused to do so. The couple moved to Paris where they had a daughter and started a salon for artists. In *The Nation* in August 1925 appeared Bryant's "A Turkish Divorce," one of her most feminist pieces, concerning Mustafa Kemal, a distinguished military commander during World War I who waged the Turkish War of Independence in 1922 and established the new Turkish state. During his presidency, Kemal embarked upon a program of political, economic, and cultural reforms. But like Wilson, he spoke for democracy and denied the rights of women, beginning with his wife whom he divorced because she was childless. In this article, Bryant wrote about his personal and political disregard for women but also about celebrated women leaders, "brilliant women, superbly educated, tolerant and progressive," especially Halide Edib Hanoum, the women's movement brightest star. Like American and Russian women, Turkish feminists faced the struggle for their own rights at a time when their new and endangered country most needed their service: "They hope to achieve woman suffrage before many years have passed, but the greater part of their time and all their money are at present being utilized in caring for the hundreds of thousands of orphans and refugees who are starving in Turkey today" (231). In 1924, Turkish women gained the right to enter civil-service employment, but Turkish women did not participate in municipal elections until 1930 and national elections until 1934.

Bryant's writing career ended because of Adiposis dolorosa, or Dercum's disease, with which she was diagnosed in 1928 though the illness began much earlier, with extreme weight gain, fatigue, and mental confusion. The

Bullitts divorced in 1930; he was able to gain full custody of their daughter, and Bryant died in 1936.

After Louise Bryant began working with the suffrage campaign in Portland, she became interested in making a difference in her country and the world. She spent her career writing about politics, especially concentrating on the principles and realities that affected women's rights around the world. As she analyzed Russian or Turkish politics, she was always also commenting on America and the slow development of women's rights, the need to continue to question authorities and advocate for equality, the progress and setbacks along the way. For Bryant, suffrage activism led to a writing career in which she described real situations so that readers could enter the life of the Other and encouraged frank and open-minded evaluation of foreign governments and her own.

Helena Hill Weed (1875–1958)

Involvement in suffrage led Louise Bryant to a long-held concern for those who Americans might judge as the Other: women seeking the vote, workers struggling for fair wages and work conditions, Russians fighting for security and civil rights. She was willing to travel to dangerous sites, as she had been willing to enter jail and hunger strike, to bring an accurate picture of justice and injustice to Americans. But Bryant, like Alice Gram Robinson, was just one of a group of suffragists for whom picketing and jail led to writing careers and especially to careers focused on investigations of governments and civil rights. Like Robinson and Bryant, Helena Hill Weed brought her own determination and belief in freedom to her writing, often about a controversial political situation, a primary subject being the status of Haiti and American foreign policy towards it. She thus, similarly, through description, frank talk, and thorough research, brought readers into new perspectives about people that the American government judged as Other.

Weed came from a respected, respectable family through which she gained an interest in politics but did not secure equality of opportunity. Her father, Ebenezer J. Hill, served in the House of Representatives from 1895 to 1913. He had studied at Yale and been a soldier in the Union Army before becoming president of the Norwalk Gas Light Company and the Norwalk Street Railway Company before entering the legislature. Hill's daughter read in his library and shared his interest in American science and progress. She studied in Paris after high school and then went on to a science degree at Vassar where she graduated in 1896. When several eastern colleges turned down her request for admission to a graduate geology program as an inappropriate choice for a woman, she enrolled in the Montana School of Mines, in Butte, Montana, where she obtained a master's degree in economic geology and began attending local political meetings. In Butte, she met her husband, Walter Harvey Weed, one of her teachers, a geologist who was conducting a survey of the state with which she began assisting him ("Helena H. Weed").

Like so many other women, Helen Hill Weed went from frustrating experiences — trying to start a separate career and trying to achieve a state suffrage amendment — to work on a federal amendment, and then to picketing and jail. She was arrested while wearing a DAR pin with bars that represented her fourteen ancestors who had given their lives in the American Revolution. Photograph dated ca. 1910, by Harris & Ewing. Photograph from National Woman's Party Records. Source: Library of Congress Manuscript Division.

After they came back east, Weed had three children between 1898 and 1903 while helping her husband with his large-scale publications, such as the *Mines Handbook* and the *Copper Handbook*. She also secured a master's degree in science in 1902 at a women's college willing to accept her, Vassar.

During this period, having seen the dearth of opportunities for women in science, as had Agnes Chase, she began to support the suffrage effort through involvement in various women's clubs. She served as a national vice-president of the Daughters of the American Revolution, urging members of this organization to take an activist stance (Davies 284). But she also joined the Equal Franchise Society in New York, Connecticut, and New Jersey and began working on state suffrage campaigns, along with her sisters, Clara and Elsie.

In these states, the power of her family made her participation all the more valuable. In New Jersey, for the vote on a state suffrage amendment in November of 1915, Weed served as a poll watcher.

The *New York Times* reported that she saw bribes offered and taken in this election. With her family connections, she contributed a powerful subtitle to a *Times* article: "Saw Votes Bought in Jersey Election; Mrs. Helena Hill Weed Says Money Was Passed Before Her Eyes in Newark." Here she is fully identified and quoted about the specifics of this further delay of justice to women: "'The respectable men in New Jersey tell me that it was the rawest political deal that was ever put over,' said Mrs. Helena Hill Weed, daughter of Representative Hill of Connecticut, who was a watcher at one of the polling places in Newark." Weed claimed that a county officeholder was at the site campaigning against the amendment, threatening those men who supported it and pulling men in from the street to vote against it. She saw "money passed for votes before her eyes." On that same November 2, a state bill had also been turned down in New York, and so Weed's harsh commentary on bad faith and fraud in the *New York Times*, printed because of her family name and influence, provided commentary on both states' treatment of their women citizens on that day.

Like so many other women, Weed went from frustrating experiences — trying to start a separate career and trying to achieve a state suffrage amendment — to work on a federal amendment, and then to picketing and jail. The NWP fully recognized the clout that came with Weed as a daughter of a well-respected and long-term member of Congress, as a national leader of the DAR, as a scientist. From her first contact with the CU in 1915, she became a regular go between with the DAR, putting official invitations to suffrage events regularly on the agenda of this well-known, conservative organization's meetings, additions to the general business that secured newspaper attention, and convincing members to embrace active involvement even though the organization would not endorse the amendment ("Colors of Suffrage"). After the picketing began, she regularly joined the line even after America's entrance into World War I. She was one of five women who on July 4, 1917, moved out from suffrage headquarters carrying banners that read "Just governments derive their power from the consent of the governed," echoing the Declaration of Independence, and "Mr. President, what will you do for woman suffrage?" with Vida Milholland carrying her sister's last words. As NWP press bulletins stressed, Helena Hill Weed was arrested while wearing a DAR pin with bars that represented her fourteen ancestors who had given their lives in the American Revolution. When the judge ruled about the punishment, she accepted three days in jail instead of paying the twenty-five dollar fine ("The United States Convicts"; "Protest for Liberty").

As picketing continued, so did Helena Hill Weed. On August 6, 1918, when one hundred women gathered at Lafayette's monument bearing the

Milholland banner as well as others condemning Wilson and the Democrats, several women, Weed included, put down their banners and gave speeches to the large crowd concerning their determination to defeat all forms of opposition and secure equal rights. ("Suffragists Again Attack"). When forty-eight women were arrested, the press viewed Weed, who refused bail and accepted the sentence of fifteen days, as a newsworthy member of the group. As she had in 1917, she demanded status as a political prisoner and began hunger striking as soon as she entered prison ("Women's Protest").

On the afternoon of February 9, 1919, when thirty-six suffragists marched to the White House to burn Wilson in effigy, Weed and Bryant were among the thirty-nine participants arrested. In late February when these women went out on the Prison Special, Helen Hill Weed made their schedule. The pin that Weed wore as a member of the DAR became an important symbol for the train and for subsequent meetings. Alice Paul and she crafted a similarly sized pin, with bars, to represent the front of a prison cell. It was worn by all of the women who spent time in jail and by others, like Mary Church Terrell, who had served valiantly on the picket line but had not been sent to jail.

For Weed, as for so many other women, picketing provided a model of activism that would lead to a writing future involving political research and analysis. After suffrage, working on her husband's books and through the DAR was no longer sufficiently engaging. She left the Republican Party to support Robert La Follette's independent candidacy for president in 1924 and then switched to the Democratic Party, from which she ran unsuccessfully for mayor of Norwalk, Connecticut, in 1927, in opposition to what she labeled "the 'boss' form of politics" as the *New York Times* commented in an article calling her "Daughter of a Late Republican Congressman" in the headline and the more radical "a Sacco–Vanzetti sympathizer, leader of woman's suffrage, and a La Follette supporter in 1924" in the first sentence of the article ("Name Woman for Mayor"). When she lost to the city treasurer, the *Times* then labeled her the more acceptable "first grandmother who ever sought the Mayoralty in a Connecticut city" ("Grandmother Beaten for Mayor"). Although she did not secure elected office, she wanted to continue her activism — by involving herself in situations in which American law was denying self-determination and freedom, as she did in the suffrage campaign. She also wanted to continue seeking the camaraderie and power of groups of activists, ones using writing to make a difference.

Weed would bring the same insistence on justice that led her to poll watching and suffrage campaigning to activism concerning Haiti, an involvement that began at the end of the suffrage campaign when she first traveled there to conduct research on copper deposits and continued through several visits and many articles into the 1930s ("Helena H. Weed"). For Weed, the group through which to make a difference concerning this issue would involve Oswald Garrison Villard, who became owner as well as editor of the *Nation* through family inheritance (Navasky). He left no doubt as to his plans for the publication's political activism. In 1917, referring to a speech that Wilson gave in Mobile in 1913, he insisted that the president adhere to his stated policy of nonintervention and mutual respect in Central and South America (Holden and Zolov 110):

> Until we live up to Mr. Wilson's promise in his Mobile speech, that we will not take any more territory to the south of us, we shall woo in vain South American business and friendship. Until we agree to respect the rights of small Caribbean nationalities and treat respectfully the citizens of them who we have annexed or purchased, our moral protests as to Serbia and Belgium must lack convincing force ["Drifting"].

Here we see in 1917, as in the suffrage campaign that same year, another use of Wilson's claims concerning his championing of democracy, what he was supposedly making the world safe for, used against him. For, while Wilson had stated principles of fairness and respect towards Latin America in 1913, he had intervened in Mexico in 1914 and 1916, and he had invaded Haiti in 1915 and the Dominican Republic in 1916 (Gilderhus).

In 1920, the *Nation* began to take the lead in "exposing the violent procedure of the Wilson administration in Haiti and the Dominican Republic" (Rippy 246; Juarez 155). At that time Villard allied the *Nation* with the NAACP and with the *Union Patriotique d'Haiti*, forming the Haiti-Santo Domingo Independence Society, with offices in New York and Washington, to carry on agitation in the United States and force a change in governmental policy. Helena Hill Weed served as the society's national secretary, doing most of the organizational work as she had done for the suffrage train. The society's plans were to argue for immediate withdrawal of the Marines from both Haiti and Santo Domingo, for equitable treaties, and for American backing of constitutional governments in both countries (Juarez 170). Weed also worked with Villard to plan a series of articles, in the *Nation* and other journals, that could galvanize support for the disenfranchised, as publicity in the *Suffragist* and in newspapers had ultimately done for suffrage.

Like the NWP at its meetings and in its written accounts, Weed employed techniques of argumentation and education that could sway Americans and cause them to act. The society raised funds through ads and benefit theater performances; they urged supporters to contact their senators and taught them how to do so effectively; they regularly published articles to acquaint Americans with the facts behind Wilson's lofty calls for democracy and mutual respect. Like Louise Bryant concerning Russia, Weed believed that Americans needed not just lofty counterclaims about Haiti and Santo Domingo, but a thorough rendition of the facts. The assassination of Haitian president Guillaume Sam in 1915, Villard and Weed believed and explained at length in the *Nation*, had only been a plausible excuse for American invasion, for scrapping all of the principles that Wilson had stated. A series of letters between Wilson, William Jennings Bryan, secretary of state, and Josephus Daniels, secretary of the navy, revealed that a new treaty giving the United States control over Haiti had been drafted in Washington as early as July 1914 and a naval landing had been planned. The Haitian government, however, then and again in early 1915, refused to yield to Wilson's pressure, maintained its independence, and vowed to mount a defense if invaded (Schmidt 42–63).

Then came the revolution of July 1915, and American troops landed, a crisis about which Weed and Villard disagreed with the American government, as they explained in the *Nation*. Haitian leaders claimed that this revolution was an almost unanimous uprising against Guillaume Sam caused by his intention to sign a treaty that would give the United States control of Haitian custom houses: since the income from customs receipts was almost the sole source of government revenue, such control meant a loss of political independence (Schmidt 64–81).

When the Marines, led by Admiral William B. Caperton, landed to take control, as the *Nation* claimed in many articles, the Haitian Congress was in session and in the process of electing a president to succeed Sam. The Congress planned to restore constitutional government but could not do so after the Marines assumed full military control of the capital, with Wilson planning to delay elections until he could find a candidate who would pledge himself to ratifying a treaty that would cede control to the United States. In Sudre Dartiguenave, Wilson finally found a candidate who professed to believe that any terms the United States might demand would be for Haiti's benefit. Under Admiral Caperton's command, both the Marines and Haitian militia quelled any dissent against Dartiguenave and American control with violence. In response to this denial of civil rights and to attacks on citizens, on November 3 the *Nation* demanded "a broad-minded committee of the ablest men in Congress — men without color prejudice" to investigate conditions there ("What to Do"). A Senate committee was appointed, but it quickly endorsed all that Wilson had done.

At this point, with Helena Hill Weed leading the effort, the society called upon other like-minded publications, such as *Current History* and the

New Republic, to join the *Nation* in educating Americans concerning the choices being made in Washington and the human rights violations being sanctioned in Haiti. These editors and writers realized, as had the members of the NWP, that there would have to be public pressure for political change to occur: as in the suffrage campaign, American citizens needed education concerning the rights of a group that their government treated as unworthy and properly subservient. In arguments for suffrage, writers had tried to combat the most common misconceptions: that men could vote for a family, that the majority of women did not seek the vote, that suffrage should remain a state matter. Similarly, these publications tried to isolate the most common negative beliefs — that the possibility of unrest or of negative effects on the American economy gave the United States the right to invade, that these peoples could not govern themselves ("President Harding's Pledge," "The Navy Department"). In both situations, Weed sought to disparage patriarchal assumptions about groups assumed to need the control of American men and force legislators to foster the self-governance that they expected for themselves and repeatedly endorsed in principle for others.

As Weed took on American prejudices, in her own many speeches and articles, she referred to testimony given and then ignored in Senate investigations and especially to the damning details about American foreign policy and intervention that the hearings had revealed. In this assessment, she involved readers as intelligent citizens who could read a detailed analysis and change their viewpoint about those commonly depicted as Other:

> Thus far, then, the hearings at Washington have disclosed that the intervention was prepared by Messrs. Bryan, Wilson, and Daniels — under whose inspiration is not yet clear — a year before it began; that no danger threatened foreigners' lives or property until after American Occupation was complete; that American military force was used to obtain, first, the election of a puppet President pledged to act under our orders, then to force acceptance of an unconstitutional and bitterly hated treaty, and finally illegally to revise the Haitian constitution so that foreigners — in particular the National City Bank of New York — might hold land; and that in six years of Occupation we have done nothing for Haiti and have not even been able to establish order, so bitter is the patriotic hostility of the Haitians to foreign intervention ["Hearing the Truth about Haiti"].

Like the writers of many *Suffragist* articles and the pickets in front of the White House, Weed tried in her *Nation* articles, such as "Hearing the Truth About Haiti" from November of 1921 and "Fresh Hope for Haiti" and "Victory in Haiti" from March 1930, as well as in the *New York Times* in "Santo Domingo Loan" in 1922, to position Americans as people who wanted liberty, who had been misled about a group that the government was opposing, one seeking the rights and independence that Americans had. She thus portrayed President Harding and Secretary of the Navy Daniels as capitalists backing moneyed interests rather than freedom, thus like Wilson and the Senate members who had opposed women suffrage; Admiral Caperton as the government factotum with a cruel streak, like Superintendent Raymond Whittaker of Occoquan Workhouse; and Haitians as peace and freedom loving peoples, like American women seeking only the right to participate in their government. Thus Haitians, like women as they were constructed in suffrage rhetoric, could be posited as desiring something noble that just a few powerful, selfish, and cruel men refused to provide.

While creating these characterizations and making these arguments in a series of *Nation* articles, Weed and Villard marshaled a select group through which to state and bolster their case, just as the NWP sought pickets, like Louisine Havemeyer and Weed herself, whose participation ceded influence. One of these speakers and writers was James Weldon Johnson, who had served as U.S. consul in Venezuela from 1906 to 1908 and in Nicaragua from 1909 to 1913. In 1916, Johnson joined the staff of the NAACP, which Villard had helped to form in 1909 along with W.E.B. Du Bois, Mary Church Terrell, Ida Wells Barnett, and other activists; in 1920, he became general secretary of the NAACP. His articles in the *Nation* stressed the proper nobility of democracy in comparison with ignoble acts perpetrated towards Haiti. The group that held meetings and published articles also included Pierre Hudicourt, a Haitian lawyer who in January of 1922 came to the United States to argue before the Senate for the withdrawal of the Marines, and Herbert Seligmann, a graduate from Harvard University, who had written articles and books advocating for the civil rights of African Americans. Sinclair Lewis was at a height of his influence and popularity when his "Devil-Dog Rule" concerning cruelties perpetrated by American officials in Haiti appeared in the *Nation* in December 1929; as biographer Mark Schorer has stated, the phenomenal success of *Main Street* from 1920 "was the most sensational event in twentieth-century American publishing history" (268). He had followed up this first great success with *Babbitt* in 1922, a novel satirizing American commercial culture, a subject matter that made him another powerful speaker for Haiti.

Through the society, her writing for *The Nation*, and her planning with Villard for an array of articles, Weed was able to keep American attention on Haiti in the twenties and thirties even with so many other concerns before the nation, a difficult feat that Alice Paul had achieved with suffrage, even during World War I. Reviewing *The Nation*'s battle for justice in Haiti, Villard wrote: "I look back upon these crusades on behalf of our Caribbean neighbors with unbounded satisfaction. They also seem to me to have justified all the time and money I put into *The Nation*" (Navasky). The United States began withdrawing from the island in 1931. In Haiti in July 1934, Franklin Roosevelt reaffirmed an August 1933 disengagement agreement. The last U.S. Marines departed in mid–August ("Haiti").

After the campaign for Haitian freedom, Weed continued to research and write about attempts by women and men to gain freedom, both in Latin America and the United States. She worked diligently to help prepare for the Inter American Commission on Women in Montevideo in December 1933, part of the Seventh International Conference of American States, at which the United States' representatives finally signed an equal opportunity act, drafted by Alice Paul, which many feminists viewed as a key protection, granting women the right to choose the country of their citizenship after marriage (Hinton). In "The Repercussions of Montevideo," a long article from which many newspapers published excerpts, Weed discussed this treaty and its probable impact throughout the Americas (Bredbenner 239–40; Lemons 198). In this piece, she also commented positively, through reference to Haiti, on the Good Neighbor Policy that Secretary of State Cordell Hull had affirmed in Montevideo: "No country has the right to intervene in the internal or external affairs of another" (LaFeber 376). From February to June 1935, along with fellow suffragist Mary Winsor, Weed traveled to Panama and Haiti, sending back reports on civil rights. Afterwards, she continued writing about Latin America, especially the effects of Franklin Roosevelt's visit to Brazil, Argentina, and Uruguay in 1936.

As an attendant at Eleanor Roosevelt's press conferences and a member of the president's press corps, Weed also analyzed American politics for various newspapers. For *Current History*, as for newspapers, she carefully considered the impact of the New Deal on women, criticizing the marital status clause in the Economy Act, which allowed for one spouse, generally the wife, to be fired from the civil service even if she was doing her job well. She also wrote about the effect on women of minimum wages, lower than those created for men, and of the restricted hours set for them on federal projects. Using statistics and examples, she argued in *Current History* in November of 1934 that only one conclusion could be drawn from these discriminatory practices as well as the lack of work projects for women workers: "For some incomprehensible reason the New Deal has regarded unemployment among women as less pitiable than that of men. Federal relief itself has been characterized by sex discrimination" ("The New Deal" 182). In this piece, Weed concludes that "seemingly the long struggle for women's right to work on an equal footing with men has not yet ended. It must go on under the New Deal even as under the old" (183). In other articles, she continued to record how women and men dealt with economic hardships. For the *New York Times* in 1935, for example, in a long article about ongoing renovations to the Capitol, she wrote about how Americans were coping "in the midst of a Depression which is profoundly altering the nature of the national life" ("Change Again" 15).

After the suffrage campaign, Helena Hill Weed was not willing to return to her work as a geologist and project assistant. She sought instead her own writing career, one centered in political critique on the national and international level, bringing to American readers a different perspective on groups judged as Other, not ceding them as lesser and thus to be controlled by a government in which they had no voice. Working through the Haiti–Santo Domingo Independence Society, a political organization like the NWP with clear activist goals, she was able to bring to bear the power of the group, as well as her own research and writing skills, to instigate change. For her activism, begun in suffrage, Haiti has named her to its national honor roll for distinguished public service ("Helena H. Weed"). When the *New York Times* wrote her obituary in 1958, its headline was "Helena H. Weed, a Suffragist, 83," and indeed the suffrage campaign had led to her career.

Beatrice Kinkead (1874–1947)

Like Robinson, Bryant, and Weed, other suffragists involved themselves in writing that had the goal of enlarging the American perspective. Beatrice Kinkead also found in suffrage an appreciation of those deemed as Other and an interest in further involving Americans in international politics and rights. But her purview was not journalism, and her audience was rarely adults. Instead, she chose work as a translator, an ultimate means of introducing Americans to another culture, and her primary audience was children and adolescents, the next generation of Americans. For her, as for so many others, suffrage and jail led to a much larger world.

She was called Minnie Belle but was born Beatrice Reynolds, in 1874, in Lake County, California. She graduated from the University of California, among the first women to do so, where she began her suffrage involvement in the campus suffrage society, witnessing the difficulties of state campaigns ("Mrs. Beatrice Kinkead"). In 1893 when a woman's suffrage bill won approval in the state legislature, the governor vetoed it as unconstitutional. While she was teaching at a high school in San Francisco and working in a city suffrage league in 1896, suffragists convinced the legislature to allow a statewide referendum, but it was defeated by a sizeable majority.

Kinkead then left high school teaching and moved east, where she taught at Vassar and at Bryn Mawr, becoming further involved with suffrage and ultimately with the NWP, having grown disenchanted with state campaigns. In 1902 she married James Alan "Lanny" Kinkead, a civil engineer from Illinois, and they moved to Montclair, New Jersey, where she had four sons between 1906 and 1911 ("Mrs. Beatrice Kinkead"). Although California finally approved a suffrage referendum in 1911, the fight for the vote was just beginning in New Jersey, President Wilson's home state, where in 1916 he voted for state suffrage, in a referendum that failed, although he still opposed a federal amendment, a decision made, NWP members like Kinkead felt, to placate suffrage supporters without offering real assistance, as the *Suffragist* argued: "In Congress, where the chances for the success of woman suffrage were good, he turned his whole party machine against it; in New Jersey, where defeat was sure, he cast a solitary vote in its favor" ("Wilson's Vote on Suffrage").

In the spring of 1917, Kinkead came from New Jersey to stand on the picket line several times, beginning with New Jersey Day in February, one of many special days used to secure publicity and volunteers. Kinkead was one of the sixteen women who went out on July 14, 1917, carrying a banner reading "Liberty, Equality, Fraternity, July 14, 1789." On July 17, at the trial for these Bastille Day offenses, the court meted out sentences of sixty days to Kinkead and the other fifteen pickets. At the trial, she maintained before the judge and packed courtroom that "the administration has ordered the conviction" ("Suffragists Take"). Kinkead did not return to the line, the experience having been a shocking one concerning American rights and justice.

Like Louise Bryant and Helen Keller, Kinkead became involved with socialism as well as the suffrage campaign as an answer to the capitalistic exploitation of women workers with no regard for their rights. On February 6, 1913, Helen Keller had given her first public speech at the Hillside School in Montclair, sponsored by the active local branch of the Socialist Party. The *New York Times* reported her thesis in its headline: "More Blind Than She, Miss Keller Says; All Are Sightless Who Do Not Open Their Eyes to Fellow-Men and Know Their Rights." Kinkead had been there that night, and afterwards she began studying communism and socialism, in principle and in practice, and especially in Russia.

After the suffrage campaign, Kinkead abandoned her teaching career and looked for a means of making an impact as a writer though employing a very different means than Louise Bryant. On several trips to Russia in 1934 she met with writers and then began translating the works of M. Il'in, or Mikhail Andreevich Il'in, a young engineer whose brother Marshak was a famous poet and storyteller. Both brothers belonged to a group of writers who were studying science, history, and Soviet life and writing books not only for children but for workers in factories and for peasants; Kinkead's long headnote in several translations presented them as good, educationally oriented folk, traits that Kinkead argued were not negated by their participation in the Red Army. "All of them work together," she wrote in her headnote, "trying to make simple stories about the real world we live in." In celebrating this group, she is asking her readers to appreciate their writing and view these authors not just as communists or factory workers but as skilled writers and historians, bringing uplifting stories to American young people.

These books, all featuring the introduction about the writer and his group while associating Russian customs and history with American traditions, became very popular in the United States. Mikhail Il'in's *What Time Is It? The Story of Clocks*, reprinted frequently in the Kinkead translation between 1932 and 1937, gives young readers a history of clocks of all types, including water, sand, and milk clocks, with Russian customs associated with Greek, Roman, and Egyptian customs, as well as with the Strasburg Cathedral clock and with Benedictine monks telling time through their ringing of bells and measured reading of the Psalms. In this translation, for American readers, Kinkead thus associates Russians with the history of the better known and more approved world.

Like the clock book, her other translations associated Russia with scientific progress. She translated, for example, Mikhail Il'in's *A Ring and a Riddle*, a large children's picture book featuring the story of Ivan, no country mentioned. Here Il'in shows how the elements of a fairy tale actually exist because of science. The action takes Ivan on a quest for riches around the world, and at the end he translates what he returns with into what moderns have via science: a magic ring is a compass; a talking horn is the radio. And new dreams of flying to other planets, controlling wind and rain, and turning the whole world into a land of plenty, the book also posits, don't have to be dreams: "The old fairy tales have come true. And the new ones will, too, if people will only continue to dream, work hard and follow the advice of Science, the wonder worker" (np). Science is here an international marvel, with progress shared by all countries, and an originally Russian "Ivan" a character that all can appreciate.

Throughout the 1930s and 1940s, Kinkead used her translations to stress the common ground between Russians and Americans, associating a frequently regarded Other with progress, science, and education — and with the entertainment of American children. At the eve of World War II, she especially stressed the need for understanding and cooperation with the Russians in the fight against fascism. As a member of a group of four hundred Americans, including fellow suffragist Sara Bard Field, Miriam Allen de Ford, Dashiell Hammett, Ernest Hemingway, Langston Hughes, James Thurber, William Carlos Williams, and Richard Wright, she participated in writing and signing an open letter, publicized widely, "calling for greater unity of the anti-fascist forces and strengthening of the front against aggression through closer cooperation with the Soviet Union" ("To All Active Supporters").

After the war, Kinkead continued with her book projects in Russia, not changing her interest in Russian learning after American views of the Soviet Union began to shift from World War II ally to Cold-War enemy. She began during the war translating a book series by M. Il'in concerning human evolution from the beginnings to cave dwellers in the first book, Egypt, Greece, and Rome in the second, and the Middle Ages and the Renaissance in the third, books labeling man as increasingly a "giant" as he evolved. And she continued with this project after the war, with volumes appearing in 1948 and 1949. In 1946 she also translated Il'in's explication of the science involved in everyday living and especially within a kitchen, *100,000 Whys: A Trip Around the Room*, this project involving significant discussion with the author as had earlier collaborations. In 1946 she worked additionally with I. Nechaev on *Chemical Elements: The Fascinating Story of Their Discovery and of the Famous Scientists Who Discovered Them*. This continued involvement with Russian writers caused her to be investigated by the House Committee on Un-American Activities when it held hearings in San Francisco in December of 1953.

In her translations through the 1930s, the war years, and the Cold War, Kinkead involved adolescent and adult readers in a larger perspective, her work imbued with the independence and critical judgment that she gained through the suffrage campaign. Like Weed and Bryant, she asked Americans to look reflectively, with open minds, at the contributions of cultures being judged as lesser and as dangerous. She thought that younger as well as older readers needed involvement with the full range of achievements, her dedication to translation having special meaning to her in the synthesis of cultures that it involved.

Martha Foley (1897–1977)

As suffragists moved into writing careers, they involved themselves in journalism, political analysis, and children's books, as editors, writers, and translators. Writers like Robinson, Bryant, and Weed attempted to expand the journalism and political commentary available to Americans; Kinkead translated scientific and historical writing aimed at adolescents and adults, involving them in the learning of Russian writers. In the field of fiction, also, a suffragist enabled a younger generation to move beyond formulas and beyond the establishment, with the suffrage movement serving as a formative experience. After her participation in the campaign, Martha Foley created a place for people to publish short stories, beyond commercial considerations, helping to forward a genre that was not the most financially viable in the coming age of the novel. She wanted to expand the power of the artist and introduce readers to the new, the experimental, to ideas that might open them to different choices and lives, as suffrage had done for her.

In her childhood, illnesses of both of her parents, in Zanesville, Ohio, led to Foley's staying, along with her brother, in Boston, "with people who either did not like or did not understand children," as she wrote in an autobiography (*The Story of* 29). Her parents, a schoolteacher and doctor, had encouraged reading and some of their library went to Boston with her, a salvation. She attended the Boston Girls' Latin School where she published stories in the school magazine; she then went on to Boston University though she was not sure of what she wanted to study there.

When she was twenty, she was visiting a friend at the Socialist Party headquarters in Boston when a member of the NWP asked her to picket at the State House. On the day of Wilson's return from the first League of Nations meeting on February 24, 1919, hundreds of thousands of people lined up for a big parade in his honor. Down the street went twenty-two suffragists carrying signs with slogans like "Taxation without Representation is Tyranny." They were warned that unless they moved on they would be arrested. They were then taken to the Tombs, a jail under the courthouse.

The next morning Alice Paul came and told them the police commissioners' plan was to try them separately and secretly because there was a mob outside of the courthouse and the police didn't want a riot. When the court officers came, the prisoners refused to move forward; officers grabbed them and began lugging them up winding iron stairs to the courtroom. Along with the others, Foley was carried into the courtroom, and there she refused to speak. She was given eight days in jail for "loitering and sauntering," a terminology that equated their public presence with prostitution. When these women entered the Charles Street prison, they began to hunger strike. They were released after three days: when Foley refused to leave the prison, she was dumped out onto the street ("Reminding the President").

Like so many other women, Foley sought to make a further impact after her frightening experience with picketing and jail made her more aware of power structures in her nation. While she had been unsure of her goals before, she now knew that she wanted a future in meaningful newspaper work: "I decided to leave Boston University to go to New York and become a newspaperwoman in earnest. I turned down all jobs as society editor or club editor or woman's page editor. I got a job as copy editor — unusual for a girl then — and as a rewrite woman and a book reviewer" (*The Story of* 35). She worked for the *New York Globe* and then the *Newark Ledger*.

Foley next went to the West Coast, intending to develop a career reporting American political realities. She was quickly hired and fired at the *San Francisco Journal*: the editor-in-chief, who had been out of town when she interviewed, found a woman working on the copy desk on his return and dismissed her. In San Francisco, she mostly worked freelance, covering stories that seemed important to her. She had the opportunity to go with Eugene Debs and Otto Branstetter, national secretary of the Socialist Party, to see Tom Mooney, who had been convicted for a bombing during a labor parade of 1916 and who would serve twenty-three years before being pardoned in 1939. She entered San Quentin prison to witness a heart-wrenching meeting between Debs and Mooney, described in her story that the *Record* featured prominently, but which didn't lead to a permanent job (*The Story of* 36–40).

After marrying writer Whit Burnett and moving with him to New York, Foley began working at the Hearst tabloid, the *Mirror*, as a caption writer, while Burnett worked at the *Times*. When he lost his job in 1927, they decided to go to France, but unable to secure employment there, they quickly returned, she to the *Mirror*. When they had saved enough money, they went back to Paris, where she worked for the *Paris Herald*, the only woman in the city room, doing all types of writing and editing.

In December 1929, they decided to go to Vienna. While doing freelance journalism, she and Burnett both wrote short stories and became concerned with the lack of places to send them for publication. They recognized that some magazines like *American Mercury*, which had featured short stories, were moving entirely to non-fiction articles; other magazines published only a few stories a year by well-known writers, works following formulas that led to commercial success (Bennett 62).

Given these conditions, Foley and Burnett decided to initiate a magazine through which they could publish their own work and that of others and thus create a larger market for the short story, especially the experimental one. Burnett decided on the title, *Story Magazine*, to make their purpose clear, and Foley decided on the plan by which, without any monetary support or experience as fiction editors, they could begin a publication that would foster a creative space for writers and readers. As they continued doing newspaper work, which paid the bills, they solicited pieces from people that they knew and respected. They mimeographed only 167 copies of their first issue and sent it out widely, its recipients including Edward J. O'Brien, editor of *The Best American Short Stories*, and newspaper reviewers. Both the *Sunday London Times Literary Supplement* and the *New York Herald Tribune* lauded the unique, new effort. As word thus got out about their publication, more stories started coming in and more readers subscribed. The only magazine devoted solely to the short story, this journal gave more than half its space to the work of new authors and the rest to work by better known writers that did not follow established formats. For Foley, the hard daily commitment to a meaningful endeavor, with little financial backing but with an enlarging group determined to bring more voices into the public sphere, reiterated the best values of the suffrage campaign (*The Story of* 117–31).

In early 1932, along with their infant son, Foley and Burnett left Vienna, where the Nazi presence was developing, and moved to Majorca, where they continued with the magazine though they had difficulties finding a printer. *Story* was published there beginning in April, an issue with stories by Erskine Caldwell and Kay Boyle as well as Foley's own "She Walks in Beauty." In 1933, Foley and Burnett returned to the United States where *Story*, which had received an enthusiastic reception from New York periodicals, would go from a bimonthly to a monthly with support from Random House ("Fiction Magazine Moves").

In the third American issue, August 1933, Foley wrote that *Story* "will continue to be the medium, and, at the present, the sole medium, for the presentation to intelligent readers of the new, significant writing in the short story form as it is being practiced (if not printed) by the significant writers in America and abroad." In 1934, in the first anniversary issue for the American publication, Foley continued a commitment to producing a magazine of "short fiction which makes no compromise with outmoded formulas and commercial demands" (9). As she sought to further authorial power and influence, she was the first to allow writers to retain rights to their printed stories, and she gave them a share in the royalties: with these decisions, she planned to enable outsiders to secure a place within the literary community and thus to change literature.

From 1921 to 1941, the magazine included stories by William Faulkner, William Carlos Williams, Gertrude Stein, Louis L'Amour, Wallace Stegner, Irwin Shaw, Aldous Huxley, Dorothy Canfield Fisher, Zora Neale Hurston, and hundreds of others who were in various degrees of just becoming known, encouraging them to stretch beyond the precepts of other publications. It was the first to publish short stories by Ignacio Silone, Meridel LeSeuer, Graham Greene, Norman Mailer, Erskine Caldwell, William Saroyan, Peter De Vries, J.D. Salinger, John Cheever, Richard Wright, James T. Farrell, Tennessee Williams, Jesse Stuart, Carson McCullers, Nelson Algren, and many others, and in their first English translations, Anton Chekhov and Luigi Pirandello.

With Foley's encouragement, here was the era of the short story. For the ten years that she edited it, *Story* was a monthly of more than one hundred pages, with eight to ten stories in each issue. It also came to include poems, adaptations of plays, photo essays, film criticism, and more than forty novellas. In the United States, circulation rose to 25,000. The magazine also ran a readers' literary service and an annual college short story collection, produced a weekly radio program called *Tonight's Best Story*, sponsored a WPA story contest that discovered Richard Wright, and founded Story Press, first with Harper and Brothers and later with Lippincott. The press' first book was Ignazio Silone's *Bread and Wine*, on the communist resistance movement in Italy in 1935 (Kenison 216).

As an established writer and editor, Foley also began teaching the short story at Columbia and at Barnard in 1945, where she worked until 1966. She told a *New York Times* interviewer that she preferred not to grade writers and not to allow destructive criticism from other students because what writers needed, as she also provided in her *Story*, was encouragement for developing their own ideas and style: "In the class, we try to be honest, we try to be critical. But no hostility — no, no, no." She often continued class at the West End Bar on Broadway so that students could fully discuss their writing plans and current literature (Saxon). When she was injured in an accident in 1966, writers continued to study with her at her home (Weinraub). Foley also wrote many prize-winning and widely anthologized stories herself, with five chosen by the Edward O'Brien *Best Stories* volumes.

Foley left *Story* in 1941 when she and Burnett divorced, and from then until her death in 1977 she edited the annual *Best American Short Stories*, published by Houghton Mifflin. She also edited three special collections: *Best of the Best American Short Stories: 1915 to 1950; Fifty Best American Short Stories, 1915–1965;* and *200 Years of Great American Short Stories*. She was proud to have recognized in the anthologies, before these writers were well known, the work of Saul Bellow, Bernard Malamud, Philip Roth, Flannery O'Connor, Vladimir Nabakov, Peter Taylor, Eudora Welty, Joyce Carol Oates, Ray Bradbury, Lionel Trilling, Shirley Jackson, Jack Kerouac, James Agee, John

Updike, Tillie Olsen, Cynthia Ozick, Raymond Carver, Russell Banks, Tim O'Brien, and Leslie Silko.

Like other suffragists after the campaign, Foley established a voice for the Other, in her case for a group of writers that lacked institutional acceptance and support. Through writing and especially editing, she was thus promoting the new, expanding the acceptable, forwarding the needs of an ignored or disenfranchised group — reforming the established literary order, on her own, beginning with a mimeograph machine.

Through their writing, this suffrage group made an impact, especially introducing Americans to people, places, and genres that they might have ignored or judged negatively. These women, including Alice Gram Robinson, Louise Bryant, Helena Hill Weed, Beatrice Kinkead, and Martha Foley, worked diligently to bring to Americans writing by and about those frequently judged as Other, engaging readers of various ages with new authors, new content and points of view, new and perhaps un-commercial genres, taking physical and financial risks to do so. After the suffrage campaign, imbued with a sense of social responsibility and with courage, they certainly did not just go home.

5

A Continuing Life of Activism

While members of the suffrage generation influenced many parts of American life, they also continued working in the realm in which they began their activism, in politics. In the political world, from whence their reputation has been the worst, their contribution has only recently begun to be noted, as was discussed in the introduction. To fully understand their involvement, we will need to look beyond who voted and who was elected to the larger sphere of political reform, to what these women sought. As in writing, education, and art, they did not just seek to join in what had gone before, at first perhaps because they were not allowed or encouraged to do so: they sought not just to enter but to re-create what they found.

By the end of the first decade after suffrage, as many journal and newspaper articles announced, the anticipated women's vote had not transformed women's political roles. By 1930, only thirteen women had gained seats in Congress, seven of them filling mid-term vacancies. In state legislatures, the showing was little better: in 1925, women won less than 150 seats in state legislatures out of approximately 7500 (Harrison 10).

Part of the problem may have been the political stance of the first candidates, reformers evidencing views outside of the mainstream, as many women did concerning war. Two ardent suffragists, Anne Martin and Jeannette Rankin, one never elected and one elected both before and after the federal amendment, opened doors for other women and also closed them as pacifism became allied with the naïve compassion of women.

The experience of suffrage prisoner Anne Martin typified the frustration of seeking political office with pacifism as a principle. She graduated from the University of Nevada in 1894 and then went to Stanford where she received a second bachelor's degree in 1896 and a master's degree in history in 1897. She headed the University of Nevada history department from 1897 to 1899. After two years' additional study at Columbia University, the Chase

School of Art in New York, and at Liepzig and London universities, she returned to the University of Nevada as a teacher of art history and then, resigning in 1903, went on to further study in Europe. Like Alice Paul and Lucy Burns, she was drawn to the Pankhursts: she was arrested in 1910 during a suffrage demonstration in England (A.B. Howard 45–62). In 1911 she returned to Nevada and became president of the state's Equal Suffrage Society, with success secured in 1914 when the state legislature approved state suffrage for women (Martin, *The Story of*). She later joined the executive committee of NAWSA, and in 1917 she became the first national chair of the NWP, as she felt ready to move beyond state campaigns, already completed for her, to the national arena.

In both 1918 and 1920, Martin ran on an independent ticket for the U.S. Senate from Nebraska but her pacifism as well as her sex was not in her favor (Smith 14). As she campaigned across Nevada in 1918, she was repeatedly interrupted as she tried to discuss civil rights and employment. Questioners, some sent by the Democratic Party, frequently yelled at her: How could she have been prepared to surrender America to the dreadful Huns? Would she not even protect women and children? Would she betray even her own sex? How could pacifist women protect democracy? In 1920, with the war won, she again faced constant criticism for her pacifism, associated with women's inability to fight for their country or make the hard decisions to insure its safety, accusations that forced her to end many speaking sessions and that overwhelmed her attempts to bring other issues before the voters. She continued working within the Women's International League for Peace and Freedom, a type of women's organization that seemed suspect, even un–American, to many of her state's residents, and did not attain political office (A.B. Howard 128–73).

While pacifism helped to keep Martin out of office, becoming a topic through which to describe the gendered weakness of women, Jeannette Rankin gained elected office but her anti-war principles, denounced in highly gendered rhetoric, made her twice seem unfit to serve. In November of 1916, she was elected to the House of Representatives as a Republican from Montana, becoming the first female member of Congress. On April 6, 1917, only four days into her term, the House voted on the resolution to enter World War I. Rankin cast a vote against it, earning her immediate vilification from the press. Although fifty members of Congress voted no, the *New York Times*, in the main article concerning the vote, led with the headline of "Seek to Explain Miss Rankin's 'No,'" and with a secondary headline labeled her as "Overcome by the Ordeal"; a much smaller fifth headline mentioned that fifty Senators voted against the resolution. The article focuses on her emotional reaction to her own decision and her inability to move forward rationally: she "threw her head back and sobbed.... Her appearance was that of a woman on the verge of a breakdown." A subheading in the article called hers "purely a woman's vote." And the next day, the article continued, as a still hysterical and unstable woman, as others continued with governing, "she remained at home, overwrought, harassed by conflicting emotions, beset by doubts as to the expediency of her course." The article described the specific actions and motivation of no other senator and thus presented her as a misguided and hysterical woman who should not be in office.

Anne Martin was a professor of history at the University of Nevada and legislative chairman for the Congressional Union and the NWP. She was arrested picketing for suffrage in Washington, D.C., on July 14, 1917, and sentenced to 60 days at Occoquan Workhouse, but pardoned by President Wilson after three days. Photograph dated ca. 1917, from National Woman's Party Records. Source: Library of Congress Manuscript Division.

In 1918, Rankin ran an unsuccessful campaign for the Republican nomination to return to the Senate, opposed for refusing to support the war as well as for supporting Butte miners who went on strike in June 1917 after a fire in a mine shaft, the worst disaster in hard-rock mining in the United States, took the lives of 167 men (Smith 127). In 1918, she chose to run an independent candidacy after the Republicans rejected her, but this bid for election also failed. For the next two decades, she worked as a lobbyist in Washington, D.C., but elected office eluded her.

In 1940, Rankin was again elected to Congress, on another anti-war platform as Americans feared an entrance into a second world war, this stance again acceptable. Following the attack on Pearl Harbor, she once again did not vote for entering war, this time as the only member of Congress to do so. When the Senate voted to declare war on Germany and Italy following their declaration of war on the United States, she voted solely as "present."

On December 9, the *New York Times* reported that Montana's Republican leaders had claimed that declaring war was the only possible choice of loyal Americans and that she needed to publicly change her vote "to redeem Montana's honor and loyalty" ("Ask Miss Rankin Recant"). With this vote, Rankin assured that she would not be re-elected — in fact, she did not run again — and made it difficult for other women to be elected during the World War II and afterwards.

Although women may have failed to gain greater political power because of their seemingly extreme positions, such as pacifism, they also failed to be elected, failed to vote for each other and to work together on campaigns because they disagreed on fundamental issues affecting women, especially protectionist legislation. This disagreement can most clearly be seen in the arguments made by two devoted suffragists, Florence Kelley and Alice Paul. While working for the vote, NWP member Florence Kelley was also striving to secure a minimum wage for women and girls, especially those working in factories. At her instigation, the counsel in *Muller v. Oregon* (1908), activist Louis D. Brandeis, submitted a lengthy brief supporting the constitutionality of an Oregon statute that limited the hours per day that women could work in laundries and other industries. While two pages discussed the legal issues, the remaining 110 pages presented evidence of the deleterious effects of long hours of labor on the "health, safety, morals and general welfare of women," data culled from medical reports, psychological studies, and public committees (Rattner 105). With this brief as evidence, Kelley worked around the country on legislation providing protection to women workers. When the NWP presented the Equal Rights Amendment in 1923, Kelley opposed it because under a system of complete equality women might lose what they had gained state by state: maximum hour laws, night work laws, minimum wage laws. She judged members of the NWP as professional women without this larger picture in mind. But Alice Paul felt that protectionist laws made women less than equal and ultimately harmed their position as workers (Trigg 272–73). Although Paul opposed protectionism, for two years she attempted to keep the NWP neutral on the issue by a construing clause that would exempt industrial protections from the ERA, an exemption that no one was sure could survive legal questioning, but this attempt did not cure the division: not only did the National Consumers' League, led by Kelley, ultimately decide to oppose the ERA, but also the American Association of University Women, the National Council of Jewish Women, the League of Women Voters, which had evolved from NAWSA, and the federal Women's Bureau, led by Mary Anderson (Fry, "Alice Paul" 11–12; Cott, "Feminist Politics" 57–60).

While some women experienced political opposition because of their stances, whether against war or against protectionist legislation, women who tried to run for office also discovered that both the Democratic and Republican parties discouraged the nomination of female candidates for an array of other reasons. With women leaving separate parties like the NWP and associating themselves with the traditional parties as they began voting, they seemed willing to vote for the nominated candidates: these parties did not have to nominate women to secure women's votes. Democratic National Committee member Emily Newell Blair observed in 1924, "I know of no politician who is afraid of the woman vote on any question under the sun" (Chafe 30). Women who attempted to seek office had difficulty raising campaign funds, especially when running against male incumbents. The traditional families, law schools, and corporations that funded political careers did not need to make room for these new participants. Carrie Chapman Catt had accurately predicted that getting the vote would not guarantee women access to the nation's legislatures. "You will see the ... door locked tight," she said. "You will have a hard fight before you get inside" ("A Different Voice").

In November of 1916, Jeannette Rankin was elected to the House of Representatives as a Republican from Montana, becoming the first female member of Congress. On April 6, 1917, only four days into her term, the House voted on the resolution to enter World War I. Rankin cast a vote against it, earning her immediate vilification from the press. Dated April 2, 1917, this photograph was published in *The Suffragist*, 5, no. 63 (April 7, 1917): 7. Photograph from National Woman's Party Records. Source: Library of Congress Manuscript Division.

These trends from the 1920s did not change measurably for a long time.

Before 1950, fewer than a dozen women had ever held seats in Congress at any one time. In 1961, there were still only 17 women in the House of Representatives and two in the Senate. Before the 1992 elections, 21 women held seats in the House of Representatives, up four seats from 1961, while only two held seats in the Senate, the same number as in 1961 ("A Different Voice"). It was not until 1992 that this trend showed signs of change: voters elected more women to Congress that year than ever before in the nation's history. Twenty-four new congresswomen (21 Democrats and three Republicans) joined 23 other women who won re-election to the House of Representatives. In the Senate, Carol Moseley Braun (D–Illinois), Dianne Feinstein (D–California), Barbara Boxer (D–California), and Patty Murray (D–Washington) were all elected to a first term. They joined Barbara A. Mikulski (D–Maryland) who was elected to a second term and Nancy Kassebaum (R–Kansas). After the election, Eleanor Smeal, past president of the National Organization of Women and then president of the Fund for the Feminist Majority, proclaimed that, "This is the first significant breakthrough for women in the history of Congress; we're cracking the political glass ceiling." Others were more cautious, pointing out that women still had a long way to go to be truly represented ("A Different Voice").

For the 110th Congress, 2007 to 2009, a record number of 16 African American women were elected to the House in the 110th Congress and a total of 91 women served: 75 in the House (55 Democrats and 20 Republicans) and 16 in the Senate (11 Democrats and 5 Republicans). Three additional women died during the first session, Juanita Millender-McDonald (D–CA), Jo Ann Davis (R–VA), and Julia Carson (D–IN) (Wertheimer). A record number of 95 women is serving in the 111th Congress: 78 in the House (61 Democrats and 17 Republicans) and 17 in the Senate (13 Democrats and 4 Republicans). Although these numbers have increased, along with women serving as governors, attorney general, and secretary of state, their participation certainly still does not reflect their over 50 percent of the population. Despite their underrepresentation in elected office, women turn out to vote at a higher rate than their men ("Record-Breaking Number").

Women moved into elected office slowly, with significant gains coming only quite recently. They voted in increasing numbers and percentages, but, for various reasons, like their male counterparts, they were voting primarily for men. But even in this sphere of politics, where they did not have the instantly countable impact that some had expected and about which they have been most maligned, suffragists mattered after 1920. Through the decades following the campaign, they were in fact heavily involved with the political process — not just joining what had already been established, but also changing the political system and American law. Imbued with the lessons that they had learned in the suffrage campaign, women like Sue Shelton White, Mary Church Terrell, Dorothy Day, and Hazel Hunkins-Hallinan worked within the larger realm of activism, seeking not just to enter but also to alter the realities they found.

Over the course of her lifetime, in Tennessee and later in Washington, D.C., Sue Shelton White was a secretary at a machine shop, a court reporter, suffragist, lawyer, equal rights advocate, and a bureaucrat at the highest levels and — always and everywhere — a strong feminist. Her early activism in suffrage, beginning in 1912, helped to hone her into a strong and influential political figure throughout the New Deal, possessed of the tact, bargaining skills, and determination that led to Tennessee being the final state to ratify the Nineteenth Amendment and helped to shape the implementation of the New Deal. Photographer Harris & Ewing, ca. 1920. Photograph from National Woman's Party Records. Source: Library of Congress Manuscript Division.

Sue Shelton White (1887–1943)

One suffragist who made a huge impact in the decades after the campaign, an impact not tied to elected office, was Sue Shelton White. Born and raised in Henderson, Tennessee, a town with a population of 1000, White was over the course of her lifetime, in Tennessee and later in Washington, D.C., a secretary at a machine shop, a court reporter, suffragist, lawyer, equal rights advocate, and a bureaucrat at the highest levels and — always and everywhere — a strong feminist. Her early activism in suffrage, beginning in 1912, helped to hone her into a strong and influential political figure throughout the New Deal, possessed of the tact, bargaining skills, and determination that led to Tennessee being the final state to ratify the Nineteenth Amendment and helped to shape the implementation of the New Deal.

Like many other women in the suffrage movement, including Agnes

Chase, Dorothy Day, and Louise Bryant, White had a difficult and uncertain childhood that led her to seek her own independent path. She had three brothers and a sister; her mother supported them all after her father, a Methodist minister, teacher, and school superintendent, died. White says of her mother, who herself died when White was thirteen:

> I have never classed my mother as a feminist, but I suspect she was one. Life would have made her one in the end if she had not been in the beginning. After my father's death she faced the necessity of supporting a large family—six of us—in a town of less than a thousand population. She taught and gave music lessons—"piano and voice." She sent local items to newspapers in nearby cities. She peddled pianos and sometimes books. Between these activities she supervised our studies, our reading, our behavior, our work; nursed her neighbors, laid out their dead, helped their children with their school essays.... In her narrow, almost primitive field, she held her position as an unusual, if sometimes a troublesome, woman—always tolerated and sometimes acclaimed ["Mother's Daughter" 49].

White's aunt took her in when her mother died, but she soon had to become self-supporting. At Georgie Robertson Christian College in Henderson and then at the West Tennessee Business School in Dyer, she secured the training she needed to begin working as a secretary in a machine shop (Huehls 30–31). From there, she progressed to being the first female court reporter in the "big city" of Jackson, Tennessee, where she worked from 1906 to 1918. In this job, like so many other suffragists, White witnessed the different treatment afforded female and male workers: "I observed that young men were encouraged to 'read.' They were taken into offices, into the trial of cases, sponsored, even fed, sometimes, by the older members of the bar; and the banks would extend them credit while they were struggling" ("Mother's Daughter" 51). Although a judge recommended her to a U.S. Senator as an assistant, she was deemed unacceptable as a woman and thus turned down.

Like other women, White turned to the campaign not just to gain the vote but to give voice to her frustration over the inequities that both she and her mother had encountered in trying to become self-supporting. As she sought greater opportunity in her career and became interested in state politics, she joined the Tennessee Equal Suffrage Association, allied with NAWSA, in 1912, and began helping to organize parades and meetings (Huehls 32). As a Southerner, White had an especially difficult path in supporting suffrage. After the Civil War, Southern leaders and writers lauded a superior Southern civilization, of the Lost Cause, representing values of an older time of which women were important vessels, creating the secure home and genteel family (Wheeler 4). Any other goals or priorities might seem an abdication of allegiance to the region. Strong Southern religious traditions also cast women as intended to help bring men to God: they needed to keep their reform work in church, not in the community or government. And then, of course, race complicated the Southern suffrage commitment. Many Southerners feared extending suffrage to African American women. Some Southern suffragists, like Kate Gordon of New Orleans, president of the Southern States' Woman Suffrage Conference, argued that African American women could be kept from voting through the Jim Crow laws enacted in individual states — literacy tests, poll taxes, and residency requirements — that kept their husbands and sons out of the ballot box; her organization advocated for voting rights for white women, with strict state control (Green 132–34).

When White first became involved with NAWSA, to seek opportunities for women workers, even though this activism seemed suspect to many of her friends and co-workers. But she ultimately switched to the even more controversial NWP because this organization, pursing national change, seemed more willing to fight for suffrage in the South. NAWSA's state-by-state efforts concentrated on those states where a positive vote was likely; thus the organization did not extend much support to Southern states such as Tennessee where a positive vote was unlikely and where a strong Klan presence and Jim Crow laws made African American voting, or even the discussion of it, potentially dangerous (Wormser 22, 64). As White's lifelong partner Florence Armstrong commented in a series of articles about White's career, written in 1958, "When the N.A.W.S.A. decided at its Indianapolis Convention not to carry on any activity in the South but to concentrate on those States having a referendum on Suffrage, Miss White was aghast and disappointed" (The Papers of). Only the NWP was regularly sending speakers to Tennessee. Impressed with this commitment, White came to the rescue of the NWP's Maud Younger in the fall of 1917, for example, helping find places for meetings when local bar associations, civic officials, and Home Defense Leagues attempted to keep her from speaking. In a letter written in 1958, Rebecca Hourwich Reyher, who came to Tennessee to set the schedule for Younger's talks, wrote that she met Sue White because she needed a stenographer and that talking with her made all the difference:

> I told her that the Mayor was beginning to think our holding our meeting at the school, because trouble was threatened, and some of the people had demanded we be run out of town. She listened, her eyes flashing.
>
> She got on the phone. She called the Mayor, and the Police Chief. She demanded that we be given the privilege of speaking, and that we have the protection we might need, and she guaranteed to stand behind us and anything we

said on her own word of honor. We were women asking for the vote, and there was nothing anyone could call *unpatriotic* in that.

At the talks, heavily attended by detractors after newspapers labeled Younger as radical and disloyal, White's presence on the stage and introduction enabled Younger to speak (Louis 173). Rebecca Hourwich Reyher described White's effect as she opened the volatile first meeting:

> I remember I was surprised to hear the deep rumble that came from that slender frame, the passion and oratory with which her words rolled out. But at the top of her voice she reminded the audience that we had all been strangers at the gates once, and the South, with its great tradition of liberty loving people owed us courtesy and a friendly welcome.
>
> She spellbound that hostile audience. The rumblings stopped, the atmosphere became friendly; we hated to leave Jackson. But Sue closed her office, and announced that as long as we were in the State on a speaking tour she would accompany us, and she did. And everywhere, thanks to her, the hostility vanished.

As they traveled the state, Reyher recorded, she found that "everyone respected and loved her," having met White as she worked as a court reporter. And Reyher recognized the sacrifice that White made by going with her from town to town: "In those days Sue lived by what she earned, and her shutting up shop to help us was a real sacrifice." When Reyher and Younger returned to Washington, they told Alice Paul that "of all the women we had met no one had the weight that Sue had." Greatly impressed by their stories of meetings across Tennessee, Paul began to recruit White, putting her in leadership roles that she had not had with NAWSA. White became chair of the NWP in Tennessee in June 1918 and then in 1919 went to Washington where she began to edit the *Suffragist*, applying her persuasive and organizational abilities to this publication and participating in protests. For Sue White, an allegiance to a principle had led from one inactive suffrage membership to another very active one, leading her from Tennessee to Washington, from the sidelines to the center of the action, and from one sort of career to another.

At the infamous moment, Sue Shelton White was the woman who as part of a demonstration in front of the White House burned an effigy of President Wilson on the afternoon of February 9, 1919. Paul's description of the scene focused on White's bravery: "I saw Sue White at the urn — the flames flashed. She gave me a nod; I knew the deed was done." White's strident statement as she burned the small figure presented the president as a tyrant: "We burn not the effigy of the President of a free people, but the leader of an autocratic party organization whose tyrannical power holds millions of women in political slavery" ("Suffragists Burn Wilson"). For this act, she was put in an abandoned jail with other women, for five days, during which time she hunger struck.

White then went on the Prison Special in February of 1919, the group relying on her oratorical powers as well as her knowledge of Southern audiences, just as Reyher and Younger had done in Tennessee. A local newspaper account of one of the train's first stops, in February of 1919, in Charleston, South Carolina, said that White's first words quieted the Southern crowd and squelched criticisms of her as unpatriotic or radical: "I come of good American stock. The blood of Thomas Jefferson and John Marshall flows in my veins. My father fought under Lee, and I have a brother in France." The crowd then listened attentively for about thirty minutes as she spoke with vehemence in support of the amendment and against the Democratic Party since, as she argued, the majority of Americans supported the measure but their leaders refused to listen, a well-calculated ploy with Southerner audiences that might be distrustful of federal power. She then exhorted her audience to question the Democratic Party's choices even if they approved of the conduct of the war and its aftermath: "A political party is a powerful thing, but no party and the leaders of no party is sufficiently strong to stand an exposure of deceit and insincerity" ("The Prison Special" Feb. 22).

As White participated increasingly in the suffrage movement, she began to see herself as able to contribute to many political reform efforts. She joined the Southern Sociological Congress, dedicated to coordinating efforts to solve a variety of Southern social problems. She was most critical of Southern race relations and institutions, which she disparaged in an unpublished letter to the editor of *Harper's* magazine expressing dismay over the conditions in which black people lived and over the closing of restaurants and theaters to avoid serving them. White also worked doggedly for state support of the blind, serving as executive secretary of the Tennessee Commission for the Blind when it was established in 1918. Additionally, working in both Nashville and Washington, she helped draft and push through the state legislature the state's first married women's property bill, a mother's pension act, and an old-age pension act (Wheeler 57).

For the suffrage ratification campaign, White returned to Tennessee from Washington and worked hard at uniting suffragists in the effort to wrest a call for a special session from the governor. By August of 1920, thirty-five states had ratified the amendment. Only one additional state legislature had to vote positively for it to become law, to make the "perfect 36," as the NWP dubbed the required total. It was White's letter to the governor that officially requested consideration of the amendment, and her skillful use of her long established contacts in Tennessee was crucial in securing passage of the amendment, by one vote, in the Tennessee General Assembly.

An example of her careful but cagy work can be seen in her handling of this letter to the governor. Opponents to ratification had tried to raise an issue of whether it was even legal for the Tennessee legislature to vote. There was a long-standing belief that the Tennessee Constitution prohibited the legislature's taking action on a federal constitutional amendment unless those legislators had been chosen in an election during the year in which the amendment had been presented to the state. When White sent her letter to the governor requesting an immediate special session to consider the amendment, she commented to the newspapers, as the *New York Times* reported:

> I discussed this matter with the Solicitor-General of the United States, W.L. Frierson, a member of the Tennessee Bar and one of the foremost lawyers of the country. His official position deters him from giving a written opinion, and I have not the authority to quote any opinion he may have expressed privately, further than to say that from my construction of all that he said, I am quite sure he has considered the question quite carefully and, if in position to express an opinion for publication, it would be to the effect that ratification by the present Tennessee Legislature would be legal and proper under the principles laid down by the Supreme Court of the United States ["Tennessee Will Act" 2].

Here, though she does not actually quote the well-respected Frierson, she does imply that he supported her efforts. At the Democratic National Convention in 1920, White and Abby Scott Baker further employed this opinion as they urged Democratic leaders to put pressure on the Democratic governor of Tennessee to convene the legislative session.

After the governor gave permission for a vote by the Tennessee legislature, White worked along with NWP organizers like Catherine Flanagan and Anita Pollitzer as well as old friends from state societies and NAWSA to plan campaigns in every congressional district in the state. As Florence Armstrong commented about White's effort, "She worked at white heat, directing the lobbyists, day by day, and hour by hour, so that at every moment they knew where the legislation stood in the Legislature." With so many strangers coming to aid the effort, and to fight against it, "her contacts, her good judgment, and her fire accomplished wonders" ("Sue Shelton White"). Betty Gram Swing, sister of Alice Gram Robinson who later taught women's history at Syracuse University, also commented on the heroic effort: "We were often together during that harrowing experience and while we worked night and day against formidable opposition, a lobby of wealthy suffragists, ostentatious liquor interests and clandestine railroad executives, we seldom had time to eat a decent meal.... I think it can be said that the date of victory might have been delayed many years but for her brilliant strategy." In a jam-packed Nashville, housing anti-suffrage as well as suffrage forces, suffrage was ratified on August 18, 1920.

Like other women involved in the suffrage campaign, Alice Paul among them, White entered law school after the campaign ended to extend her ability to help others secure their civil rights. White also viewed the degree as further qualifying her for a position in politics. In 1923 she earned a law degree from Washington College of Law, and from 1920 to 1926 she served as administrative secretary to Tennessee senator Kenneth McKellar, a Democrat, running his Washington office. This senator, a suffrage supporter, hired White, as Florence Armstrong commented, "in recognition of her record" ("Sue Shelton White").

After passage of the 19th Amendment, it was Sue Shelton White to whom Alice Paul gave the credit for writing "a blanket bill" that could be introduced in Congress and in state legislatures to eliminate sex discriminations in all legal codes, an early form of the Equal Rights Amendment, unveiled by Paul in 1923 at the seventy-fifth anniversary of the 1848 Seneca Falls Convention. While attempting to achieve federal legislation, Paul, White, and other NWP members worked, as they had not before, on changing state laws. By the end of the 1920s, these women could point to about three hundred state laws changed out of six hundred that they had advocated for reform (Fry, "Alice Paul and the ERA" 12). She ultimately broke her connection with the NWP, however, as government work drew her into a strong Democratic Party affiliation.

White never attempted to run for office, but she took on influential government positions, employing the organizational skills, speaking ability, and confidence that she gained from suffrage. She returned to Jackson in 1926 and opened the law firm of Anderson and White. From 1930 to 1933, she worked in New York and Washington as executive secretary of the Women's Division of the Democratic National Committee. Along with the division's director, Nellie Tayloe Ross, former governor of Wyoming, she helped to organize Roosevelt's first campaign for the presidency (Armstrong, "Sue Shelton White"). She felt "extremely proud" of her influence on some of his first appointments: Lucille Foster McMillan of Tennessee as a civil service commissioner; Lucy Somerville Howorth of Mississippi as a judge in the Court of Appeals; Nellie Tayloe Ross as director of the Mint; Ruth Bryan Owen as minister to Denmark, and Frances Perkins, secretary of labor (White, "Women in Public Office"; Armstrong, "Sue Shelton White").

In 1934 White took on the first of a series of government jobs that would involve her in implementing the New Deal. She first served as assistant to the chair of the Consumers Advisory Board of the National Recovery Administration, setting up county consumer councils that sent in reports on prices and practices to guide federal legislation. She ran this board during the illness and after the death of its chair, Mary Harriman Rumsey. After the court held the National Recovery Act unconstitutional in 1935, she joined the first legal staff of the Social Security Board, and eventually became principal attorney and assistant to the general counsel of that agency, Jack B. Tate, who when he was dean of the Yale Law School described the challenging situation that they faced and White's ability to cope with it: "It is difficult enough to organize and plan the basic foundations for the administration of any broad scale legislative program. With this program it was more difficult than usual. One forgets how controversial, how radical, this program, which is now accepted as right and essential, was considered to be in its infancy. Perhaps it is just as well to forget that it was a major issue in a Presidential campaign; that voters were told by the political strumps that they would have to wear dog tags. In any event, Sue rolled up her sleeves and went to work. She was at home with the most idealistic social worker fresh from college and with the most cynical politician from, or aspiring to be from, legislative halls." While setting up a brand new system of allocation for the elderly and disabled and dealing with an often hostile public, she also worked to insure reasonable profit levels for industry as well as equitable treatment of workers. These efforts led to the Federal Fair Labor Standards Act of 1938, which established a national minimum wage, guaranteed time and a half for overtime in certain jobs, and prohibited most employment of minors (Pfeffer 50). Cooperating with the National Emergency Council, White also established new requirements for fuller corporation reports and stock evaluation to help the government craft the best means of avoiding another stock crash.

From the time she entered the suffrage movement through her years as a principal counsel for the Social Security Administration, White developed public speaking, networking, and planning skills that enabled her to do the difficult work of politics that is not as noticeable as winning the election: implementing legislation so that it makes a difference in individual lives. With the New Deal, so many legislative decisions happened quickly, with acts approved and rescinded, and much less well known than Roosevelt are the people who actually made the change happen. White's network of associates and her own good judgment and ability, demonstrated and developed through suffrage, made her one of the most powerful women in Washington, D.C. She died of cancer at age fifty-five in 1943.

Mary Church Terrell (1863–1954)

Many women like Sue Shelton White entered local, state, and national politics after the suffrage campaign, perhaps not through the more noticeable route of elected office but through highly influential positions where they did the hard work that could create change. Their contribution might escape notice in a summing up of elections and voting, but it was quite real nevertheless.

After the suffrage campaign, other women sought to continue working for reform through their own organizations, not to implement government programs or maneuver within the system but to radically change what they found. For Mary Church Terrell, becoming a suffrage activist led her from being an educator to leading a campaign of civil disobedience. She looked at election to office within the existing system as too limited, not enough: she sought not the mainstream political involvement concerning which suffragists are often measured but something bigger, a well-crafted effort to secure fundamental social change.

Terrell was born in Memphis, Tennessee, to Robert Reed Church and Louisa Ayers, both former slaves. After the Civil War, he became a saloon keeper and soon acquired a hotel, opened the largest theater for blacks in the United States, as well as an amusement park and bank, and thus became a self-made millionaire. Terrell's mother also became a successful entrepreneur, opening a store to sell hair products and wigs in Memphis and later in New York on Sixth Avenue (Jones 8).

Though her parents provided monetary support, she experienced an insecure childhood, like so many other activists who asserted their own separate strength through the suffrage campaign. Terrell's parents separated when she was six and later divorced. After her mother moved away, her parents sent her by herself to the Antioch College Model School in Yellow Springs, Ohio, for her elementary and secondary education, where she boarded with local families (Terrell, *A Colored Woman* 18).

When Terrell continued her education at Oberlin College, studying Greek and English literature in the classical curriculum, she was an African American woman among mostly white male students, as she had been in the lower-school grades, but she was not intimidated and immediately became a campus leader. The freshman class elected her class poet, and she joined two of the college's literary societies and participated in their debates. In her freshman year, she wrote an essay entitled "Resolved, There Should Be a Sixteenth Amendment to the Constitution Granting Suffrage to Women" (Terrell 144). In her senior year, Terrell served as an editor of the *Oberlin Review.*

When she earned her bachelor's degree in 1884, she was one of the first African American women to earn a college degree. Next, in 1888, Terrell earned a master's degree from Oberlin. She then took a position at Wilberforce University near Xenia, Ohio, teaching French and mineralogy at the college and reading and writing in the preparatory department, against her father's wishes. He wanted her to come home to Memphis (Sterling 127–28).

Although Terrell did not return to Memphis, she did accede to another plan that the father had for his daughter: he sent her to Europe, where she stayed for two years, boarding with families, in Lausanne, Berlin, and Florence. This travel made her more keenly aware of the racial prejudices that she had faced in the United States, more aware of what needed to be changed. Though she had opportunities in Europe, for marriage and for further study, as she wrote, "I knew I would be much happier trying to promote the welfare of my race in my native land, working under certain hard conditions, than I would be living in a foreign land where I could enjoy freedom from prejudice, but where I would make no effort to do the work which I then believed it was my duty to do" (*A Colored Woman* 99).

When she returned, she took a job at a Washington high school teaching Latin and German. Because her future husband, a lawyer who became the first black municipal court judge in the district, lived in Washington, she turned down an offer to be the registrar at Oberlin, what was "my duty to do," though she ultimately did not go.

In Washington, though, Terrell sought through suffrage activism an opportunity to do the duty she sought for herself (McKay xxiii). She began attending meetings of the Women's Suffrage Committee of Washington. While working for the vote, this group also pursued other political involvements for women. After the committee won a six-year court battle to allow women to serve on the District of Columbia Board of Education, it pushed for the appointment of Terrell, who served from 1895 to 1906. In this position, she advocated for a director of music, for qualified teachers, and for better facilities in African American schools (*A Colored Woman* 127; Jones 49). Terrell saw better education and women's suffrage as well as fair voting laws for African Americans as key to righting American wrongs and creating the more equitable system that she had seen in Europe.

In Washington, Terrell also became involved in African American women's organizations spreading through the country in the early 1890s that combined suffrage activism with responsibility for family and community. She joined the Colored Woman's League, founded in Washington in 1892, a group that merged with another new organization to form the National Association of Colored Women in 1896. Terrell was elected president of this new group and held the position to 1901. Through this organization, she worked for suffrage and helped to form and coordinate Mothers' Clubs, training schools for nurses, clubs for young working women, homes for the aged and infirm, musical clubs, and temperance organizations (Jones 26–28).

At meetings in Washington of a variety of women's groups, Terrell got to know Anthony, Shaw, Stone, Blatch, and other leaders of the national suffrage campaign, and she eased into public speaking as so many other women did. She spoke at the NAWSA convention held in Washington in 1890 and said the following to turn these activists' attention to the prejudices facing African American suffragists: "A White Woman has only one handicap to overcome — a great one, true, her sex; a colored woman faces two — her sex and her race. A colored man has only one — that of race" (Jones 3). In 1900, at another convention meeting in Washington, she vehemently opposed the group's neglect of the injustices suffered by black women. From 1895, she traveled extensively as a popular lecturer at Chautauqua assemblies and universities, stressing racial pride and the achievements of her race. She represented African American women at the International Congress of Women in Berlin in 1904, speaking in English, French, and German. She was one of two African American women (Ida B. Wells-Barnett was the other) invited to sign the Call and to speak at the organizational meeting of the National Association for the Advancement of Colored People (NAACP). Along with her at the founding in 1909 were many other suffragists, including Mary White Ovington, Inez Milholland, Jane Addams, Harriet Stanton Blatch, Mary Dreier, Francis Grimke, Florence Kelley, Leonora O'Reilly, and Lillian Wald. After 1910, as her letters now housed at the Library of Congress reveal, she was regularly giving speeches for the NAACP as well as the American Missionary Association, the eastern and southern Lyceum Bureaus, African American women's groups, Chautauqua assemblies, peace societies, churches, and universities, combining discussion of African American civil rights with suffrage (Terrell, Letters). Though speaking bureaus and colleges, as well as magazines and newspapers, welcomed what she had to say about education, child care, women's organizations, and community betterment, they often found her controversial when she segued to lynching, to other realities faced by her race, and to suffrage, as she discussed in her autobiography: "Nobody wants to know a colored woman's opinion about her own status or that of her group. When she dares express it, no matter how mild or tactful it may be, it is called 'propaganda,' or is labeled 'controversial'" (*A Colored Woman* 224). Like Helen Keller when she advocated for suffrage and socialism, Terrell was less acceptable as a speaker and writer when she went further as a reformer than some groups wanted her to go.

As a resident of Washington, with no state within which to gain the vote, Terrell was a natural candidate for not just local efforts but work on a federal amendment. Washington residents, both men and women, had no voting representatives in either the House or Senate; a state-by-state progression of woman's suffrage might not gain the women there any voting rights. In 1913, as Terrell wrote about in detail in her autobiography, she marched in the pre-inaugural parade staged by NAWSA and Alice Paul, one in which Paul feared that African American marchers might cause others to boycott, as Terrell discussed in her autobiography: "I once marched in a parade in Washington which was arranged by women who thus expressed their desire and their determination to secure suffrage. At the head of the procession on a snow white horse rode Inez Milholland, a vision of loveliness, an example and an inspiration to the young womanhood of the United States. When some of the suffragists objected to having the colored girls of Howard University march in the parade, it was Inez Milholland who insisted that they be given a place with the pupils of the other schools" (*A Colored Woman* 212). Each year, Terrell kept attending meetings of both the NWP and state suffrage committees, especially with those suffragists who attempted to achieve a state amendment in New York in both 1915 and 1917. In March of 1916, for example, she bought a box for a suffrage dance at Madison Square Garden that drew 10,000 people, a crowd so large that the doors had to be closed against more entrants because of fire regulations ("Suffrage Dancers").

Terrell was willing to parade in 1913 and attend meetings afterwards, but it would be her war experiences that would propel her to greater activism. After Wilson declared war, as she wrote in her autobiography, she began working as a clerk for the War Risk Insurance Bureau, keeping records concerning ill soldiers, placed in a room with white women, mistakenly, where the women themselves were all "very cordial and pleasant indeed." There she witnessed, even with the war rhetoric of togetherness and citizenship displayed around her on posters, the prejudice still facing African American women workers. She felt that she was accused of bad performance, of numerous mistakes that she had not made, because of her race: "It was a case of 'framing' a colored woman.... I realized that I was treading on thin ice all the time, and I was very careful to do the work exactly as I was instructed... . I knew that the slightest error on my part meant embarrassment and loss of my job" (*A Colored Woman* 252–53; Batker 66). Other women there would inform her of policy changes so she could do the work correctly since the managers kept new instructions from her. She chose not to fight back but instead resigned because of her husband's position as a judge in the Municipal Court: "It was one of the most galling experiences of my life."

She went from there to the Census Bureau, where she found white and black clerks separated. She resigned after seeing light-skinned African American clerks, hired to work in the white section and doing exemplary work there, being moved after their race was discovered. Before she resigned, she got rescinded the standing order that black women could only use the restroom at certain times, when no white women were there (*A Colored Woman* 256).

With these experiences making all too clear to Terrell the lack of rights in this country, she embraced a greater level of suffrage activism, the militant movement standing for her, as for so many other women, as a bold affirmation of women's rights. Ida Wells Barnett did not engage with the CU and NWP after the pre-inaugural parade in 1913 because of the dispute about African American marchers and her belief that Alice Paul cared for nothing but voting rights, but Terrell joined the CU, attended meetings, and stood on the picket line frequently, bringing her daughter Phyllis with her, as she recorded in her autobiography:

> The National Woman's Party, led by Alice Paul, used to picket the White House in the afternoon when the departments were closing and the clerks passing by on their way home. On a bitter cold day the phone would ring and a voice from Headquarters, which were then at Jackson Place, opposite Lafayette Square, would inquire, "Will you come to picket the White House this afternoon?" As a rule, I complied with the request and several times Phyllis would come with me to swell the number. Sometimes it was necessary to stand on hot bricks supplied by a colored man employed expressly for that purpose to keep our feet from freezing [*A Colored Woman* 316].

Her continued commitment to the NWP and to picketing angered some women with whom she worked in African American women's organizations, an example of which occurred after an attack by an angry white mob in East St. Louis, Illinois, on July 2, 1917, left at least forty dead, hundreds injured, and entire neighborhoods burned. In protest on July 28, New Yorkers, led by W.E.B. Du Bois and James Weldon Johnson of the NAACP, walked in silence leading ten thousand marchers down Fifth Avenue, Terrell among them (Rudwick 135). Early that fall Terrell received a letter from Eslanda Cordozo Goode about the failure of white New York suffragists to join in the parade and to denounce Illinois suffragists for ignoring the violence. Goode, whose grandfather was the first African American treasurer of South Carolina and who after graduation from Columbia had become the head histological chemist of Surgical Pathology at New York-Presbyterian Hospital, asked Terrell to quit working for suffrage because the movement's leaders denied the rights of black women: "Please do not speak in favor of Suffrage as the Negro Women of Harlem are fighting Suffrage this year because the

Suffrage Party of N.Y. State in conference at 171 Madison Ave. this city on Wed. Thurs. & Friday last refused to come out in the Asso. Press and denounce the actions of their white sisters in East St. Louis." Terrell continued, however, to work with both African American women's associations and with the NWP.

After war was declared, Terrell continued to stand in the White House picket line even though she knew that jail held a considerably greater risk for her than for white women, but she was not able to come on one day when women were taken to jail, as she wrote in her autobiography: "But once it was impossible for me to respond to this call, and as Fates would have it, on that very day several women were arrested for picketing and sent to Occuquan, the workhouse, when I was absent from my post." For her regular service and her dedication to the cause, the NWP considered her as one of those who sacrificed, and the distinction mattered to Terrell. In her autobiography, she included the letter sent to her about being granted a prison pin at an NWP banquet:

> The following letter, dated January 20, 1921, notified me that a pin was to be presented to me, along with others, for the service I had rendered the cause of woman suffrage. It read:
>
> "Dear Fellow Picket:
>
> "The National Woman's Party wishes to present to each woman who has ever picketed, whether she was imprisoned or not, a picket pin in memory of our picket days together. We will present these pins on the evening of February 18th during our national convention, which meets in Washington, February 15th, and lasts through February 18th. We hope to make the ceremony of giving the pins a dignified and impressive one and want, by this ceremony, to show appreciation of the militant workers in our campaign of whom we are all proud. We ask each picket to wear this evening a white dress, if possible, white shoes and stockings. A room will be provided adjoining the hall in which wraps may be left during the ceremony."
>
> And so it happened that on February 18, 1921, my daughter, Phyllis, and myself were each presented a pin at the Washington Hotel by the National Woman's Party because we helped picket the White House as a protest against the disenfranchisement of women. There is no doubt that this gesture on the part of determined women called attention to the injustice perpetrated upon them by denying them the suffrage and hastened the passage of the nineteenth amendment the year before [*A Colored Woman* 316–17].

After her activism as a picket, Terrell did not give up or go home: she looked at the attainment of the vote as a step along the way. She was appointed director of the Eastern Division among Colored Women of the Republican National Committee in September 1920, a position through which she could keep African Americans informed about pending legislation, work on their securing full voting rights throughout the South, and involve them further in activism. As she said in public addresses, black women especially needed to vote and actively work for change: "By a miracle the 19th amendment has been ratified. We women now have a weapon of defense which we have never possessed before. It will be a shame and a reproach to us if we do not use it. However much the white women of the country need suffrage, for many reasons which will immediately occur to you, colored women need it more" (*A Colored Woman* 310). In 1922, she asked Republican Party and NWP members to organize writing campaigns for the Dyer Anti-Lynching Bill, which would have made lynching a federal felony. Although the bill passed the House of Representatives in 1922, it was defeated in the Senate because of a filibuster by the white Southern Democratic block, a sign of the significant work still to be done, as were the continued occurrences of lynching and the lack of prosecution, an attack on residents of the African American town of Rosewood, Florida, in 1923, and a huge Ku Klux Klan parade through Washington in 1926 ("Racial Violence").

In each decade, Terrell took on other discriminatory practices while still speaking against racial violence. During the Depression, she criticized racial and gender discrimination in governmental policies, especially the differing standards in public relief and welfare benefits, in wages, in hours, and in opportunities in federal programs (Jones 61). During World War II, she fought discrimination against African Americans in industry and in the armed services. In 1946 she was turned down for membership in the American Association of University Women in the Washington chapter, and she resolved to fight: "I thought I'd be a coward unless I opened the way for the colored women" (Jones 66). In June 1948, the national convention instituted a new by-law stating there would be no discrimination on racial, religious, or political grounds and that individual branches could not be in conflict with the national.

After World War II and the death of her husband, after years of not enough progress being made, she abandoned her post-suffrage combination of committee work and public speaking to sympathetic groups and again embarked on the militancy and civil disobedience she had first engaged in with suffrage picketing. While she lobbied for the ERA, she began planning sit-ins to protest segregated restaurants and other facilities. In these events and the subsequent court struggle, Terrell was requesting enforcement of laws on the books in the District, from 1872 and 1873, that required "all eating-place proprietors to serve any respectable well-behaved persons regardless of color, or face a $100 fine and forfeiture of their license for one year."

Her small group visited with restaurant owners, informed them of the law, and promised to initiate boycotts, picket, and stage sit-ins if they refused to comply. As a test case, an interracial group of four requested service at Thompson's Restaurant in Washington in February of 1949. When the owner denied service to the three African Americans, including Terrell, they filed affidavits and the District Commissioners prosecuted a clear violation of the law, instigating a three-year court battle, which they lost when the judge decided that the laws had been "repealed by implication." During the battle and after, Terrell conducted a survey of restaurants, for which 145 black and white volunteers tested 99 downtown restaurants, going 316 times to places not previously known to serve African Americans. Of the 99 businesses surveyed, 63 refused service initially, and 28 refused to do so after the first test under pressure from other owners (Jones 72, 76; Shepperd 59). At no time was there any protest from patrons concerning the presence of African American customers, just from owners.

As Terrell circulated information on restaurants, she also began calling attention to department stores, like Kresge's, that admitted African Americans to the store but not to the lunch counter. When this store would not change its policy in December of 1950, she organized picketing: after six weeks, Kresge's changed its policy. In July of 1951, pickets also surrounded Hecht's with signs and pamphlets claiming that African Americans spent half a million dollars there a year and asking patrons to boycott. The store finally capitulated in January of 1952 after four months of picketing, and then she went on to Murphy's Dime Store in September of 1952. As she fought each battle, she also helped to shepherd the Thompson case to the Supreme Court, where *District of Columbia v John Thompson* became during the spring of 1953 a "national symbol of the fight against segregation in the United States." On June 8, 1953, Chief Justice William O. Douglas declared the laws from 1872 and 1873, requiring patrons to be served "regardless of color," to be still in force, as "part of the governing body of laws applicable to the District of Columbia" (Jones 84–85).

As biographer Beverly Jones wrote, "this anti-segregation drive that Mary Church Terrell led in the early 1950s popularized the strategies that brought black Americans the most profound and far reaching desegregation movement in their history" (91). Just as she did in the suffrage campaign, when organizations and committee meetings failed to produce the desired results, Terrell moved beyond moral suasion and dialogue to the direct action of picketing, boycotts, and sit-ins, all techniques again used in the Montgomery bus boycott of 1955–56, at North Carolina lunch counters in 1960, and in the Selma to Montgomery marches in 1965. Terrell lived to see the

Supreme Court's decision in *Brown v. Topeka Board of Education*. She died two months later at the age of ninety, on July 24, 1954, a week before the NACW was to hold its annual meeting at her home in Annapolis, Maryland. Throughout her life, Terrell had worked diligently to end discrimination based on gender and race. In the suffrage movement she learned the tools of non-violent activism that she brought to the civil rights movement in 1949, when Martin Luther King was still in divinity school, six years before the Montgomery bus boycott.

Dorothy Day (1897–1980)

At twenty years old, another woman who picketed and went to jail was Dorothy Day, who later founded the *Catholic Worker* and the Catholic Worker Movement. And like Louisine Havemeyer, Rhoda Kellogg, Agnes Chase, and so many other women, she viewed her suffrage experience as life changing, not because she was allowed to vote after the amendment passed or to enter a traditional political life. Instead, like many others, Day found that the experience infused her with a sense of the injustices around her and led her toward a group involvement that could rectify those injustices. Her parents were not activists — she came from a traditional family — and she believed that "we're born with a temperament, and it's our temperament that pushes us to do the work we do" (Coles 24). But it is also opportunity — who we meet, where we go, what we see — that strengthens and demarcates a commitment, as it did for Dorothy Day. After her picketing and prison experience, she viewed it as the individual's and the group's responsibility to work for change, to refuse to thoughtlessly succumb to the entrenched values of any government or institution. For her, this dedication to the right ideals defined the best form of impracticality: "You people are impractical, they tell us, nice idealists, but not headed anywhere big and important. They are right. We *are* impractical, as one of us puts it, as impractical as Calvary" (Coles 97). In two autobiographies and a novel and in numerous articles written throughout her life, Day returned to her suffrage experience as transformative — to her view of American justice and the status of the dispossessed and to her confidence that she could change the current social situation as well as the Catholic Church's role in it.

As a child, moving from California to Illinois, Day witnessed differences of class and religious affiliation. Her parents were solidly middle class, from New York, her father a journalist and later a founder of Hialeah, the first race track in Florida. Her two older brothers became respected, respectable journalists. After surviving the San Francisco earthquake in 1906, her family lived in Berkeley and Oakland, her father working as a sports editor. After he lost his job, the family moved into a tenement flat on Chicago's South Side, a big step down in the world. In that neighborhood, Day learned about Catholicism from her poor neighbors while attending the local, more affluent Episcopal church with her parents. She would later recall her discovery of a friend's mother, a devout Catholic, praying at the side of her bed. Without embarrassment, the woman looked up at Day, told her where to find her friend, and returned to her prayers, religion a natural and daily part of her life. "I felt a burst of love toward [her] that I have never forgotten," Day recalled (Forest, "A Biography").

Day won a scholarship to the University of Illinois in the fall of 1914 and launched into an uncertain voyage to find something to do that mattered. A reluctant scholar, she generally read radical political works instead of her assignments. She joined the Socialist Party, avoided campus social life, and insisted on supporting herself rather than living on money from her father. In the summer of 1916 when her father began to work for the *Morning Telegraph* in New York, she moved with her parents to the city, found work at the *Call*, and entered the Greenwich Village scene, looking for meaningful work and alliances.

In Greenwich Village, she met activists like Louise Bryant who were involved in an array of causes, one of which was suffrage. In her autobiographical novel *The Eleventh Virgin*, published in 1924, Day describes her heroine June's attraction to associating with activists who had entered prisons to support their beliefs: "Everyone in the radical movement had gone to jail at some time or another for at least a few days, if not a few years. June had not yet had that experience, but she had heard many talk of it" (180). In the novel, June's friend Billy warns her that guards could get violent when jailed suffragists insisted on their rights as political prisoners. Yet June becomes especially attracted to the suffragists' cause when her friend Ivan praises this willingness to withstand violence, in the "first time in the history of America that political prisoners have fought for their rights" (187). Like Day herself, June decides to join the picket line, not for the sake of suffrage but for an entrance into broader social action: "This is a time for fighting and here's the chance for me. I've been feeling rotten to be out of it when all my friends are risking arrest for conscientious objection and for writing and working for radical magazines and publications. I'll go. Not for suffrage exactly, but for the rights of political prisoners of the United States" (187).

In this novel, when June arrives in the Washington suffrage headquarters, she comments on the two women who led the organization. Jane Worth is her Alice Paul: "There was something compelling about Miss Worth's eyes. It was said around headquarters that she could make a fractious devotee do anything she wished by just looking at her, backing up her steady gaze in a most ladylike tone of voice. June thought at first that these remarks arose from admiration, but the more she saw of the suffragists, the more she realized that it was something more than just admiration in the attitude of her followers towards her. There was a quality of blind adoration" (190). Unlike Jane Worth, Grace Drummond, the book's Lucy Burns, running the headquarters and picketing when Worth went to jail, was more vigorous and "brought with her the atmosphere of combat.... She was a type that appealed to June far more than little Miss Worth with her quietly compelling and assured eyes" (190). For June as for Dorothy Day, these two leaders, with their fierce dedication and devotion, stood at the head of a group with an unfailing desire for justice: "They merely reflected the religious zeal which was undercurrent in the entire organization" (189).

The picketing that Day described in *The Eleventh Virgin* and her autobiographies led to her sentence of a month in Occoquan Workhouse, where she took part in the "Night of Terror," November 15, 1917. As she recorded in *The Long Loneliness*, an autobiography from 1952 that contains another lengthy description of picketing and incarceration, when she tried in the prison reception hall to move over where her friend Peggy Baird was, "four guards jumped upon me as though they were indulging in a football game and I were the football. Other women arose to my assistance, and immediately there was a mad scuffle, a most disgraceful scene where dignified women tore at the guards, bit and kicked and were belabored in turn" (83). The violence continued as guards pulled the women down the hall to the cells, a cruel encounter that remained in Day's memory: "It seems impossible to believe, but we were not allowed to walk, were all but lifted from the floor, in the effort that the men made to drag, rather than lead us to our place of confinement for the night" (75).

When guards flung Lucy Burns into the cell with Day, they shared the one bed and discussed Joseph Conrad to pass the long night. The next day they had to enter solitary confinement after they began to hunger strike: both of them refused to eat for ten days. In this understaffed facility, the guards did not have the manpower to force-feed everyone, and so they just shoved hoses down the throats of the leaders: "Thank God I wasn't a leader!" Day wrote in another autobiography, *From Union Square to Rome*, that described these prison days. "The woman in the next cell was forcibly fed and I could hear her struggles as the four guards held her down on the bed and the doctor and his assistant forced a tube down her throat through which they poured beaten egg and milk" (85).

Though Day received a sentence of thirty days, she was released after sixteen when Wilson signed a pardon for the group. Although Day frequently stated that for her the specific cause of suffrage had not greatly mattered to her, she did recognize the prison experience as profound. There, as she recorded concerning June in *The Eleventh Virgin*, she had a highly affecting experience with injustice and suffering: "She lost all feeling of her own identity. She was no longer June Henreddy who regarded the obstacles of life as things to be met with a lifted chin and a smile. She could not throw back her head and shrug her shoulders and cast pain from her. A dull weight of it had descended upon her, the weight of the sorrow of all the world" (207). This experience made Day especially aware of people caught within the prison system, as she wrote in another autobiography, *From Union Square to Rome*: "In spite of the fact that I was with scores of other women I felt a sense of complete solitude lying behind the bars. I felt keenly the misery of all those others in jail for criminal offenses. My own sentence of thirty days seemed interminable and when I thought of long sentences and even six months seemed terribly long, I was overcome by the misery of those about me.... They were enduring punishment which would not cure them or deter them from future crimes, and they were being punished by men not much better than themselves, indeed, far worse in some cases" (86). In a capitalistic society, she wrote, jails seemed primarily filled with poor people — "prisoners throughout the country, victims of a materialistic system" — who were guilty of crimes, but also victims of the system itself (86; O'Connor 35).

During the days in jail, as her autobiographies and novel testify, Day recognized the distance of this capitalistic reality from Christian values: "I truly suffered that first week and the reading of the Bible intensified that suffering. I felt that we were a people fallen from grace and abandoned by God. I felt that we were indeed children of wrath and that a personal conversion was necessary before any revolution could be successful." As a young revolutionary, however, she questioned whether her longing for a stronger Christian faith within American society and within herself was a sign of weakness and conventionality: "I distrusted my own emotions, feeling that they arose from my long fast and the imprisonment, and besides I felt a sense of shame in turning to God in despair. There was in my heart that insinuation of my college professor that religion was for the weak and those who needed solace and comfort, who could not suffer alone but must turn to God for comfort — to a God whom they themselves conjured up to protect them against fear and solitude" (*From Union Square to Rome* 87).

While Day constructed her time in jail as causing her to question her own attraction to Christianity, she also wrote that it helped her consider a new role for the church, moving it beyond "solace and comfort" for the individual stuck in an unjust world. In *The Eleventh Virgin*, she spoke of the religious calling inherent in social activism such as picketing. About the suffragists' heading out toward the White House, she wrote that "there was a religious flavor about the silent proceeding and a holy light shone in the faces of the suffragists" (193). That "holy light shone" because these women were risking everything for their fellow human beings as those truly led by Christ would do. In *The Eleventh Virgin*, she also wrote of her own desire for a meaningful social commitment: "Sitting in the solitary confinement cell for five days made me think — made me want to perform so useful labor instead of frittering away my time as I have been doing. I want to really and honestly work" (216). On the sixteenth day, these pickets were released but "some yeast of revolt was in her" (217).

Day's second jail experience, which occurred in Chicago in 1920 when she was staying in an IWW house with a friend who had tried to kill herself, again caused her to focus on the powerlessness of the poor, especially of poor women. After a police raid, she and her friend were charged with being inmates in a disorderly house, thus as prostitutes. Not allowed to use the phone, they entered a cell housing twenty women, mostly prostitutes, with six beds and with men passing in front all the time. These women seemed to her "like any other group of working girls, these young women, who had turned to this hideous way of earning a living.... The women did not disgust me, it was their profession that disgusted me." Day encountered there the "horror of the police and the police matron," who employed frequent strip searches and seemed bent on denigration. In this locale, she furthered her commitment to the poor and to institutional change, thinking of Eugene Debs' words: "While there is a lower class, I am of it, and while there is a criminal element, I am of it, and while there is a soul in prison, I am not free" (*From Union Square to Rome* 102, 104–05).

As she further reflected on her experiences, Day was moving through towns and jobs, not yet sure of how she could alter American institutions, as she later declared: "If you want to think of me in my twenties, think of someone drifting — I won't deny it — but drifting on water. I hadn't asked *whose* water until I was in my later twenties" (Coles 7). She was going from job to job to eke out a living while also writing for newspapers on how courts treated juveniles and prostitutes. "I did not know in what I believed," she later wrote, "though I tried to serve a cause" (*The Long Loneliness* 11).

Prison had readied her for action; joining forces in 1932 with Peter

Maurin would finally provide her with the means of taking that action. A former Christian Brother, he had left France for Canada in 1908 and made his way to the United States. When he met Day, he was working as a handyman at a Catholic boys' camp in upstate New York. What Day should do, Maurin told her, was start a newspaper to begin teaching about inequality and to urge the Catholic Church to enact the values of Christ through political and industrial reform. Day embraced his ideas.

For *The Catholic Worker*, Day determined the price, chose a press, and covered the first printing costs, going ahead with no backing, as had Martha Foley and Alice Gram Robinson. She wanted a one-cent affordability so that anyone who wanted to read the paper could do so. Like Alice Paul with the *Suffragist*, Day was starting with the concrete choice of a newspaper, one of her own forming, citing a descriptor of a person involved, not The Suffragist but The Catholic Worker, finally enacting her goal instigated during her suffrage incarceration: "I want to really and honestly work" (*The Eleventh Virgin* 216). The Paulist Press printed 2,500 copies of the first eight-page issue, and Maurin and Day began distributing *The Catholic Worker* on May Day, 1933. By December, 100,000 copies were being printed each month (Forest, "A Biography").

For the first half year, *The Catholic Worker* was only a newspaper, but as winter approached, homeless people began to seek out Day and Maurin, asking them to enact their principles. Maurin's essays in the paper called for renewal of the ancient Christian practice of hospitality to the homeless. In this way followers of Christ could enable others to re-enact Jesus' words: "I was a stranger and you took me in." Surrounded by people in need and attracting volunteers excited about ideas they discovered in *The Catholic Worker*, the editors decided to move from theory to practice: Day's apartment became the harbinger of many houses of hospitality to come (Forest, "A Biography").

By wintertime, Day and Maurin rented an apartment with space for ten women; soon afterwards, they established another place for men. Next came a house in Greenwich Village and then two buildings in Chinatown. Throughout the 1930s, Day wrote, most of their residents were "grey men, the color of lifeless trees and bushes and winter soil, who had in them as yet none of the green of hope, the rising sap of faith." Together Day and Maurin began encouraging the formation of other houses across the United States. By 1936, the depths of the Depression, there were thirty-three Catholic Worker houses across the country. Day and Maurin also experimented with farming communes, starting with one on Staten Island, and then in Pennsylvania and upstate New York (Forest, "A Biography").

In all of these houses, from their beginning, Day encouraged a seamless existence between the poor and those that came to live and work with them, not one group enabling another, but a unit working to end inequities, like suffragists serving jail terms together, protecting each other, and striving for national reform. In contrast with most charitable centers, at a house of hospitality all the residents, both the needy and those that volunteered to help them, worked together to serve the group. Like Alice Paul and Helen Keller, Day sought not to provide aid but to alter the lot of the dispossessed; otherwise her volunteers would be "mere philanthropists, doling out palliatives" ("Aims and Purposes" 31). Day viewed the model of the houses as revolutionary, creating a new equality, a seamlessness between helper and helped so that self-respect and engagement could be the result and society would change.

Like Alice Paul, Jeannette Rankin, Anne Martin, and many other suffragists, Day was dedicated to the difficult choice of pacifism, her commitment to social justice rendering warfare an anathema. Following Japan's attack on Pearl Harbor and America's declaration of war, Day announced that the *Catholic Worker* would maintain its pacifist stand. Opposition to the war, she maintained, had nothing to do with sympathy for America's enemies. "We love our country.... We have been the only country in the world where men and women of all nations have taken refuge from oppression" (Wogaman and Strong 247). But the Catholic Worker movement's means of action involved works of mercy rather than works of war.

In the 1950s, the New York Catholic Worker community continued its pacifism by refusing to participate in the state's annual civil defense drill, a form of picketing as in the suffrage campaign. Any preparation for attack seemed to Day part of an attempt to promote nuclear war as survivable and winnable and to justify spending billions on the military. When sirens sounded on June 15, 1955, Day was among a small group sitting in front of City Hall, refusing very publicly to take cover inside during a citywide drill. "In the name of Jesus, who is God, who is Love, we will not obey this order to pretend, to evacuate, to hide. We will not be drilled into fear. We do not have faith in God if we depend upon the Atom Bomb," a *Catholic Worker* leaflet explained. Day described her civil disobedience as an act of "penance for America's use of nuclear weapons on Japanese cities" (Forest, "A Biography").

Entering prison regularly in the 1950s, she could describe prison life as routine by the time of the July-August 1957 edition of *The Catholic Worker* when she had again been incarcerated, this time for opposing the drill: "We get out of our cells at 6:30. Good showers night and morning. Work from

8–11 and 1–3. Recreation on the roof so we get fresh air. Not much inside. I'll have a prison pallor when I get out" ("Dorothy Day"). But, just as she did concerning her suffrage incarceration, she reflected on the power of prison to elucidate the weaknesses of capitalistic society: "One comes out from jail into a world where everyone has problems, all but insoluble problems, and the first thing that strikes me is that the world today is almost worse than jail" ("Thoughts after Prison" 5). As she first did at Occoquan Workhouse, Day continued to see people as too often imprisoned by their own few choices, by their lack of meaningful work, their own minimal sense of purpose and responsibility within a system in which no trust or respect was ceded to them. But, like so many other suffragists combining the one with the group, she thought that the individual could still embody and seek to change this system: "It begins with each one of us" ("After Prison, Part 2" 19).

While Day continued with public picketing and jail sentences as she sought social justice, she also continued with the pleas for political-prisoner status and with the hunger-striking that had been a part of the suffrage movement. Each time that she entered jail she asked for this unrecognized status and encouraged others to do so. In 1965, Day went to Rome to take part in a hunger strike expressing "our prayer and our hope" that the Second Vatican Council would issue "a clear statement, 'Put away thy sword'" to oppose warfare and especially the war in Vietnam. Day saw this hunger strike as a "widow's mite," a sign of total dedication from the humble individual, like the widow's gift of her two mites in the Gospels of Mark and Luke (Forest, *Love Is* 156). Those who fasted had reason to rejoice in December when the bishops approved the Constitution on the Church in the Modern World. This document described as "a crime against God and humanity" any act of war "directed to the indiscriminate destruction of whole cities or vast areas with their inhabitants." The church called on states to make legal provision for conscientious objectors while describing as "criminal" those who obeyed commands that condemned the innocent and defenseless (Stone 92).

Day lived long enough to see her achievements honored. In 1967, when she made her last visit to Rome to take part in the International Congress of the Laity, she was one of two Americans invited to receive Communion from the hands of Pope Paul VI. On her seventy-fifth birthday, the Jesuit magazine *America* devoted a special issue to her, finding in her the individual who best exemplified "the aspiration and action of the American Catholic community during the past forty years." Notre Dame University presented her with its Laetare Medal, thanking her for "comforting the afflicted and afflicting the comfortable." Long before her death on November 29, 1980,

Day found herself regarded by many as a saint. No words of hers are better known than her brusque response, "Don't call me a saint. I don't want to be dismissed so easily" (Forest, "The Living Legacy"). Nonetheless, she is a candidate for inclusion in the calendar of saints: the Claretians have launched an effort to have her canonized, and the Vatican has given its approval to the process.

After her jailing for suffrage, and in her subsequent work with Maurin, Day dedicated herself to further activism, taking from the experience a commitment to the rights and needs of the poor. She believed, like Alice Paul in forming the NWP, that change began in the self-respect and commitment of those seeking change, in creating a strong group that could fight for equal rights. The commitment to justice that began for her with suffrage shaped her life.

Hazel Hunkins-Hallinan was a graduate of Vassar, and later professor of History at the University of Missouri. During the summer of 1916, suffragist Anna Louise Rowe came to her hometown, organizing for the National Woman's Party, and, in Hunkins-Hallinan's words, "I fell for it hook, line and sinker." When on August 6, 1918, one hundred women gathered at Lafayette's monument, at the head of the line of women was Hunkins-Hallinan, carrying the American flag, When arrested, she refused to give the police her American flag and walked into the courtroom leading the women and carrying it. In the courtroom, she contested the right of the judicial system to sentence these women, telling the judge, "Women cannot be lawbreakers until they are law-makers." Photograph dated ca. 1917; photographer Congressional Union. Photograph from National Woman's Party Records. Source: Library of Congress Manuscript Division.

Hazel Hunkins-Hallinan

As suffragists left the campaign, they worked to achieve social justice and to alter the status of women through social and religious activism as well as governmental positions. Like many others, Hazel Hunkins-Hallinan believed that a radical change for women could occur as they moved beyond the suffrage campaign and took charge of their bodies, homes, and communities. In *The Female Eunuch* (1970), Gemaine Greer concluded that, unlike the other "old suffragettes" who were "ever dwindling, ever more respectable," Hazel Hunkins-Hallinan "welcomed the younger militants and even welcomed their sexual frankness" (11). For Greer, echoing Marsha Lear's arguments from 1968, Hunkins-Hallinan was the one exception that proved the rule about the bankrupt suffrage generation. In 1983, in *There's Always Been a Women's Movement This Century,* Dale Spender discussed the difficulty of finding out information about Hunkins-Hallinan, noting about women's traditions and lives, "the way they so readily and so easily become invisible in our society" (11). Spender recognized that she had been indoctrinated, in histories written by women and men, "to see any women's protest at the beginning of this century as a fleeting — and flighty — phase, as exhibitionism associated with getting the vote, and as very peripheral to fundamental and serious political issues" (12–13). Studying Hunkins-Hallinan, Spender writes, drawing a conclusion different from Greer's, "eliminated forever from my consciousness the simplistic belief that middle-class and 'bourgeois' women were not interested in radical change" though Hunkins-Hallinan is the only representative of the American suffrage movement that she interviewed (13).

This lone exemplar — or equal member of an activist group — was born in 1890, in Aspen, Colorado. Hunkins-Hallinan's family settled in Billings, Montana, in 1903, where she graduated from high school in 1908. She then attended Mount Ida School in Newton, Massachusetts, for a year of college preparatory classes, and next went to Vassar, graduating in 1913, after which she began teaching at the University of Missouri and working on a master's degree in chemistry. But then her mother became ill and asked her to come home to do the caring job expected of daughters and not of her brother who was living in her hometown: "I was just stuck there" ("A Revolution Unfinished" 14). When she applied for a high school teaching job in chemistry and physics, she encountered the gender prejudices of the scientific community, as had Agnes Chase and Helena Hill Weed, a situation that to her seemed unbelievable, as she wrote in 1968:

> I had spent years being trained as a chemist. I had taken every chemistry course there was at Vassar and I thought I'd be able to teach chemistry. Then I discovered, "Oh, no, we only have *men* teaching chemistry and physics — you will have to teach geography and botany." I knew nothing about botany. I knew nothing about geography. But that's what I had to teach. Only men had chemistry and physics — and so that was one of my first real blows about the limita-

tions that were placed on women. It wasn't very tragic, but to a young girl it was tragic ["A Revolution Unfinished" 15].

In the summer of 1916, when she was twenty-six and able to leave home, she applied for jobs around the nation as an industrial chemist and got back only negative responses, along with notices that these firms did not hire any women for such positions. It was "a summer of despair and unhappiness" ("A Revolution Unfinished" 15).

Then, for Hunkins-Hallinan, as for so many other women, suffrage work happily intervened. During the summer of 1916, suffragist Anna Louise Rowe came to her hometown, organizing for the National Woman's Party, and, in Hunkins-Hallinan's words, "I fell for it hook, line and sinker." She found in this movement, as did so many other women, the chance to oppose the injustices she had encountered, as she succinctly described: "Anna Louise Rowe offered me a chance to *do* something, not just for myself but also for all those other women who had been stopped like I had. And so it turned from a summer of despair into a summer of great happiness" ("A Revolution Unfinished" 16).

Hunkins-Hallinan began making speeches in that year, especially about the boycott of the Democrats. At first, like many others, she was sent out to begin drawing a crowd, with a better speaker coming out as the numbers grew. This involvement led to longer speeches and then to a paid position with the NWP, working as an organizer in Montana, California, Utah, and New York.

In 1917, she left this position to work for the National War Labor Board in Washington as a researcher and union investigator, seeking to contribute to the war effort as did Mary Church Terrell. While she was living in Washington, during the winter and spring of 1917, she participated in the picket lines regularly. When Dale Spender interviewed her in 1982, Hunkins-Hallinan remembered well the banners echoing Wilson's declarations on democracy and the harsh reaction of crowds of men, especially after America entered the war and banners bore the Kaiser Wilson remarks: "The crowds were very unfriendly. We used to grit our teeth for the insults. When the civil servants came out from work at 4:00 pm 'Dirty bitches—what are you doing here?' they would shout. Sometimes it was even worse than that. The men in the street would become hostile and violent, and banners were torn from the pickets' hands and their clothes ripped from their backs." The police didn't seem much better. "I had my shirt waist torn off me once," she told Spender. "The police would drag you off and throw you around if they felt like it. And their language was abusive too" (21). What impressed Hunkins-Hallinan that summer and fall was the dedication of Alice Paul and the large number of women who joined her: "Alice Paul made women's position a burning political issue. Women came from all over the country to take part in the demonstrations and pickets. They came and were attacked by mobs and clubbed by police; and they kept on coming!" (Spender 40).

When on August 6, 1918, one hundred women gathered at Lafayette's monument, at the head of the line of women was Hunkins-Hallinan, carrying the American flag, her militant actions demonstrating her growing confidence and commitment to equal rights ("Suffrage Demonstration "). Several women, including Hunkins-Hallinan, Helena Hill Weed, and Lucy Burns, attempted to give speeches to the large crowd. As Hunkins-Hallinan began—"Here at the statue of Lafayette, who fought for the liberty of this country and under the American flag, I am asking for..."—she was immediately arrested (Stevens, *Jailed* 142). She refused to give the police her American flag and walked into the courtroom leading the women and carrying it. In the courtroom, she contested the right of the judicial system to sentence these women, telling the judge that "women cannot be law-breakers until they are law-makers" (Irwin, *The Story of* 358). She was one of twenty-six then sentenced to ten days ("Suffragists Again"). The women immediately declared themselves political prisoners and instigated a hunger strike.

After the vote was won, in July 1920, Hunkins-Hallinan moved to England and tried to make a difference there. The American Railway Union sent her there to find out all she could about the Co-operative Movement in England, through which workers were opening their own stores, initiating adult education and social clubs, and buying land together, ventures that American unionists hoped to emulate (Gurney 62–65). Her union research job enabled her to meet with activists and theorists from the London School of Economics, where she frequently attended lectures to learn more about government and labor, as had Alice Paul. During the 1920s and 1930s she worked as a journalist, often for the *Chicago Tribune*, writing a column under the pseudonym Ann Whittingham about English society, with a focus on Americans in England, while she also attended Fabian meetings where she met economist and social activist Beatrice Webb, with whom Paul had studied in 1908 and 1909. In London, she married suffrage and ACLU activist Charles Hallinan, financial editor for UPI, and they had three children before they married at the end of the 1920s at the request of the children and her mother (Cottrell 50–51).

After Hunkins-Hallinan moved to England, while working as a journalist, she continued to organize women for change, as she had done through suffrage. In 1921, she participated with Margaret Haig, the Viscountess

Rhondda, a successful business leader, in creating the Six Point Group. After activists in England achieved limited franchise in 1918 — women over the age of thirty could vote — they immediately began working for the full franchise, achieved in 1928. They also began to isolate their first goals for moving beyond the ability to vote, stated as six points:

1. Satisfactory legislation on child assault
2. Satisfactory legislation for the widowed mother
3. Satisfactory legislation for the unmarried mother and her child
4. Equal rights of guardianship for married parents
5. Equal pay for teachers
6. Equal opportunities for men and women in the civil service

As legislation began to address some of these inequities, the group used its label to indicate six general points of equality for women — political, occupational, moral, social, economic, and legal — that could describe their changing priorities. As Hunkins-Hallinan noted of the continuing relevance of the name and effort, "You could just go on and on, adding more points to work for" (Spender 30).

Hunkins-Hallinan believed that in working toward equality, she needed to help with the education of women within their homes, to help them make their own decisions. In 1922, she wrote the fifth edition of *To Wives and Mothers: How to Keep Yourselves and Your Children Well and Strong* for London's National League for Health, Maternity and Child Welfare, greatly changing the tone of earlier editions, changes that remained in it subsequently. In this version "brought up-to-date" as the preface says, she declared that motherhood "starts with the necessity of the mother keeping proper care of her own health" (np). Here she advocates recognition of a mother's personal needs and time, the priorities of the mother's own lives that must be honored for positive parenting. She also reviews specifics of dealing with the child for women who return to work as well as those who stay at home as well as for involving both father and mother in the daily responsibilities of child rearing.

In Hunkins-Hallinan's analysis, the on-going education and interaction of women would naturally lead beyond the home to political action that would better the situation of all women. In frequent talks that might include help with child care, she focused on the listeners' ability not just to improve their home life but to reach larger political goals, like those of the Six Point Group. When the Scottish birth-control campaigner Marie Stopes set up the first English birth-control clinic in 1921, the Six Point Group supported her efforts. During the 1920s, it was active in urging the League of Nations to pass an Equal Rights Treaty written by Doris Stevens and supported by the NWP (D'Itri 154–57).

Like the NWP in seeking reform, the Six Point Group relied on a journal, *Time and Tide*, made deputations to government officials, and organized public rallies in support of equal rights laws, and not protective legislation, as well as the extension of the franchise to all English women. Beginning in 1933, the Six Point Group helped to spearhead the movement for the right of married women to work, opposing suggested legislation that would have led to the firing of married women in hard economic times (Graves 121–29). In 1935, through their lobbying, married women in England gained the full right to assume personal liability for the contracts in which they entered (Shanley 73–75).

During World War II, the Six Point Group continued its work for women, as the NWP had continued to work for suffrage during World War I. Through deputations to government ministers, public rallies, and letters to major newspapers, as well as articles in *Time and Tide*, the group fought the policy of paying women in the Civil Defense Services only two-thirds of what men received. The Six-Point Group also encouraged women to do their part as leaders within their neighborhoods. Hunkins-Hallinan served as an air raid warden and patrolled the streets. When houses around her were gutted by a bomb, as she wrote much later, "My lungs got blasted, and I breathed in all that rotten air. I was in a hospital for eleven months" (Spender 35). She finally evacuated with two of her children to the United States and there served on a committee attempting to evacuate British children. After the war when she returned to England, she continued "fighting behind the government scene," achieving much of what she sought, slowly, first in individual cities and counties and then through Parliament: the Matrimonial Proceedings and Property Act of 1970, the Equal Pay Act of 1970, and the Sex Discrimination Act of 1975 (Butler and Sloman 308; Spender 31).

In 1968, she published *In Her Own Right* as a discussion document of the Six Point Group and in her introduction commented on changes over the century, especially the hard fought campaign to actually induce the government to remove legal disabilities facing women, not just legislate their removal and avoid enforcement (*In Her Own Right* 14). With the American Equal Pay Act of 1963, for example, she had been disappointed in her expectation of huge changes: she argued that the American government has purposely failed to provide the resources to enact such legislation, a tactic culled from Prohibition. In making the comparison to Prohibition, with England on the brink of passing similar legislation, she contended that English women had to insure that the new laws included plans and funding for full enforcement.

While building political influence through elected office, government jobs, and party committees, suffragists continued to engage in direct social action. Women like Sue Shelton White, Dorothy Day, Mary Church Terrell, and Hazel Hunkins-Hallinan looked at the vote as a symbol of citizenship and equal rights, but they certainly were not naïve enough to think that it would change everything. They dedicated their lives to equality of race and gender, to the needs of the poor and of children, to radical change in the social structure. For them, the suffrage campaign was a significant step into a life of fully committed activism.

6

After 1920: The Lives of Other Suffragists

Although this study cannot consider the life choices of all the women who stood in picket lines and went to jail, there are many other stories that deserve to be told. A short discussion of several other members of this group can give a greater feel for the whole.

Pauline Adams, born in Ireland in 1874, moved to Norfolk, Virginia, with her husband, a Navy doctor. She helped bring to Norfolk well-known suffrage speakers, such as Anna Shaw; served as president of the Equal Suffrage League of Norfolk; and became an officer in the state suffrage organization. She participated in the pre-inaugural parade in 1913. For her picketing, Adams went to Occoquan in November 1917, where she demanded political prisoner status. Her letter to her son, Forsty (Edward Forstall Adams), dated September 30 revealed that on Sunday, although they did not go to church, the women had to attach white caps and collars and cuffs to their prison dresses with five straight pins. "Uplifters" came on Sunday to hand out leaflets, as Adams described, "with Lost Sheep pictures on them." In these speeches, Adams commented, with tongue in cheek, one imagines, "drink and drugs are the causes of all the down falls I've seen. And you know men invented them therefore 'Votes for Women.'" A letter from Adams to her son, Walter, dated October 23 and smuggled out of federal prison, declared that she had been kept from "the privilege of incoming or outgoing mail for over the past week and am now locked in a small cell in 'solitary.'"

In 1921, Adams passed the bar examination and became Norfolk's second woman qualified to practice law. A Norfolk newspaper's editorial tribute at the time of her death in 1957 noted that Adams "believed so thoroughly that woman's place was not only in the home, but also in public affairs, that she became a practicing attorney to prove it to herself and to others." She specialized in fighting for women in the divorce courts. Throughout her life, she remained active in civic and cultural affairs and worked tirelessly to establish museums and parks in Norfolk ("Pauline Adams").

Dollee Chevrier was an independent and assertive woman at a time in Canada when Franco-Catholic women were largely restricted to family related activities in the home. She spent her youth in Manitoba, where she attended St. Mary's Academy. In 1910, she left her restrictive community for what she considered the more modern and progressive America, where she became active in the suffrage movement and exchanged her birthname of Lorena for Dollee. She participated in the 1913 pre-inaugural parade and went to jail as a picket in 1917.

After the suffrage campaign, Chevrier traveled independently to Europe and China. She was particularly struck by the rich cultural tradition and the natural beauty of China, its business opportunities, as well as its poverty and social tensions. She worked there with foreign missionaries, her emphasis on food and health care rather than saving souls (Payment).

Sarah Tarleton Colvin wrote in her autobiography that "my greatest need, as a girl, was to feel some sense of importance — that is, to know that just because I existed I mattered.... The tremendous effort used to compress a woman's individuality into a uniform mold, be she rich or poor, is appalling" (51). She found that "sense of importance," of mattering, in suffrage. For participating in the watchfire demonstrations of January 1919, she was sentenced to five days in jail and then participated in a hunger strike, "a most unpleasant experience" (*A Rebel in Thought* 135). After she was brought into the cell, as she recalled in 1949, "the sound of that closing door caused me a greater sense of fear than I ever experienced again. I was never so near to panic. There was no knob on my side of the door, and I could not get out. For the first time in my life I was behind bars and 'in the clutches of the law'" (135). As she described this experience, she wrote of a change in her personality that Dorothy Day also echoed: "Life in a prison is indescribably revolting. For the first time in my life I was relieved of all responsibility for good conduct. I was under duress and entitled to do anything I could get away with, and under control of people completely irresponsible in their treatment of me, provided they did not kill me" (136–37).

After her suffrage activism, Colvin became a Minnesota Farmer Labor Party activist, working to insure that the populace had better knowledge of the issues, and she also became a member of the state board of education through which she lobbied for better science education for girls and boys, equal pay and status for women teachers, and nursery school funding, especially for poor children, as well as better training and status for nurses.

Rebecca Winsor Evans. Arrested at a watchfire demonstration with two of her sisters in January of 1919 and sentenced to five days in jail, Evans continued with a political life after the campaign ended. In 1923, she served as a member of the Amnesty Committee for Political Prisoners, with the focus on IWW members. In 1942, she co-authored *Land, Labor, Wealth*, a dictionary of economic terms intended to educate readers about the realities of labor exploitation in a capitalist country, with her sister Ellen, an early NAACP supporter who wrote for the *Crisis* and had been jailed for suffrage with Rebecca. As a Quaker and pacifist, during World War II Rebecca Evans served on a national committee to oppose conscription and to assure observance of conscientious-objector rights. Together the sisters provided funds to defend and secure the release of imprisoned I.W.W. leaders such as E.F. Doree, to help support struggling artists like Julius Thiengen Bloch and writers like libertarian critic Albert Jay Nock, and to establish an ongoing scholarship fund for African American students at Bryn Mawr (Rosen 107; Powell).

Inez Haynes Gilmore Irwin. The author of *The Story of the National Woman's Party* (1921), Irwin, who worked as a consultant for the Schlesinger Library, wrote a popular series of children's books, the *Maida* stories, from 1909 to 1955. Maida grows in these sentimental yet lively books from pampered invalid to shop assistant in Charleston, helping the poorer members of her neighborhood: "The consciousness of a new strength and a new power made a different child of her" (Showalter 34). The twelve books recount her adventures with a new group of young friends, on an island, at a camp, and in school, locations in which girls and boys become independent together. Irwin also wrote popular mysteries as well as *Angels and Amazons: A Hundred Years of American Women* (1933), concerning American women's long involvement in activist organizations. Her presentation of suffrage history angered Carrie Chapman Catt, who thought it unfairly biased toward the contribution of the NWP. Indeed, as Irwin admitted to fellow NWP member Maud Wood Park, "It is perhaps beyond my poor powers to be impartial on what was after all the most precious civic experience of my life" (Des Jardins 212).

Ernestine Hara Kettler, a socialist who supported strikes called by the IWW, described being jailed for suffrage an experience that would haunt her for the rest of her life: "I felt horrified by the different things that could happen to you in prison.... That was one reason why I decided not to go back again on the picket line and then be tried again and sentenced again" (Gluck 262). She also recognized the judgments of her morality made even by family and friends: "If you were a jailbird, you were a fallen woman" (Hara in Gluck 264). Coming to the United States from Rumania as a young girl, she lived in tenements and worked in clothing factories. She had a long involvement in the labor movement following her participation in the suffrage struggle. In the 1930s, she joined the Socialists Workers Party and worked for the Office Employees Union. She joined the National Organization for Women in 1968 and during the Jubilee Celebration of Woman's Suffrage, August 26, 1970, was one of the principal speakers, describing in moving terms the jail experience that had remained all too vivid for her.

Alice Mary Kimball, sentenced for fifteen days in the District Jail in August 1918, worked as a labor investigator, journalist, and librarian. Her collection of poems, *The Devil Is a Woman* (1929), presents portraits of valiant village women, facing constant work for their families and joining in women's organizations, the younger with the older, to work for reform. In her descriptions of individuals, she discusses the possible choices that a woman might make. For "Stasia Whitsett," marriage has aspects she would not stoop to; she is "too dignified and elevated" ("The Mating Flight of Stacia Whitsett" 24). Stasia finds her way through the help of her woman's club, whose members, like Jane Proudfoot, the chair who is "so white-haired and so wise and scholarly," are listed in the poem (30). Before the book publication, these poems had appeared in prominent journals, such as *The American Mercury* and *The Liberator* (Showalter 52–53).

Maud Malone was first arrested in November of 1912 in New York at the Academy of Music where Wilson was giving a lecture on tariffs. Officers took her away when she stood on her seat and yelled out "What about votes for women?" and remained standing as she awaited a reply that was not forthcoming ("Maud Malone Asks"). When she was arrested on the picket line in November of 1917, she sought political prisoner status along with Pauline Adams in Occoquan. That fall, she became the main spokesperson in the first labor union for librarians, a group that existed from 1917 to 1929, a group in which she stressed activism through solidarity, an approach that she frequently spoke of as arising for her in the suffrage campaign (Kuzyk).

Edna Purtell, as a very young woman, went to prison as a stand-in on the picket line for Katharine Houghton Hepburn, the actress' mother, who wasn't able to attend a protest in Lafayette Square in August of 1918. Purtell had been working in Connecticut and going to state suffrage meetings. After the suffrage campaign, she became a federal labor investigator, her work concentrating on the rights and health of farm laborers in the tobacco industry and especially the elimination of child labor. She was active as a speaker for

Robert LaFollette and the Progressive Party in the 1924 campaign. In 1941, she wrote "Working and Living Conditions on Connecticut Tobacco Plantations, as Industrial Investigator, Department of Labor and Factory Inspection, Hartford." In 1979 she was given the Susan B. Anthony award by the Connecticut Federation of Democratic Women's Clubs, which she had led in the 1930s (Nichols).

Doris Stevens. In 1928, the International Conference of American States established the Inter-American Commission of Women (IACW) to study the civil and political status of women in the Americas. Doris Stevens, who was jailed repeatedly as an NWP leader, was appointed the first chair of the commission of twenty-one members, one from each country in North, Central, and South America. This was the first inter-governmental body to address issues related to the status of women. In 1933, the IACW prepared, and its member governments adopted, the Montevideo Convention on the Nationality of Married Women. The IACW also prepared the 1938 Declaration of Lima in Favor of Women's Rights. At this time, the IACW encouraged its member governments to establish women's bureaus, revise discriminatory civil codes, and take women's initiatives regarding these issues to the League of Nations (Pietila). In 1939, Women's Bureau officials removed Stevens from the commission chairmanship because it wanted to emphasize protectionist legislation instead of the equal rights treaties that Stevens favored (D'Itri 158; Sklar). Afterwards, Stevens, like Alma Lutz, worked on expanding the teaching of women's history in American universities while giving frequent lectures and composing songs.

Many women did many things after the suffrage campaign, certainly, but several threads unite their choices. The most active of activists came into the campaign not with the narrow goal of achieving the vote, but instead with large and long-range goals, of enriching their own lives and of securing more opportunities for women and other dispossessed members of society—of making a difference. They found in suffrage a model for activism that affected them for the rest of their lives: the campaign confirmed for them that they could and did matter; that they could take on risks to their bodies and reputations; that they could impact who Americans credited as approved and unapproved, as worthy and unworthy; and that they could extend to others the choices that they had sought for themselves. After the campaign for the vote, in fields as diverse as art, education, science, publishing, international affairs, and church doctrine, they continued to advocate for the rights and place of women as well as other groups that a profession or school or country might choose to deny: they thus fought for the rights of women within larger contexts, as activists with many types of work to do. Certainly the suffrage movement was not the only influence on their lives — it would be Jonathan Swift's "Roguery and Ignorance" of historians to claim so. But it reoriented and guided a large group of women in a highly influential manner, enabling them to do the work they chose, thus enriching their own lives and their country.

Works Cited

Abir-Am, Pnina, and Dorinda Outram. *Uneasy Careers and Intimate Lives: Women in Science, 1789–1979*. New Brunswick, NJ: Rutgers University Press, 1987.

Adams, J.F.A. "Is Botany a Suitable Study for Young Men?" *Science* 9.209 (1887): 116–17.

Adams, Katherine H., and Michael L. Keene. *Alice Paul and the American Suffrage Campaign*. Urbana: University of Illinois Press, 2008.

Adams, Nicholas, and Bonnie G. Smith. *A History and Texture of Modern Life: Selected Essays*. Philadelphia: University of Pennsylvania Press, 2001.

"The Administration Versus the Woman's Party." *Suffragist*, 25 August 1917: 6–7.

Andersen, Kristi. *After Suffrage: Women in Partisan and Electoral Politics before the New Deal*. Chicago: University of Chicago Press, 1996.

Ardis, Ann L., and Leslie W. Lewis. Introduction. *Women's Experience of Modernity, 1875 to 1945*. Baltimore: Johns Hopkins University Press, 2002. 1–10.

Armstrong, Florence A. "The Papers of Sue Shelton White." Box 1. Sue Shelton White Papers, Schlesinger Library, Radcliffe Institute, Harvard University.

_____. "Sue Shelton White (1887–1943)." Box 1. Sue Shelton White Papers, Schlesinger Library, Radcliffe Institute, Harvard University, Cambridge.

"'Art and Artists,' by Mrs. Havemeyer; Discusses Mary Cassatt and Edgar Degas and Their Work with a Critical Taste." *New York Times* 7 April 1915: 7. *Historical New York Times*, 20 June 2009.

"Art at Home and Abroad: Paintings by El Greco and Goya Now on Exhibition." *New York Times*, 7 April 1912: SM15. *Historical New York Times*, 19 June 2009.

"Art Exhibit for Suffrage: Paintings of El Greco and Goya Loaned for the Purpose." *New York Times*, 15 April 1912: 8. *Historical New York Times*, 20 July 2009.

"Art Exhibit for Suffrage: A Rubens among Old Masters' Paintings at Knoedler's." *New York Times*, 6 April 1915: 10. *Historical New York Times*, 12 June 2009.

"Art for Woman's Suffrage: Exhibition of Goya and El Greco Paintings at Knoedler Galleries." *New York Times*, 2 April 1912: 12. *Historical New York Times*, 14 May 2009.

"Art in the Current Exhibitions of Paintings." *New York Times*, 10 December 1922: 106. *Historical New York Times*, 4 June 2009.

"Ask Miss Rankin Recant." *New York Times*, 9 December 1941: 8. *Historical New York Times*, 20 May 2009.

Bank, Barbara J., Sara Delamont, and Catherine Marshall. *Gender and Education: An Encyclopedia*. 2nd vol. Columbus: University of South Carolina Press, 2007.

Barber, Lucy G. *Marching on Washington: The Forging of an American Political Tradition*. Berkeley: University of California Press, 2004.

Batker, Carol J. *Reforming Fictions: Native, African, and Jewish American Women's Literature and Journalism in the Progressive Era*. New York: Columbia University Press, 2000.

Beard, Mary. "Have Americans Lost Their Democracy?" *Pearson's Magazine* 1913. Microform. Reel 5, National Woman's Party Papers, Library of Congress.

_____. *On Understanding Women*. New York: Grosset and Dunlap, 1931.

_____. *Woman as a Force in History: A Study of Traditions and Realities*. New York: Macmillan, 1946.

Beard, Mary, and Nancy F. Cott. *A Woman Making History: Mary Beard Through Her Letters*. New Haven: Yale University Press, 1991.

Bennett, Patrick. *Rough and Rowdy Ways: The Life and Hard Times of Edward Anderson*. College Station: Texas A&M University Press, 1988.

Benvenuti, Francesco. *The Bolsheviks and the Red Army, 1918–1922*. New York: Cambridge University Press, 2009.

Berkshire Conference of Women Historians (1930–1977), Archival Papers. Schlesinger Library, Radcliffe Institute, Harvard University.

"Betsy G. Reyneau Exhibits: Artist's Portraits Include Her Grandfather, Chief Justice Graves." *New York Times*, 5 December 1922: 19. *Historical New York Times*, 20 April 2009.

Bhavnagri, Navaz Peshotan, and Sue Krolikowski. "Home-Community Visits during an Era of Reform (1870–1920)." *ECRP: Early Childhood Research and Practice* 2.1. n.d. 10 July 2009.

Bindley, Barbara. "Helen Keller—'Why I Became an IWW.'" *New York Herald Tribune*, 15 January 1916. *Industrial Workers of the World: A Union for All Workers*, 15 July 2009.

Blatch, Harriot Stanton, and Alma Lutz. *Challenging Years: The Memoirs of Harriot Stanton Blatch*. New York: Putnam, 1940.

"Breaking Racial Barriers: African Americans in the Harmon Foundation Collection." *National Portrait Gallery*. 9 September 2009.

Bonta, Marcia Myers. *American Women Afield: Writing by Pioneering Women Naturalists*. College Station: Texas A&M University Press, 1995.

_____. *Women in the Field: America's Pioneering Women Naturalists*. College Station: Texas A&M University Press, 1991.

"Botanical Expedition to Brazil." *Explorations and Field-Work of the Smithsonian Institution in 1925*. 78.1. Smithsonian Miscellaneous Collections. Washington, DC: Smithsonian Institution, 1926. 48–54.

Bredbenner, Candace Lewis. *A Nationality of Her Own: Women, Marriage, and the Law of Citizenship*. Berkeley: University of California Press, 1998.

Bruno, Maryann, and Elizabeth A. Daniels. *Vassar College*. The College History Series. Charleston, SC: Arcadia, 2001.

Bryant, Louise. "American Ambulance Corps Enters the Fray." *New York American*, 19 August 1917: 52–2.

_____. "From the Tower." *The Masses*, 8.61 (July 1916): 22.

_____. *The Game: A Morality Play*. *The Provincetown Plays: First Series*. New York: Shay, 1916. 27–42.

_____. Letter to Jack Reed. 19 February 1919. Folder II. Jack Reed Papers. Harvard University Press.

_____. *Mirrors of Moscow*. New York: Seltzer, 1923.

_____. "The Poets' Revolution." *The Masses*, 8.61 (1916): 29.

_____. *Six Red Months in Russia: An Observer's Account of Russia before and during the Proletarian Dictatorship*. New York: Doran, 1918.

_____. "A Turkish Divorce." *Nation*, 121 (26 August 1925): 231–32.

_____. "Woman Tells Liner's Fight with U-Boat." *New York American*, 8 July 1917: 52–3.

Burns, Lucy. Letter to Alva Belmont. 24 July 1917. Reel 44. National Woman's Party Papers. Library of Congress.

_____. "The Indomitable Picket Line." *Suffragist*, 9 June 1917: 6.

Burrell, Barbara. *Women and Political Participation: A Reference Handbook*. Santa Barbara, CA: ABC Clio, 2004.

Butler, David, and Ann Sloman. *British Political Facts, 1900–1979*. New York: St. Martin's, 1980.

Cassatt, Mary. Letter to Louisine Havemeyer. 8 December 1909. Letters by Mary Cassatt, 1908–1910. Library of Congress.

Catt, Carrie Chapman, and Nettie Rogers Shuler. *Woman Suffrage and Politics: The Inner Story of the Suffrage Movement.* New York: Scribner's, 1923.

Chafe, William. *The American Woman.* New York: Oxford, 1972.

Chase, Agnes. "Eastern Brazil through an Agrostologist's Spectacles." *Annual Report of the Smithsonian Institution for 1926.* Washington, DC: GPO, 1927. 383–403.

_____. *First Book of Grasses: The Structure of Grasses Explained for Beginners.* 1922. Washington, DC: Smithsonian Institution, 1959.

Chase, Agnes, and Alfred S. Hitchcock. *Grass.* Washington, DC: Smithsonian Institution, 1931.

_____. *The North American Species of Panicum.* Washington, DC: GPO, 1910.

Circular Letter to the Membership, On Picketing in Wartime. May 1917. Microfilm. Reel 42, National Woman's Party Papers. Library of Congress.

Clinton, Hillary. "U.S. Election: Full Text of Hillary Clinton's Speech in Denver." Democratic National Convention. 27 August 2008. *Guardian.co.uk*, 19 July 2009.

"Colby Proclaims Woman Suffrage." *New York Times*, 26 August 1920: 1. *Historical New York Times*, 20 September 2009.

Coles, Robert. *Dorothy Day: A Radical Devotion.* Reading, MA: Addison-Wesley, 1952.

"Colors of Suffrage at D.A.R. Meeting." *New York Times*, 23 April 1915: 13. *Historical New York Times*, 21 September 2009.

Colvin, Sarah Tarleton. *A Rebel in Thought.* New York: Island Workshop, 1944.

Comments of the Press. *Suffragist*, 12 November 1917: 10.

Committee on Woman Suffrage. Hearing before the Committee on Rules, House of Representatives, Sixty-Third Congress. December 3–5, 1913. Washington, DC: GPO, 1914.

Congressional Digest Corporation: An Impartial View of Controversial Issues. 7 July 2009.

Cott, Nancy. "Feminist Politics in the 1920s: The National Woman's Party." *Journal of American History* 71 (1984): 43–68.

_____. *The Grounding of Modern Feminism.* New Haven: Yale University Press, 1989.

_____. "Putting Women on the Record: Mary Ritter Beard's Accomplishments." *A Woman Making History: Mary Beard Through Her Letters.* Mary Ritter Beard and Nancy F. Cott, eds. New Haven: Yale University Press, 1991. 1–62.

Cottrell, Robert C. *Roger Nash Baldwin and the American Civil Liberties Union.* New York: Columbia University Press, 2001.

"Courage." *New York Times*, 4 February 1955: 20. *Historical New York Times*, 20 June 2009.

Crocco, Margaret, and Ozro Luke Davis. *"Bending the Future to Their Will": Civic Women, Social Education, and Democracy.* New York: Rowman & Littlefield, 1999.

Davies, Wallace Evan. *Patriotism on Parade: The Story of Veterans' and Hereditary Organizations in America, 1783–1900.* Cambridge: Harvard University Press, 1955.

Day, Dorothy. "After Prison, Part 2." *Liberation*, October 1957: 17–19.

_____. "Aims and Purposes." February 1940. *A Penny a Copy: Readings from the Catholic Worker.* Thomas C. Cornell, Robert Ellsberg, and Jim Forest, eds. Maryknoll, NY: Orbis, 1995. 31–32.

_____. "Dorothy Day Writes from Jail." *The Catholic Worker*, July-August 1957: 3.

_____. *Eleventh Virgin.* New York: Albert and Charles Boni, 1924.

_____. *From Union Square to Rome.* New York: Arno, 1978.

_____. *The Long Loneliness.* 1952. Chicago: Saint Thomas More, 1993.

_____. "Thoughts after Prison." *Liberator*, September 1957: 5–7.

Dearborn, Mary V. *Queen of Bohemia: The Life of Louise Bryant.* Boston: Houghton Mifflin, 1996.

"The Demonstration of February 9." *Suffragist*, 22 February 1919: 10–12.

Dervaux, Isabelle. *Manet, Monet, and the Gare Saint-Lazare*. Washington, DC: National Gallery of Art, 1998.

Des Jardins, Julie. *Women and the Historical Enterprise in America: Gender, Race, and the Politics of Memory, 1880–1945*. Chapel Hill: University of North Carolina Press, 2003.

"A Different Voice: Women in Congress." *Constitutional Rights Foundation. Bill of Right in Action*. Summer 1993 (9:3 and 9.4). Updated July 2000. 21 July 2009.

D'Itri, Patricia Ward. *Cross Currents in the International Women's Movement, 1848–1948*. Bowling Green, OH: Bowling Green University, 1999.

Dodge, Alice Madeline. "Louisine Havemeyer's Art and Activism: From the Domestic Interior to the Woman's Suffrage Movement." Master's thesis, University of California Davis, 2005.

"Drifting in the Caribbean." *Nation*, 8 February 1917: 152–53.

Du Bois, Ellen Carol. *Harriot Stanton Blatch and the Winning of Woman Suffrage*. New Haven: Yale University Press, 1999.

Einhorn, Lois J. *Helen Keller, Public Speaker: Sightless but Seen, Deaf but Heard*. Great American Orators Series, No. 23. Westport, CT: Greenwood, 1998.

Eisner, Elliot W., and Michael D. Day. *The Handbook of Research and Policy in Art Education*. Mahwah, NJ: Erlbaum, 2004.

Elizabeth Schlesinger, 1887–1997: A Staunch Advocate and a Dear Friend. Boston: The Arthur and Elizabeth Schlesinger Library in the History of Women in America, 1978.

Evans, Rebecca Winsor, and Ellen Winsor. *Land, Labor, and Wealth: A Handbook of Economic Terms*. Caldwell, ID: Caxton, 1942.

"Exhibition for Suffrage Cause: Pictures Representing Many Phases of the Art of Edgar Degas and Mary Cassatt in Exhibition for the Suffrage Cause." *New York Times*, 4 April 1915: SM14. *Historical New York Times*, 9 April 2009.

"The Exhibition of the H.O. Havemeyer Collection." *Metropolitan Museum of Art Bulletin* 25.3 (1930): 53–76.

Faber, Doris. *Petticoat Politics: How American Women Won the Right to Vote*. New York: Lothrop, Lee and Shepard, 1967.

"Fiction Magazine Moves." *New York Times*, 6 February 1933: 13. *Historical New York Times*, 27 August 2009.

Field, Sara Bard. Letters to Louise Bryant. Box 3, Folder 36. Louise Bryant Papers. Yale University Library.

Fine, Elsa Honig. *The Afro-American Artist: A Search for Identity*. New York: Holt, 1973.

Fishbein, Leslie. *Rebels in Bohemia : The Radicals of the Masses, 1911–1917*. Chapel Hill: University of North Carolina Press, 1982.

Fitzpatrick, Sheila. *The Russian Revolution*. New York: Oxford University Press, 2008.

Fleming, Tuliza K. *Breaking Racial Barriers: African Americans in the Harmon Foundation Collection*. San Francisco: Pomegranate Art Books, 1997.

Flexner, Eleanor, and Ellen Fitzpatrick. *Century of Struggle: The Woman's Rights Movement in the United States*. 1959. Enlarged ed. Cambridge: Harvard University Press, 1996.

Foks-Apelman, Theresa. *Draw Me a Picture: The Meaning of Children's Drawings and Play from the Perspective of Analytical Psychology*. Atlanta: BookSurge, 2007.

Foley, Martha. *200 Years of Great American Short Stories*. Boston: Houghton, 1975.

_____. *The Best of the Best American Short Stories, 1915–1950*. Boston: Houghton, 1952.

_____. *Fifty Best American Short Stories, 1915–1965*. Boston: Houghton, 1965.

_____. *The Story of Story Magazine: A Memoir by Martha Foley*. New York: Norton, 1980.

Foner, Philip S. Introduction. *Helen Keller: Her Socialist Years*. Foner, ed. New York: International, 1967. 7–18.

Ford, Linda G. *Iron-Jawed Angels: The Suf-*

frage Militancy of the National Woman's Party, 1912–1920. Lanham, MD: University Press of America, 1991.

Forest, Jim. "A Biography of Dorothy Day." *Catholic Worker Home Page*, 24 July 2009.

_____. "The Living Legacy of Dorothy Day." *Claretian Publications*, 1 August 2009.

_____. *Love is the Measure: A Biography of Dorothy Day*, Maryknoll, NY: Orbis, 1994.

Fortieth Anniversary Report: The Arthur and Elizabeth Schlesinger Library of the History of Women in America. Cambridge: Radcliffe College, 1983.

Fosberg, F. Raymond, and Jason R. Swallen. "Agnes Chase." *Taxon* 8.5 (1959): 145–51.

Freedman, Estelle. "Separatism as Strategy: Female Institution Building and American Feminism, 1870–1930." *Feminist Studies* 5.3 (1979): 512–29.

_____. "Separatism Revisited: Women's Institutions, Social Reform, and the Career of Miriam Van Waters." *U.S. History as Women's History: New Feminist Essays*. Linda K. Kerber, Alice Kessler-Harris, and Kathryn Kish Sklar, eds. Chapel Hill: University of North Carolina Press, 1995. 170–88.

Fry, Amelia R. "Alice Paul and the ERA." *Rights of Passage: The Past and Future of the ERA*. Joan Hoff-Wilson, ed. Bloomington: Indiana University Press, 1986. 8–24.

_____. "Conversations with Alice Paul: Woman Suffrage and the Equal Rights Amendment. November 1972 and May 1973." *Suffragists Oral History Project, University of California at Berkeley*. 5 August 2009.

Gallagher, Robert S. "I Was Arrested, of Course." *American Heritage*, February 1974: 17–24+.

Gardner, Virginia. *"Friend and Lover": The Life of Louise Bryant*. New York: Horizon, 1982.

Gelb, Barbara. *So Short a Time: A Biography of John Reed and Louise Bryant*. New York: Norton, 1973.

Gilderhus, Mark T. "Revolution, War, and Expansion: Woodrow Wilson in Latin America." *Reconsidering Woodrow Wilson: Progressivism, Internationalism, War, and Peace*. John Milton Cooper, Jr., ed. Baltimore: John Hopkins University Press, 2008. 165–88. Print.

Glaspell, Susan, and Jig Cook. *Suppressed Desires: A Comedy in Two Episodes*. Boston: Baker, 1924.

Gluck, Sherna Berger. *From Parlor to Prison: Five American Suffragists Talk About Their Lives*. New York: Vintage, 1976.

Goode, Eslanda Cordozo. Letter to Mary Church Terrell. Microform. Reel 4, Papers of Mary Church Terrell. Library of Congress.

"Grandmother Beaten for Mayor." *New York Times*, 4 October 1927: 31. *Historical New York Times*, 29 April 2009.

Graves, Pamela M. *Labour Women: Women in British Working Class Politics, 1918–1939*. New York: Cambridge University Press, 1994.

Green, Elna C. *Southern Strategies: Southern Women and the Woman Suffrage Question*. Chapel Hill: University of North Carolina Press, 1997.

Greene, William M. *Louise Bryant: An Informal Biography of an Activist*. http://louisebryant.com. Accessed 9 August 2009.

Greer, Germaine. *The Female Eunuch*. London: MacGibbon and Kee, 1970.

"Guilty of—?" *Suffragist*, 1 February 1919: 4.

Gurney, Peter. *Co-operative Culture and the Politics of Consumption in England, 1870–1930*. Manchester: Manchester University Press, 1996.

"Haiti—The United States Occupation, 1915–1934." *Haiti, a Country Study. Nations Encyclopedia*. 8 September 2009.

Hallowell, Anna Davis. *James and Lucretia Mott: Life and Letters*. Boston: Houghton, 1890.

Hamburger, Robert. *Two Rooms: The Life of Charles Erskine Scott Wood*. Lincoln: University of Nebraska Press, 1998.

Harper, Ida Husted. Letter to the Editor of

the *Chattanooga Times*, January 3, 1917. Box 2, Ida H. Harper Papers, Huntington Library.

_____. *The Life and Work of Susan B. Anthony*. Indianapolis: Hollenbeck, 1898.

Harper, Ida Husted, Elizabeth Cady Stanton, Susan B. Anthony, and Matilda J. Gage, eds. *History of Woman Suffrage*. 6 vols. New York: Little and Ives, 1881–1922.

Harrison, Cynthia. "The Changing Role of Women in American Society." *U.S. Society and Values* 2.2 (1997): 10–12. 9 September 2009.

"Havemeyer Art Gift Valued at $3,489,461." *New York Times*, March 1931: 18. *Historical New York Times*, 2 July 2009.

Havemeyer, Louisine W. "The Prison Special: Memories of a Militant." *Scribner's Magazine* 71 (1922): 661–76.

_____. *Sixteen to Sixty: Memoirs of a Collector*. 1961. New York: Ursus, 1993.

_____. "The Suffrage Torch. Memories of a Militant." *Scribner's Magazine* 71 (1922): 528–39.

"Helen Keller a Militant; Blind Girl Believes Suffrage Will Lead to Socialism." *New York Times*, 6 May 1913: 2. *Historical New York Times*, 18 July 2009.

"Helen Keller at Radcliffe: The Blind Deaf-Mute Passes the Examination and Is Admitted." *New York Times*, 8 October 1900: 1. *Historical New York Times*, 18 September 2009.

"Helen Keller, Back, Is 'Dismayed' by Events in Italy and Germany." *New York Times*, 29 September 1934: 17. *Historical New York Times*, 18 July 2009.

"Helen Keller Hits at Two Dictators." *New York Times*, 20 September 1934: 24. *Historical New York Times*, 18 July 2009.

"Helena H. Weed, a Suffragist, 83." *New York Times*, 26 April 1958: 19. *Historical New York Times*, 26 August 2009.

Henson, Pamela M. "Invading Arcadia: Women Scientists in the Field in Latin America, 1900–1950." *The Americas* 58.4 (2002): 577–600.

_____. "'What Holds the Earth Together': Agnes Chase and American Agrostology." *Journal of the History of Biology* 36.3 (Fall 2003): 437–60.

Hinton, Harold B. "Washington Group Jubilant." *New York Times*, 21 December 1933: 1. *Historical New York Times*, 26 August 2009.

"History of SDSU Women's Studies." *San Diego State University Women's Studies*. 10 September 2009.

Holden, Robert H., and Eric Zolov. *Latin America and the United States: A Documentary History*. New York: Oxford University Press, 2000.

Hothersall, David. *History of Psychology*. New York: McGraw Hill, 2003.

"How Woman Suffrage Works." *New York Times*, 8 March 1924: 10. *Historical New York Times*, 20 June 2009.

Howard, Anne Bail. *The Long Campaign: A Biography of Anne Martin*. Reno: University of Nevada Press, 1985.

Howard, Harold S. "Suffrage and College Women." *New York Times*, 16 March 1909: 5. *Historical New York Times*, 20 June 2009.

Howells, Dorothy Elia. *A Century to Celebrate Radcliffe College: 1879–1979*. Cambridge: Radcliffe College, 1978.

Hudicourt, Pierre. "Before the Pan-American Bar." *Nation* 117 (18 July 1923): 54–55.

Huehls, Betty Sparks. "Sue Shelton White: The Making of a Radical." *West Tennessee Historical Society Papers* 48 (1994): 24–34.

Hunkins-Hallinan, Hazel. Foreword. *In Her Own Right: A Discussion Conducted by the Six Point Group*. London: Harrap, 1968. 7.

_____. "A Revolution Unfinished." *In Her Own Right: A Discussion Conducted by the Six Point Group*. London: Harrap, 1968. 9–17.

_____. *To Wives and Mothers: How to Keep Yourselves and Your Children Well and Strong*. 5th ed. London: National League for Health, Maternity and Child Welfare, 1922.

"Impressions from the District Jail." *Suffragist* 25 January 1919: 12.

"In Prison." *Suffragist* 24 August 1918: 7.

Introduction. *The Opulent Interiors of the Gilded Age: All 203 Photographs from Artistic Houses*. With new text by Arnold Lewis, James Turner, and Steven McQuillin. New York: Dover, 1987. 1–29.

Irwin, Inez Haynes. *Angels and Amazons: A Hundred Years of American Women*. Garden City, NY: Doubleday, 1934.

_____. *Maida's Little Shop*. New York: Grosset and Dunlap, 1909.

_____. *The Story of Alice Paul and the Woman's Party*. New York: Harcourt, 1921.

Jewell, Edward Alden. "Negro Art Shown in Two Exhibits." *New York Times*, 6 November 1945: 26. *Historical New York Times*, 2 May 2009.

"Jo Davidson Heads Unit for Roosevelt." *New York Times*, 24 August 1944: 32. *Historical New York Times*, 29 June 2009.

Johnson, James Weldon. "The Truth about Haiti: An N.A.A.C.P. Investigation." *Crisis* 5 (September 1920): 217–24.

_____. "Self-Determining Haiti: The American Occupation." *Nation* 111 (28 August 1920): 237.

Jones, Beverly Washington. *Quest for Equality: The Life and Writings of Mary Eliza Church Terrell, 1863–1954*. Darlene Clark Hine, ed. Brooklyn: Carlson, 1990.

Josephson, Hannah Geffen. *Jeannette Rankin, First Lady in Congress: A Biography*. New York: Bobbs-Merrill, 1974.

Juarez, Joseph Robert. "United States Withdrawal from Santo Domingo." *Hispanic American Historical Review* 42.2 (May 1962): 152–90.

Jung, Carl. *Mandala Symbolism*. Trans. R.F.C. Hull. Princeton: Princeton University Press, 1959.

"Kaiser Wilson." *Suffragist* 18 August 1917: 6.

Keller, Helen. "An Apology for Going to College." *Out of the Dark: Essays, Letters, and Addresses on Physical and Social Vision*. New York: Doubleday, 1920. 83–106.

_____. "Blind Leaders." *Outlook* 105 (September 27, 1913): 231–36.

_____. "An Epic of Courage: 'Seen' by Helen Keller." *New York Times*, 6 January 1946:

SM3. *Historical New York Times*, 21 August 2009.

_____. "The Heaviest Burden on the Blind." *Out of the Dark*. New York: Doubleday, 1920. 213–20.

_____. "How I Became a Socialist." *Out of the Dark*. New York: Doubleday, 1920. 18–29.

_____. "A Letter to an English Woman-Suffragist." *Out of the Dark*. New York: Doubleday, 1920. 115–20.

_____. Letter to Nella Braddy Henney. 18 September 1944. Henney Collection. Perkins School for the Blind.

_____. *Midstream: My Later Life*. New York: Greenwood, 1968.

_____. "The Modern Woman." *Out of the Dark*. New York: Doubleday, 1920. 36–82.

_____. "My Future as I See It." *Ladies Home Journal* 20 (November 1903): 11.

_____. "The New Woman's Party." *Helen Keller: Her Socialist Years*. Philip S. Foner, ed. New York: International, 1967. 87–88.

_____. "Our Duties to the Blind." *Out of the Dark*. New York: Doubleday, 1920. 125–40.

_____. "Preventable Blindness." *Out of the Dark*. New York: Doubleday, 1920. 160–73.

_____. "To Senator Robert M. La Follette." *Helen Keller: Her Socialist Years*. Philip S. Foner, ed. New York: International, 1967. 113–15.

_____. "What Might Be Done for the Blind." *The World's Work* 14 (April 1907): 9259–64.

_____. "Why Men Need Woman Suffrage." *Helen Keller: Her Socialist Years*. Philip S. Foner, ed. New York: International, 1967. 64–68.

Kellogg, Rhoda. *Analyzing Children's Art*. Palo Alto, CA: National Press Books, 1969.

_____. *Babies Need Fathers, Too*. New York: Comet, 1953.

_____. *Children's Drawings/Children's Minds*. New York: Avon, 1979.

_____. *The Crucial Years*. Daphne Plaskow, ed. London: Society for Education Through Art, 1972.

_____. Journal Notes, Rhoda Kellogg Collection. Box 1 and 2. California Historical Society.

_____. "Montessori Today." *Commentary* 38.5 (November 1964): 20–22.

_____. *Nursery School Guide: Theory and Practice for Teachers and Parents*. Boston: Houghton, 1949.

_____. "Understanding Children's Art." *Theory and Practice in the Teaching of Composition: Processing, Distancing, and Modeling*. Miles Myers and James Gray, ed. Urbana, IL: NCTE, 1983. 67–74.

_____. *What Children Scribble and Why*. Palo Alto, CA: N-P Publications, 1955.

Kellogg, Rhoda, and Scott O'Dell. *The Psychology of Children's Art*. New York: CRM–Random House, 1967.

Kenison, Katrina. "Martha Foley." *Notable American Women: A Biographical Dictionary, Completing the Twentieth Century*. Susan Ware and Stacy Braukman, eds. Cambridge: Belknap Press of Harvard University Press, 2005. 216–17.

Kerber, Linda. *Toward an Intellectual History of Women*. Chapel Hill: University of North Carolina Press, 1997.

Kettler, Ernestine Hara. "In Prison." *From Parlor to Prison: Five American Suffragists Talk About Their Lives*. Sherna Berger Gluck, ed. New York: Vintage, 1976. 241–86.

Kimball, Alice Mary. *The Devil Is a Woman*. New York: Knopf, 1929.

Kinkead, Beatrice, trans. *100,000 Whys: A Trip around the Room*. By Mikhail Andreevich Il'in. London : Routledge, 1946.

_____. *Black on White: The Story of Books*. By Mikhail Andreevich Il'in and Nikolai Iustinovich Lapshin. Philadelphia: Lippincott, 1932.

_____. *Giant at the Crossroads: The Story of Ancient Civilization*. By Mikhail Andreevich Il'in and E. Segal. New York: International, 1948.

_____. *The Giant Widens His World: The Middle Ages and the Renaissance*. By Mikhail Andreevich Il'in and E. Segal. New York: International, 1949.

_____. *How Man Became a Giant*. By Mikhail Andreevich Il'in and E. Segal. Allahabad: Kitabistan, 1945.

_____. *Men and Mountains: Man's Victory over Nature*. By Mikhail Andreevich Il'in and Nikolai Iustinovich Lapshin. Philadelphia: Lippincott, 1935.

_____. *A Ring and a Riddle*. By Mikhail Andreevich Il'in and E. Segal. Philadelphia: Lippincott, 1944.

_____. *What Time Is It? The Story of Clocks*. By Mikhail Andreevich Il'in. Philadelphia: Lippincott, 1932.

Kohlstedt, Sally Gregory. "Women in the History of Science: An Ambiguous Place." *Osiris* 10 (1995): 39–58.

Koster, Joan Bouza. *Growing Artists: Teaching Art of Young Children*. Albany: Delmar, 1997.

Kuzyk, Raya. "Hats Off to You, Maud Malone (1873–1951)." *LJ Insider*, 27 February 2008. LibraryJournal.com. Accessed 3 September 2009.

LaFeber, Walter. *The American Age: U.S. Foreign Policy at Home and Abroad, 1750 to the Present*. 2nd ed. New York: Norton, 1994.

Lane, Ann. "Mary Ritter Beard: An Appraisal of Her Life and Work." *Making Women's History: The Essential Mary Ritter Beard*. Mary Beard and Ann J. Lane, eds. New York: Feminist, 1977. 1–72.

Lash, Joseph P. *Helen and Teacher: The Story of Helen Keller and Anne Sullivan Macy*. Reading, MA: Addison-Wesley, 1980.

"The Later Demonstrations." *Suffragist* 24 August 1918: 5.

Lear, Martha Weinman. "What Do These Women Want: The Second Feminist Wave." *New York Times Magazine*, 10 March 1968: 24–33. *Historical New York Times*, 20 June 2009.

Lemons, J. Stanley. "Feminists against Feminists." *The Woman Citizen: Social Feminists in the 1920s*. Urbana: University of Illinois Press, 1973. 181–208.

Lerner, Gerda. "New Approaches to the Study of Women in American History." *The Columbia Documentary History of*

American Women Since 1941. New York: Columbia University Press, 2003. 231–39.
_____. *The Woman in American History.* Menlo Park, CA: Addison-Wesley, 1971.
Lewis, Sinclair. *Babbitt.* New York: Harcourt, 1922.
_____. "Devil-Dog Rule." *Nation* 129 (18 December 1929): 751.
_____. *Main Street.* New York: Harcourt, 1920.
Locke, Alain. "Color: Unfinished Business of Democracy." Special issue of *Survey Graphic,* November 1942.
_____. "Harlem: Mecca of the New Negro." Special issue of *Survey Graphic,* March 1925.
_____. *The New Negro: An Interpretation.* New York: Arno, 1925.
Louis, James P. "Sue Sheldon White and the Woman Suffrage Movement in Tennessee, 1913–1920." *Tennessee Historical Quarterly* 22 (1963): 170–190.
Lunardini, Christine A. *From Equal Suffrage to Equal Rights: Alice Paul and the National Woman's Party, 1910–1928.* New York: New York University Press, 1986.
Lutz, Alma. *Created Equal: A Biography of Elizabeth Cady Stanton, 1815–1902.* New York: Day, 1940.
_____. *Crusade for Freedom: Women of the Antislavery Movement.* Boston: Beacon, 1968.
_____. *Emma Willard: Daughter of Democracy.* Boston: Houghton Mifflin, 1929.
_____. *Mary Baker Eddy Historical House, Rumney Village, New Hampshire, the Rumney Years.* Brookline, MA: Longyear Foundation, 1940.
_____. "To the Vassar Alumnae Magazine." Folder 2.26. Alma Lutz Papers, 1912–1971. Vassar College Libraries.
_____. *Susan B. Anthony: Rebel, Crusader, Humanitarian.* Boston: Beacon, 1959.
_____. *With Love, Jane: Letters from American Women on the War Fronts.* New York: John Day, 1945.
_____. Women's History Courses. Folder 2.26. Alma Lutz Papers, 1912–1971. Vassar College Libraries.
Martin, Anne. Letters to Supporters. July 1917. Reel 44, National Woman's Party Papers. Library of Congress.
_____. *The Story of the Nevada Equal Suffrage Campaign.* Austin E. Hutcheson, ed. Reno: University of Nevada, 1948.
Martin, George Madden. "American Women and Public Affairs." *Atlantic Monthly* (February 1924): 169–71.
Mather, Frank Jewett, Jr. "The Havemeyer Pictures." *The Arts* 16 (March 1930): 450–83.
"Maud Malone Asks in Vain to Be Fined." *New York Times,* 13 November 1912: 34. *Historical New York Times,* 3 September 2009.
McKay, Nellie Y. Introduction. *A Colored Woman in a White World.* 1940. New York: Hall, 1996. xv–xxxvi.
Mcniff, Shaun. *Art Heals: How Creativity Cures the Soul.* New York: Shambhala, 2004.
"Militants to Picket Today." *New York Times,* 23 July 1917: 9. *Historical New York Times,* 1 July 2009.
Miller, William D. *Pretty Bubbles in the Air: America in 1919.* Urbana: University of Illinois Press, 1991.
"More Blind Than She, Miss Keller Says; All Are Sightless Who Do Not Open Their Eyes to Fellow-Men and Know Their Rights." *New York Times,* 7 February 1913: 3. *Historical New York Times,* 7 April 2009.
Morris, Mildred. "The New Year Demonstration." *Suffragist* 11 January 1919: 4–5.
"Mrs. Agnes Chase, Botanist, Is Dead." *New York Times,* 26 September 1963: 35. *Historical New York Times,* 20 June 2009.
"Mrs. Beatrice Kinkead." *New York Times,* 12 November 1947: 27. *Historical New York Times,* 8 September 2009.
"Mrs. Havemeyer, Art Patron, Dies." *New York Times,* 7 January 1929: 25. *Historical New York Times,* 12 June 2009.
"Mrs. Whittemore to Tell of Arrest." *Detroit Free Press,* 19 July 1917: 16.
Munk, Michael. *Jack Reed and Louise Bryant.* 23 August 2009.
Murphy, Darin, librarian and archivist at the School of the Museum of Fine Arts,

Boston. Telephone interview, 6 August 2008.

"Mutual Responsibility." *Suffragist* 21 April 1917: 3.

"Name Woman for Mayor." *New York Times*, 14 September 1927: 6. *Historical New York Times*, 9 June 2009.

National Women's Studies Association. 20 August 2009.

Navasky, Victor. "Oswald Garrison Villard." *The School of Cooperative Individualism*. 7 June 2009.

"The Navy Department Admits." *Nation* 7 September 1921: 255.

Nechaev, I. *Chemical Elements: The Fascinating Story of Their Discovery and of the Famous Scientists Who Discovered Them*. Trans. Beatrice Kinkead. London: Lindsay, Drummond, 1946.

"Negro Art Show." *New York Times*, 7 November 1945: 22. *Historical New York Times*, 11 March 2009.

Neugeboren, Jay. Introduction. *The Story of Story Magazine: A Memoir by Martha Foley*. New York: Norton, 1980. 7–24.

"New Members of the Advisory Council." *Suffragist*, 20 February 1915: 3.

Nielsen, Kim, and Harvey J. Kaye. *The Radical Lives of Helen Keller*. New York: New York University Press, 2004.

Nolan, Mary A. "That Night of Terror." *Suffragist*, 1 December 1917: 7+.

"Nurse Portrait Unveiled." *New York Times*, 23 January 1953: 12. *Historical New York Times*, 4 June 2009.

NWP Press Release. 6 August 1918. Microform. Reel 91, National Woman's Party Papers. Library of Congress.

O'Connor, June E. *The Moral Vision of Dorothy Day: A Feminist Perspective*. New York: Crossroad, 1991.

O'Neill, Eugene. *Bound East for Cardiff, a Sea Play. The Provincetown Plays: First Series*. New York: Shay, 1916. 5–25.

O'Neill, William L. *Everyone Was Brave: The Rise and Fall of Feminism in America*. New York: Quadrangle, 1969.

_____. *The Woman Movement: Feminism in the United States and England*. New York: Barnes and Noble, 1969.

Paul, Alice. Letter to Louisine Havemeyer. 1918 n.d. Microfilm. Reel 67, National Woman's Party Papers. Library of Congress.

_____. Letter to Mary Beard. 28 June 1913. Microfilm. Reel 2, National Woman's Party Papers. Library of Congress.

_____. "The Woman Suffrage Movement in Great Britain." *Significance of the Woman Suffrage Movement*. Philadelphia: American Academy of Political and Social Science, 1910. 23–27.

"Pauline Adams — Champion of Women's Rights." Virginia Department of Historical Resources. 11 September 2009.

Payment, Diane P. "'Dollee Chevrier (1878–1948): A Franco-Manitoban Suffragette and 'Modern' Woman." *Manitoba History* 44 (Autumn-Winter 2002–03). The Manitoba Historical Society. 5 August 2009.

Pfeffer, Paula F. "Eleanor Roosevelt and the National and World Woman's Parties." *Historian* 59 (Fall 1996): 39–57.

"A Phenomenal Child: Acquirements of Little Deaf, Dumb, and Blind Helen Keller." *New York Times*, 25 May 1890: 3. *Historical New York Times*, 11 June 2009.

Pietila, Hilkka. "The Unfinished Story of Women and the United States." *SARPN: South African Regional Poverty Network*. 8 July 2009.

Ploski, Harry A., and Ernest Kaiser. *The Negro Almanac*. 2nd ed. New York: Bellwether, 1971.

"Portrait of a Man of Genius." *New York Times*, 4 May 1944: 18. *Historical New York Times*, 20 July 2009.

Powell, Jim. "Albert Jay Nock: A Pen for Radical Individualism." *The Freeman: Ideas on Liberty* 47.3 (March 1997). 3 September 2009.

"President Harding's Pledge." *Nation*, 21 June 1922: 748.

"President Ignores Suffrage Pickets." *New York Times*, 11 January 1917: 13. *Historical New York Times*, 1 June 2009.

"President Onlooker at Mob Attack on Suffragists." *Suffragist*, 18 August 1917: 7.

"President's Words Burned as Suffragists Protest in Front of White House." *Suffragist*, 28 September 1918: 6–7.

Press Bulletin. 6 August 1918. Microfilm. Reel 91, National Woman's Party Papers. Library of Congress.

Press Release. 9 January 1918. Microfilm. Reel 91, National Woman's Party Papers. Library of Congress.

"Prison — and the Reaction." *Suffragist*, 7 July 1917: 9.

"Prison Lulls 'Suffs.'" *Detroit Free Press*, 18 July 1917: 1.

"The Prison Special." *Suffragist*, 1 February 1919: 10.

"The Prison Special." *Suffragist*, 22 February 1919: 3–4.

"Protest for Liberty Answered with Sixteen More Suffrage Arrests." *Suffragist*, 21 July 1917: 4–5.

Pruitt, Mary. "Bertha Berglin Moller." *The Privilege for Which We Struggled: Leaders of the Woman Suffrage Movement in Minnesota*. Heidi Bauer, ed. St. Paul, MN: Upper Midwest Women's History Center, 1999. 135–38.

_____. "Sarah Tarleton Colvin." *The Privilege for Which We Struggled*. 105–09.

"Publisher, Writer Alice G. Robinson Dies in Virginia at 88." *Washington Post*, 28 January 1984: C6.

Rabinow, Rebecca A. "The Suffrage Exhibition of 1915." *Splendid Legacy: The Havemeyer Collection*. Alice Cooney Frelinghuysen, et al., eds. New York: Metropolitan Museum of Art, 1993. 89–98.

"Racial Violence and Terror." *Plantation to Ghetto*. Section 6. *Amistad Digital Resource*. 28 August 2009.

Rattner, Faye. *Reform in America: Jacksonian Democracy, Progressivism, and The New Deal*. Chicago: Scott, Foresman, 1964.

"Record-Breaking Number of Women Will Serve in the 111th Congress." *Women in Government Relations: Advancing and Empowering Women*. 17 July 2009.

Reds. Warren Beatty, dir. Warren Beatty, Diane Keaton and Edward Herrmann, perf. Paramount, 1981.

"Reminding the President When He Landed in Boston." *Suffragist*, 1 March 1919: 6–9.

Resolution Passed by the Convention of the National Woman's Party and the Congressional Union, March 1917. Microfilm. Reel 87, National Woman's Party Papers. Library of Congress.

Reyher, Rebecca Hourwich. Letter to Florence Armstrong, 26 September 1958. "The Papers of Sue Shelton White." Box 1, Sue Shelton White Papers, Schlesinger Library, Radcliffe Institute, Harvard University.

"Rhoda Kellogg Child Art Collection." *Golden Gate Kindergarten Association*. 5 September 2009.

Rice, Stuart D., and Malcolm M. Willey. "American Women's Ineffective Use of the Vote." *Current History* 20 (1924): 641–47.

Riegel, Robert. *American Feminists*. Lawrence: University of Kansas Press, 1963.

Riis, Jacob A. *The Children of the Poor*. 1892. New York: Garrett: 1970.

Rippy, J. Fred. *The Caribbean Danger Zone*. New York: Putnams, 1940.

Roosevelt, Eleanor. "My Day." 4 May 1944. *Eleanor Roosevelt Papers*. 24 July 2009.

Rosen, Ellen Doree. *A Wobbly Life: IWW Organizer E.F. Doree*. Detroit: Wayne State University Press, 2004.

Ross, Elizabeth. *The Kindergarten Crusade*. Athens: Ohio University Press, 1976.

Rossiter, Margaret W. *Women Scientists in America: Struggles and Strategies to 1940*. Baltimore: Johns Hopkins University Press, 1982.

Rudwick, Elliott. *Race Riots at East St. Louis, July 2, 1917*. Urbana: University of Illinois Press, 1982.

Rupp, Leila J., and Verta A. Taylor. *Survival in the Doldrums: The American Women's Rights Movement, 1945 to the 1960s*. Columbus: Ohio State University Press, 1990.

Russell, Charles Edward. "Is Woman-Suffrage a Failure?" *Century Magazine* 107 (March 1924): 724–30.

Salmon, Lucy. *Domestic Service*. New York: Macmillan, 1897.

_____. Research for Women." *A History and Texture of Modern Life: Selected Essays*. Nicholas Adams and Bonnie G. Smith, eds. Philadelphia: University of Pennsylvania Press, 2001. 169–81.

_____. *Why Is History Rewritten?* New York: Oxford University Press, 1929.

"Saw Votes Bought in the Jersey Election; Mrs. Helena Hill Weed Says Money Was Passed before Her Eyes in Newark. " *New York Times*, 21 October 1915: 4. *Historical New York Times*, 12 February 2009.

Saxon, Wolfgang. "Martha Foley Dies, Editor and Teacher." *New York Times*, 7 September 1977: 55. *Historical New York Times*, 22 March 2009.

Schatzki, Stefan C. "Medicine in American Art: Dr. Charles Richard Drew." *American Journal of Roentgenology* 165 (1995): 1372.

Schmidt, Hans R. *The United States Occupation of Haiti, 1915–1934*. New Brunswick, NJ: Rutgers University Press, 1995.

Schorer, Mark. *Sinclair Lewis: An American Life*. New York: McGraw-Hill, 1961.

Scott, Anne Firor, and Andrew Scott. *One Half the People: The Fight for Woman Suffrage*. Philadelphia: Lippincott, 1975.

Scott, Joan Wallach. "Experience." *Feminists Theorize the Political*. Scott and Judith Butler, eds. New York: Routledge, 1992. 26–27.

Scott, William B., and Peter Rutkoff. *New York Modern: The Arts and the City*. Baltimore: Johns Hopkins University Press, 2001.

"Seek to Explain Miss Rankin's 'No.'" *New York Times*, 7 April 1917: 4. *Historical New York Times*, 20 February 2009.

"Settlement Near in Garment Strike." *New York Times*, 8 July 1916: 18. *Historical New York Times*, 14 July 2009.

Shanley, Mary Lyndon. "Suffrage, Protective Labor Legislation, and Married Women's Property Laws in England." *Signs: Journal of Women in Culture and Society* 12.1 (Autumn 1986): 62–77.

Shaw, Anna Howard. *The Story of a Pioneer*. New York: Harper, 1915.

Shepperd, Gladys Byram. *Mary Church Terrell: Respectable Person*. New York: Human Relations Press, 1959.

Sherwood, John. "The Tradition." *The Magnificent Foragers: Smithsonian Explorations in the Natural Sciences*. Washington, DC: Smithsonian Exposition Books, 1978. 11–27.

Sklar, Kathryn Kish. "Why Were Politically Active Women Opposed to the ERA in the 1920s?" *Rights of Passage: The Past and Future of the ERA*. Joan Hoff-Wilson, ed. Bloomington: Indiana University Press, 1986. 25–35.

Smith, Norma. *Jeannette Rankin, America's Conscience*. Helena: Montana Historical Society Press, 2002.

Spender, Dale. *There's Always Been a Women's Movement This Century*. London: Pandora, 1983.

Stanton, Elizabeth Cady. *Eighty Years and More (1815–1897): Reminiscences of Elizabeth Cady Stanton*. New York: European, 1898.

Sterling, Dorothy. *Black Foremothers: Three Lives*. New York: Feminist Press, 1993.

Stevens, Doris. *Jailed for Freedom: American Women Win the Vote*. New York: Boni and Liveright, 1920.

_____. "Justice: As Seen at Occuquan." *Suffragist*, 11 August 1917: 7–8.

Stewart, Jeffrey Conrad. "Paul Robeson: Icon or Hero." *Paul Robeson: Essays on His Life and Legacy*. Joseph Dorinson and William Pencak, eds. Jefferson, NC: McFarland, 2002. 194–212.

Stone, Elaine Murray. *Dorothy Day: Champion of the Poor*. Mahwah, NJ: Paulist, 2004.

Stuhler, Barbara. "Clara Hampson Ueland (1860–1927)." *The Privilege for Which We Struggled: Leaders of the Woman Suffrage Movement in Minnesota*. Heidi Bauer, ed. St. Paul: Upper Midwest Women's History Center, 1999. 111–15.

Stuyvesant, Elizabeth. "Staying Free." *These Modern Women: Autobiographical Essays from the 1920s*. Elaine Showalter, ed. Old Westbury, NY: Feminist Press, 1978. 92–97.

"Suffrage Dancers Overflow 'Garden.'" *New York Times*, 8 March 1915: 5. *Historical New York Times*, 2 June 2009.

"Suffrage Demonstration before White House Planned." *Suffragist*, 3 August 1918: 5.

"Suffragists Again Attack President." *New*

York Times, 7 August 1918: 1+. *Historical New York Times*, 1 February 2009.

"Suffragists Burn Wilson in Effigy." *New York Times*, 10 February 1919: 1+. *Historical New York Times*, 7 March 2009.

"Suffragists Take 60-Day Sentences; Won't Pay Fines." *New York Times*, 18 July 1917: 1+. *Historical New York Times*, 7 March 2009.

"Suffragists Wait at the White House for Action." *Suffragist*, 17 January 1917: 7.

"'Suffs' Resume Silent Vigil." *Detroit Free Press*, 22 July 1917: 8.

Swift, Jonathan. *Gulliver's Travels*. New York: Penguin, 2003.

Swing, Betty Gram. "A Brief Accolade to Sue S. White, the Intrepid Feminist." Box 1, Sue Shelton White Papers. Schlesinger Library, Radcliffe Institute, Harvard University.

Tate, Jack B. "Sue White: An Appreciation." Box 1, Sue Shelton White Papers. Schlesinger Library, Radcliffe Institute, Harvard University.

"Tennessee Will Act on Suffrage." *New York Times*, 24 June 1920: 1–2. *Historical New York Times*, 5 April 2009.

Terrell, Mary Church. *A Colored Woman in a White World*. 1940. New York: Hall, 1996.

_____. Letters about Speaking Engagements. Box 4, The Papers of Mary Church Terrell. Library of Congress.

Tinterow, Gary. "The Havemeyer Pictures." *Splendid Legacy: The Havemeyer Collection*. Alice Cooney Frelinghuysen, et al., eds. New York: Metropolitan Museum of Art, 1993. 3–88.

"To All Active Supporters of Democracy and Peace." *Soviet Russia Today* 8.5 (September 1939): 24–25, 28.

"To Picket Wall Street." *New York Times*, 11 December 1919: 12. *Historical New York Times*, 20 February 2009.

"Training: Experiment Proved?" *Time*, 20 September 1943: 66, 68.

Trigg, Mary Kathleen. "Four American Feminists, 1910–1940: Inez Hayes Irwin, Mary Ritter Beard, Doris Stevens, and Lorine Pruette." Ph.D. diss. Brown University, 1989.

"The United States Convicts Eleven More Women for Demanding Democracy." *Suffragist*, 14 July 1917: 4–5.

Vandewalker, Nina C. *The Kindergarten in American Education*. New York: Macmillan, 1908.

"Vassar Girl Suffragette." *New York Times*, 1 March 1909: 14. *Historical New York Times*, 12 April 2009.

"Vassar Students Are Now Radical." *New York Times*, 9 May 1909: 8. *Historical New York Times*, 20 April 2009.

Walsh, Frank P. "American Imperialism." *Nation*, 1 February 1922: 115.

Ware, Susan. *Beyond Suffrage: Women in the New Deal*. Cambridge: Harvard University Press, 1981.

"The Watchfire." *Suffragist*, 11 January 1919: 6.

Weed, Helena Hill. "Change Again Presses on the Capitol." *New York Times*, 28 April 1935: SM 6–7+. *Historical New York Times*, 26 August 2009.

_____. "Fresh Hope for Haiti." *Nation*, 19 March 1930: 342–44.

_____. "Hearing the Truth About Haiti." *Nation*, 9 November 1921: 114.

_____. "The New Deal That Women Want." *Current History*, November 1934: 179–83.

_____. "The Repercussions of Montevideo." Series V, Subseries E, 109.8, Doris Stevens Papers. Schlesinger Library, Radcliffe Institute, Harvard University.

_____. "Santo Domingo Loan." *New York Times*, 7 May 1922: 101. *Historical New York Times*, 20 April 2009.

_____. "Victory in Haiti." *Nation*, 26 March 1930: 378–80.

Weed, Walter Harvey. *Mines Handbook, An Enlargement of the Copper Handbook*. New York: Weed, 1918.

Weed, Walter Harvey, and Horace J. Stevens. *The Copper Handbook*. Houghton, MI: Stevens, 1911.

Weinraub, Bernard. "A Writing Class Comes to Its Disabled Teacher: Wednesdays at Martha Foley's." *New York Times*, 3 March 1966: 35. *Historical New York Times*, 29 September 2009.

Weitzenhoffer, Frances. *The Creation of the*

Havemeyer Collection. Ph.D. diss. City University of New York, 1982.

_____. *The Havemeyers: Impressionism Comes to America*. New York: Abrams, 1986.

"Welcome Dr. Shaw with Tea and Dance." *New York Times*, 18 April 1915: 14. *Historical New York Times*, 17 June 2009.

Wells, Ida B. *Crusade for Justice: The Autobiography of Ida B. Wells*. Chicago: University of Chicago Press, 1970.

Wertheimer, Linda. "Women Bring New Power, Perspective to Congress." National Public Radio, www.npr.org. 26 June 2009. 17 May 2009.

"What to Do in Haiti." *Nation*, 3 November 1920: 493.

Wheeler, Marjorie Spruill. *New Women of the New South: The Leaders of the Woman Suffrage Movement in the Southern States*. New York: Oxford, 1993.

White, Sue Shelton. Letter to the editor of *Harper's Magazine*. Box 33, Sue Shelton White Papers, Schlesinger Library, Radcliffe Institute, Harvard University.

_____. "Mother's Daughter." *These Modern Women: Autobiographical Essays from the Twenties*. Ed. Elaine Showalter. New York: Feminist Press, 1979. 46–52.

_____. "Women in Public Office." Box 31, Sue Shelton White Papers, Schlesinger Library, Radcliffe Institute, Harvard University.

Wilson, Edith Bolling. *My Memoirs*. New York: Bobbs-Merrill, 1938.

Wogaman, J. Philip, and Douglas M. Strong. *Readings in Christian Ethics: A Historical Sourcebook*. Louisville, KY: Westminster John Knox Press, 1996.

"Woman Suffrage Declared a Failure." *Literary Digest*, 12 April 1924: 12–13.

"Women's Protest against Disenfranchisement Broken Up by Federal Police." *Suffragist*, 17 August 1918: 5.

"Wonders of Patient Teaching: How Helen Keller, without Sight or Hearing, Learned to Speak." *New York Times*, 29 December 1891: 9. *Historical New York Times*, 7 April 2009.

"Work for Blind Urged: Continue Their Employment in Peacetime, Helen Keller Pleads." *New York Times*, 7 October 1945: 4. *Historical New York Times*, 22 August 2009.

Wormser, Richard. *The Rise and Fall of Jim Crow*. New York: St. Martin's, 2007.

Younger, Maud. "Revelations of a Woman Lobbyist." *McCall's Magazine*, September-October-November 1919: passim.

Index